PORTRAIT OF GLASGOW

Portrait of
GLASGOW

MAURICE LINDSAY

ROBERT HALE · LONDON

ISBN 0 7091 3078 3

Robert Hale & Company
63 Old Brompton Road
London S.W.7

PRINTED IN GREAT BRITAIN
BY EBENEZER BAYLIS AND SON LTD.
THE TRINITY PRESS, WORCESTER, AND LONDON

CONTENTS

ILLUSTRATIONS

PHOTO CREDITS

Annan of Glasgow: Nos. 15, 16; Oscar Marzaroli: 23, 28, 29, 30, 33; John Watt, *Scottish Field*, 18; *The Scotsman*: 17, 19, 20, 24, 27, 31; *The Glasgow Herald*: 25, 26; W. Ralston Ltd: 32.

ACKNOWLEDGEMENTS

Nobody who sets out to re-tell Glasgow's story can do so without the help of those who have previously recorded its details in various forms. To the historians and chroniclers of times past, I make grateful acknowledgement. Where I have quoted specific points, my sources, both primary and secondary, are acknowledged by footnotes throughout the text.

I am grateful to Mr. James Milligan and Dr. John Butt of the University of Strathclyde, both of whom read my typescript and made valuable suggestions regarding facts and statistics relating to Glasgow's sociological and industrial history. I must also warmly thank Miss Morven Cameron and Mr. Jack House who were kind enough to read my proofs; Mr. Douglas McLeman, who advised me upon some controversial points; and Miss Margaret Miller, who typed the manuscript. Anyone who wishes to write about Glasgow must necessarily visit the Glasgow Room of the Mitchell Library. My frequently perplexing requests were unfailingly met with a kindness and a practical helpfulness entirely typical. I should also like to thank Mr. Oscar Marzaroli, several of whose effective camera studies of Glasgow enrich these pages; Mr. James Rae of Glasgow Corporation Planning Department, who drew my attention to the aerial photograph of a part of Glasgow by W. Ralston; and the Assistant Director of the Scottish Civic Trust, Mr. John Gerrard, for the coloured view of Glasgow from the Inner Ring Motorway which adorns the dust-jacket.

On page 244, in connexion with the founding of Scottish Opera, I should certainly also have specifically acknowledged the part enthusiastically played by my umquhile school-fellow Ainslie Millar, I do so now.

MAURICE LINDSAY

TO ALEXANDER GIBSON,

*Musical Director, The Scottish National Orchestra
and Artistic Director, Scottish Opera*

I used to think when I was young that one day
people in Glasgow would grow tired of pitching
Reformation and Boyne through football bets:
        but I was wrong.

I used to think when I was young that one day
Glasgow people would grow imagination
to deck the air with music, hear through silence
        the poet's tongue.

Now that I'm middle-aged it doesn't seem to
matter much if Buber's I and Thou-It
is labelled music, bingo, God or football;
        the heart's engaged.

Yet, being middle-aged, this could be error,
my toleration tired complacency,
the truer values those against whose enemies
        in youth I raged.

Perhaps when I'm old I'll know; but meantime, Alex,
this portrait's yours, with thanks for all the pleasure
your music's given me; small recompense
        for what I owe.

MAURICE LINDSAY

INTRODUCTION

Opinion as to what constitutes a fair portrait has varied from age to age. In pre-photographic days, a detailed reliable physical likeness was generally regarded as being the essential characteristic. Later, the advent of Impressionism and the movements which followed it produced portraits where character, or symbols for it, rather than facial accuracy was aimed for. Later still, portraits were subjected to the theories of Cubism or Abstraction.

Today, the painter of a portrait on canvas is, in one sense, a curiously isolated creature. Abstraction has currently swept all before it, in varying fashionable terms; yet you can rarely practise abstraction on a human face and produce something likely to satisfy the sitter. So the portrait-painter has to find his own individual answer, without the collective reassurance of being part of the mood-movement of his contemporaries. He has, in fact, to find a largely personal solution.

The writer, attached to words, is faced with a somewhat similar problem. One can think of several contemporaries who might paint a poetic word-portrait of Glasgow, abstracting this or that aspect which suited their particular literary purpose or political bent. However fascinating, possibly the result might not be recognizable to those familiar with, or anxious to identify, the sitter.

If a portrait is to have any merit at all, it must surely depict the measure of experience reflected in the features of its subject. In this portrait of Glasgow, I have therefore adopted a highly subjective approach, through which the present reflects the past. Clearly, my Glasgow may not be the same as another man's; but at least my portrait of it sets down my native city as I have come to know it, either through the imaginations or reportings of past observers, or through my own senses. My range of enjoyments is, I hope, sufficiently wide to have allowed me convey to those who do not know Glasgow—and perhaps also to those who, though they may have lived much of their lives within the city's boundaries, know only their own local sub-division of it—something of the life and the physical quality of a city that is, and long has been, unique in Europe.

I

THE SUBJECTIVE CITY

The visitor who arrives in Glasgow for the first time is likely to receive a series of shock impressions, particularly if his native environment is that of a Continental town. He will almost certainly notice the dark-grey colour of most of the stone buildings, encased in the sooting of an obsolete coal-burning age, which, for political reasons, has been kept with us long after it has outlived its economic usefulness. If he arrives by any approach other than by road from the west, he may be appalled at the grim spectacle of crumbling tenements squaring up to each other across grimy streets and carrying the chalked or painted slogans of twentieth-century urban illiteracy. He may be surprised at the number of abandoned and derelict buildings awaiting demolition, but astonished to see the new concrete-and-glass Glasgow tearing its way through the old.

If our visitor comes from an environmentally advanced country such as Sweden or Denmark, where even the mean average of architectural standards is high, he will probably notice that much of the new Glasgow, cleaner and more spacious than the old and purified by the adoption of smoke-free zones, is made up of relatively undistinguished ingredients: high-rise housing straight off a prefabricated production line; office sprawls manipulated into convenient shapes, like blocks of children's Lego; much, in fact, that reflects the higher standards of hygiene enjoyed by, or at any rate available to, the modern Glaswegian, but little, very little, that reflects taste or even distinction in private or public buildings.

In the older parts of the city he may look more closely, and find that amongst much that is decrepit and debilitated an extraordinary number of confident Victorian buildings survive, some of them already cleaned and restored, others still fulfilling a modern function beneath their grimed exteriors.

The fact is that Glasgow has a Victorian heritage of sheer

Western
Infirmary

Glasgow
University

KELVINGROVE

Kelvingrove
Museum &
Art Gallery

Kelvin
Hall

PARK

PARK
CIRCUS

Trinity
College

PARK C.A.

Theat

GREAT WESTERN ROAD

Charing
Cross

SAUCHIEHA

King's Theatre

Mitchell Library

BLYTHEWO

ST VINCENT CRESCENT

ST VINCENT ST.

QUEEN'S
DOCK
(Closed)

ANDERSTON

R I V E R

*

C.D.A

PRINCE'S
DOCK

Ore
terminal

C L Y D E

A

Kingston
Bridge

G O V A N

B

PAISLEY RD.

MORRIS

ROAD

WEST

KINNING PARK C.D.A.

PAISLEY   ROAD

J.
PK.

PLANTATION

| Comprehensive Develop-
ment Area | C.D.A. |
| Conservation Area | C.A. |

0   Mile   ½

exuberance and flourish second to none in the United Kingdom. Some years ago, certain city fathers who, for charity, shall be nameless—members of that fellowship of functional illiterates which our democratic system so regularly, profusely and disastrously throws up into public office—disassociated themselves from an excursion round Glasgow by the Victorian Society, on the grounds that the resulting publicity could not be good for the city's 'progressive image'. The Glasgow councillors' view of progress over the past half century or so has been the need to achieve more jobs for the city, new houses and higher rateable values, the first two objectives relating to the dignity of the individual. Unfortunately in striving towards these aims, laudable in themselves, false antitheses have been created, reflected in meaningless catch-phrases like "Jobs before Snobs" and "People before Buildings".

'Progress' has in fact, become the misunderstood god of the functional illiterate. The honest functional illiterate uses the word to justify any act of vandalism which his poverty of imagination may lead him to support. He fails to reflect that true progress must always mean a conscious going towards; and that those who simply mumbo-jumbo the parrot-cry are all too often merely lurching forward aimlessly, like lemmings.

A number of buildings of importance which should not have been pulled down fell before the obduracy of our democratically-elected lemmings in the post-Second World War decade. Today the passing of the Civic Amenities Act, with its enlightened concept of the Conservation Area, and certain provisions in the Planning Act (Scotland) 1969, have helped to encourage a change of attitude. To all but the most thick-headed lemming, the psychological benefits, to say nothing of the hard-cash tourist benefits, of conserving what is best in our stone-and-mortar heritage alongside our new developments, is now apparent.

Our visitor, having sought out for himself the delights of the best buildings in Glasgow's central area, may recollect that the cathedral and the university were both founded in medieval times. Where, he may ask himself, can he find eighteenth and seventeenth-century Glasgow? Apart from a very few individual buildings, or surviving fragments of buildings, the answer unfortunately is: in the records of times past. For elected lemmings were busy in Glasgow long before our own day; moved, first of all, by the then socially acceptable desire for the gathering of

Archepiscopal Palace and Glasgow Cathedral in 1790
The Old Merchant's Hall in the Briggate, 1872

industrial fortunes, and later by the dawning twinges of social conscience disturbed by the human misery out of which their own prosperity had been built.

It is impossible fully to appreciate Glasgow today without understanding those forces which moulded it from a convenient ford over the River Clyde into a medieval centre of piety and learning, then into an expanding centre of international trade, a place of growing manufacturing importance, a power-house for international heavy engineering products and a cradle for the building of the major proportion of the world's ships. While still the second city of the British Empire the power faltered, and Glasgow tumbled into the trough of the depressed years of the late 1920s and 30s. When painfully she climbed out again, it was to find the once-unique importance of her strong skills gone, copied by countries whose needs she had formerly met; her too-long-maintained trust in heavy industries putting her at a disadvantage in a fast-changing technological age; her housing conditions the most densely over-crowded in Europe.

The changes that are reshaping Glasgow in the closing decades of the twentieth century are no less dramatic than those of the expansionist years of the mid-nineteenth, when rows of rose- or honey-coloured tenements encroached upon the hills that surrounded the Glasgow Daniel Defoe knew, and engulfed the green fields beyond and the distant surrounding villages. These at least were changes growing up out of virgin soil. The enormous magnitude of the ensuing background of overcrowding, social squalor and economic collapse out of which Glasgow has had to pull itself accounts for some contemporary mistakes, but is also the measure of the city's determined reassertion.

One of the curiosities which those who venture into the heady delights of the Scottish way of life quickly discover is that, on the whole, it is difficult for Glaswegians to be dispassionate either about themselves or their city. Scottish pride—"Here's tae us. Wha's like us? Damn few, an they're aa deid!"—is a national characteristic, manifesting itself as a kind of empty-chested swagger in the Lowlands, and in the Highlands as a belief that there is something special about blood and breeding; so special, in fact, that for years the tourist industry has been hampered by the reluctance of those in possession of it to give anything so demeaning as courteous service to foreigners who come expecting it and who pay for it.

2

A view of the Clyde, 1830
Blythswood Place, St. Vincent Street, circa 1830

Glasgow is a city with a large admixture of Celtic blood. Its connections with Ireland go back to pre-medieval times. It welcomed Irishman and Highlander to its industrial heart in the mad expansionist days. Even in these transitional times of numerical decline, when redevelopment to lower densities is forcing it to overspill population around older expanded neighbouring towns and specially-built new ones, it still retains a comparatively large Gaelic-speaking population, probably somewhat over ten thousand.

Like most other urban areas which developed rapidly during the nineteenth century, it has a stratified society. True, its land-owning aristocrats moved out to cleaner air when the industrialists moved in. But the captains of the cotton mills, the ironmasters and the kings of heavy engineering and shipbuilding, in turn formed a new elite. From them, the drive and the energy came. When the world outside eventually widened to burst asunder the bounds and the values of Empire, these leaders had left behind them a solid middle-class of professional people: lawyers, chartered accountants, merchants and business men who built the churches, endowed the schools and hospitals, and patronized the arts.

It is common Marxist practice to distort the achievements of these men, applying to their age through the factual advantages of hindsight later standards which could have had no meaning or relevance in such a context. They existed at a time when commercial opportunity offered itself for the taking; and they took it. Without their energies, there would have been no job-possibilities for Highlanders forced to leave their crofts by the Clearances, or for Irishmen driven to emigration by the potato famines. However grim conditions of livelihood and labour may have been, the only alternative could well have been death by starvation. On the other hand, without this steady nineteenth-century Celtic supply of cheap labour, there might have been no modern Glasgow as we know it.

The stratification which the evolution of these conditions caused is still apparent, though perhaps now less obvious than in pre-Second World War days. Football is, to use the Victorian term, largely a 'working-class' passion. The arts, in so far as they are supported, still rely on the middle classes. Until television sapped the popular theatre's economic foundations, music-hall, pantomimes and plays designed solely to amuse attracted substantial support from those who felt they came somewhere in between.

Happily, anti-semitism and anti-Catholicism, both common enough in the 20s and 30s, have declined, the tolerance which an infusion of Pakistanis into the Glasgow community has fostered becoming overstrained only on those occasions when a match between Celtic and Rangers stirs up meaningless outworn prejudices.

Although some Glaswegians still prefer to educate their children at private schools, and stoutly defend their free right of choice to do so, educational opportunities have widened. Social stratification no longer denies the opportunity of university or other forms of higher education to anyone adequately qualified to receive it. There are some who regret those halcyon days when it was possible for a future playwright or an aspiring politician to take ten leisurely years over the getting of a degree. Others with views perhaps less dilettante may doubt whether, technology apart, the breadth and quality of what is imparted is quite what it was in more selective days.

Since radio, television, telstar, jet aircraft and moon landings have shrunk whatever was left of distance out of our world, most of the western fashion-cults sooner or later wash up on Glasgow; usually later rather than sooner. Bingo offers its vicarious thrills mostly to middle-aged women, who presumably find in it escape from dullness. Drinking, of a dark intensity which puts Glasgow high on the list of European cities where alcoholism is a serious disease, still retains its escapist popularity. But drug-taking, though undoubtedly indulged in, and the accompanying hippie way of life, has lost much of its fashionable force on its way north to the Scottish knuckle-end of Europe. Perhaps the rainy climate of Glasgow encourages a certain measure of conformity, if only out of self-protection. For similar reasons, student protest thrives better in hot climes than in cold. There was the visit of Tariq Ali to Glasgow, come to rouse our students to a righteous sense of the sins of their fathers, many of whom were paying towards the cost of their offspring's education. The fiery Tariq found that he had to fulminate to empty seats, most students preferring a different kind of rousing with a Scottish National Party folk group.

In a sense, Glasgow has always done its thing. Naturally, climatic conditions and other related circumstances have made of it a different thing from London's, Amsterdam's, or San Francisco's. The essential point is that if your thing is anything, it must be intense. Glasgow has always been, and still is, nothing if not that.

II

RELIGION BY THE CLYDE

Although Stone Age remains have been found on the Clyde, and canoes in crannogs unearthed in St. Enoch Square in 1780, Stockwell Street in 1824 and Victoria Dock in 1875, and we know that when the Romans were here the Clyde Valley was peopled by a Druidical tribe, the Damnii, it is virtually impossible accurately to trace Glasgow's origins further back than the Middle Ages. The present city lies in an area that was just inside the Antonine Wall, built by the Romans as an outpost to contain the fierce northern Caledonians. Presumably the Romans had a fort there. A Roman ford crossed the Clyde near the site of the Old Glasgow Bridge, and another fort was excavated at Balmuildy, on the northern boundary of the modern city, just before the First World War.

When St. Ninian arrived in Scotland from Rome early in the fifth century, he is said to have founded a cemetery roughly where Glasgow Cathedral was later to rise.

About A.D. 525, a hundred years or so after Ninian's death, the King of Lothian, who no doubt had ambitious matrimonial plans for his daughter, discovered that she was pregnant. According to legend the culprit was a prince to whom the lady had secretly given herself. The King is thereupon supposed either to have set his erring child adrift in a currach on Aberlady Bay, from where she was blown ashore at Culross and found and cared for by St. Serf; or to have tossed her from the top of Trapain Law, where she and her unborn child Kentigern (or Mungo, as he has become popularly known) were miraculously saved from death.

Whichever unfatherly if unverifiable tradition you settle for, the boy grew up in Fife, a holy man credited with a reputation for achieving miracles. Later he moved westwards, serving under the venerable Abbot Fergus in Carnoch, Stirlingshire. This Fergus, so the old story goes, had a curious whim. His disciple had to promise Fergus that when he died his body should be put on a cart drawn by two untamed bulls, and buried at the spot where they first rested. In due course Mungo found himself called upon to fulfil this unusual promise. The obliging creatures stopped just outside Ninian's cemetery, by the Molendinar burn; so there Fergus was buried, and there Mungo set up his own religious community, calling it Glaschu, which is thought to mean 'the church within the enclosed space'.

King Rhydderch of Strathclyde gave Mungo whatever was then the equivalent rank of bishop, and Christianity flourished, until counter-action by a pagan king called Morken forced Mungo to flee. He sought safety with St. David in Wales, and founded the monastery of St. Asaph. In 573 the Strathclyde Christians under King Rhydderch won the Battle of Arderyd and called Mungo back. He apparently spent some time in Dumfriesshire before returning to Glaschu, where he died about the year 590.

Glasgow's armorial bearings, designed by a lawyer, Andrew MacGeorge, in 1866, refer to events in Glasgow's early Christian history. The bird is a pet robin owned by St. Serf, but restored to life by Mungo. The tree represents the now fully-grown bough which, when frozen, Mungo blew into a living flame that lit St. Serf's monastery lamps. The fish and the ring are reminders of the virtues of fidelity and honesty. Queen Languoreth, forgetting the former, gave a ring she had received from the King to a courtly lover. Coming upon the sleeping man the King noticed the ring, removed it from the man's finger, threw it into the Clyde and ordered the Queen to show it to him. In a panic the Queen went to Mungo for help. The saint told her to cast a line into the Clyde. The salmon she caught had the ring in its mouth, thus enabling the Queen to fulfil her lord's command. The bell represents one brought back by Mungo from Rome, and the mound on which the tree grows was miraculously raised by Mungo for him to stand upon when preaching a sermon on his return from Rome.

"Let Glasgow flourish by the preaching of the Word" was the ancient motto arising out of all this: but by 1866 the good MacGeorge, his Freudian slip showing, established the motto as "Let Glasgow flourish".

At that time Glaschu can only have been a village with a holy cemetery and a convenient ford over the Clyde. The old capital of Strathclyde was Dumbarton, further down the river. It was not until Scotland had come together more or less as a single entity under David I that the next step forward was achieved. Anxious to bring Scotland into line with European civilization, with its organization of abbeys and bishoprics, the King by-passed the Archbishop of York and in 1110 persuaded the Pope to appoint the former royal tutor, John Achaius, Bishop of Glasgow. Glasgow thus became an acknowledged centre of religion and learning, a position confirmed in 1188 when Bishop Jocelin got from Rome the Pope's decision that the Scottish bishops were directly dependent on the Holy See, and further confirmed in 1488, when Glasgow became an archbishopric.

Bishop Achaius built the first cathedral over the tomb of St. Mungo. It was consecrated in 1136, but burnt down about 1190. No trace of it has survived. Rebuilding went ahead, and under Bishop Jocelin a new cathedral was re-consecrated in 1197, though it may perhaps have been in an unfinished state at the time of the ceremony. Although there was substantial rebuilding between 1233 and 1258 under Bishop William de Bondington, there are grounds for believing that part of the south-west section of the lower church and some of the lower walls of the nave may well have been put up by Jocelin's masons.*

As it has come down to us today, it has been succinctly described by Ronald G. Cant and Ian G. Lindsay in their pamphlet *Old Glasgow* (1947).

> In plan, the building consists of a nave and eight bays, a central tower and transepts, and a choir of five bays with eastern chapels beyond. Under the choir is the lower church, and its north-east angle is the chapter-house. The transepts extend no further than the line of the nave and choir aisles, save on the crypt level, where the Fergus aisle forms a prolongation of the South transept. The centre spire, by far the most ambitious of its kind in medieval Scottish architecture, rises to a height of about 220 feet above the crossing. The style employed throughout most of the Cathedral is the form of early Gothic known in Scotland as First Pointed.

Though not a big church by European standards, in its hey-day Glasgow Cathedral was the second largest Gothic church in

---

*Anyone who wishes to trace the somewhat confused history of Glasgow Cathedral should see John Honeyman's essay in *The Book of Glasgow* (1898), edited by George Eyre-Todd, and *Architecture of Glasgow* (1968) by Andor Gomme and David Walker.

Scotland, with an internal length of 285 feet. Only the Cathedral of St. Andrews, destroyed by the Reformers, must certainly have been larger.

Glasgow Cathedral might well have shared the melancholy fate of St. Andrews, for towards the close of the sixteenth century the lead was stripped from its roofs, and its altars and statues were destroyed—what Scott's Andrew Fairservice described in *Rob Roy* as "an old dog shaking itself free of fleas". Fortunately, someone less barbaric than his fellows persuaded the Trades to halt the damage. The fabric was restored and turned into three Protestant churches made out of nave, chancel and crypt, with added galleries and, later, plaster ceilings which were to be removed in subsequent restorations.

The west front of the nave was once flanked by two towers of different size and character. Between 1833 and 1846, the year of the old towers' removal, various schemes were drawn up to provide the cathedral with suitable new towers. A committee under the then Lord Provost, and with an enthusiastic Dr. Cleland as secretary, drew up admirable proposals, raised a lot of local money and secured a government grant; but by some mischance, the old towers came down and the new did not go up, so that the cathedral has since been left with its present somewhat shorn appearance.

Once the cathedral was established, the next important event was the building of Old Glasgow Bridge, a fine stone erection of eight arches, which Bishop Rae and Lady Lochow caused to be put across the Clyde in 1345 at the Stockwell shallows, on the site of an earlier wooden bridge mentioned by Blind Harry in his poem "Wallace" as "Glasgow bryg that byggy★ was of tree." Old Glasgow Bridge was a toll bridge. Those who were unwilling to pay still used the ancient ford. So solidly did the masons put the bridge together that, with minor alterations of various kinds, it carried traffic for more than five centuries, being replaced only in 1847.

Medieval Glasgow, protected from the marauding Norsemen by its position up-river and the sandy shallows of the Clyde, developed around the cathedral its criss-cross pattern of streets. To the south-west, there were buildings connected with the cathedral: the palace or castle of the bishops, and later archbishops, with its great hall built by Bishop John Cameron

★Built.

between 1426 and 1446, added to by Archbishop James Beaton
early in the sixteenth century and by Gavin Dunbar about 1540;
and in the surrounding streets the prebendary manses of the
cathedral canons. Their houses in Drygate, Rottenrow, Kirk
Street and Castle Street all had orchards and gardens. Only one
has survived, Provand's Lordship, the manse of the prebendary of
Barlanark, whose alternative title was Laird of Provan. Built
about 1470, with wings added or adapted two centuries later, it is
Glasgow's only surviving domestic medieval building. Yet the
medieval city played an important part in Scottish life, some of
its bishops being made Chancellors of their country. But the
development of trade with the Continent gradually gave the
east coast greater political importance. Thus the ecclesiastical
centre moved to St. Andrews, where Scotland's first university
was established half a century before Glasgow's, and Edinburgh
eventually became the Scottish capital.

However, the founding of Glasgow University by Bishop
William Turnbull in 1451, on a site in Rottenrow, made it
certain that, whatever temporary set-back in trade the move to
the east might have produced, the city's future importance was
assured. The university later moved to the site south of the
cathedral, where it graced the city until the seventeenth century.

So far as can now be established, medieval Glasgow, with land
to spare, did not feel any need to emulate Edinburgh's cramped-
up towering tenements or 'lands'. Many of Glasgow's houses
were single-storeyed thatched cottages; others had wooden upper
storeys, rather like Edinburgh's Huntly House in the Canongate.
After 1450, the bounds of the city extended. Stretching at that
time from the Cathedral in the north, south to the Blackfriars
Monastery, and from Drygate in the east to what became in
Victorian times Balmano Street on the west, several extensions
were made: one, south from Blackfriars Monastery to the Cross
along the line of High Street; another to the east, over the Gallow
Muir in the line of the Gallowgate; and a third westwards as far
as the Tron, named after the 'trone' or weighing machine put up
towards the end of the fifteenth century. Although the town was
not walled, it did have ports at the end of its principal streets.

The older name for the Trongate had been St. Thenew's Gate,
named after the well and chapel dedicated to Mungo's mother,
on what is now St. Enoch Square (the modern name being a
corruption, through the halfway stage at St. Tennoch, of Saint

Thenew). One of the many other medieval chapels or churches that have disappeared without trace was the Collegiate Church of the Blessed St. Mary, on the south side of Trongate (where the Tron Kirk now stands), founded in the 1520s by a sub-dean of Glasgow, James Houston, and destroyed by fire in 1793. A little to the west of it was the Sang Schule, run by one of the prebendaries.

St. Nicholas Hospital, founded by Bishop Muirhead in 1460, which survived until 1808, stood on the west side of Castle Street. Glasgow Green, tree-covered, was then the Bishop's Forest. On the other side of the river stood that necessary adjunct to life in the Middle Ages, the Leper Hospital.

Isolated on their ends of islands, the Scots have traditionally cared little for their environment. Until the national character began to decline in the twentieth century under such pressures as the speeding-up of means of communication and the consequent tendency for United Kingdom government to become more firmly centralized in London, Scots energies were convulsed first by long-drawn-out differences of religious opinion, and then by the quasi-religious fever and fervour of industrial and commercial expansion. As with some other countries where Reformers carried the day, the sense of environment was all but swept away along with the aesthetic associations of the old Catholic forms of worship. The favoured god became Mammon, euphemistically dubbed Progress, regardless of what course he might eventually lead his worshippers.

The Archbishop's Castle was badly damaged by the Reformers, and, though restored by Archbishop Spottiswoode in 1611 (when he also put lead back on the Cathedral roof), was in ruins by the end of the century. In 1755 the magistrates sanctioned its use as a quarry, and its foundations disappeared to make way for Robert Adam's Royal Infirmary in 1792. Several disastrous fires, one early in the seventeenth century lasting three days, removed some of the surrounding domestic buildings. Most of what was still left disappeared between 1864 and the late 1880s, when the university moved to Gilmorehill and the City Improvement Trust swept all before it in an enthusiastic sustained wave of zealous social, if architectually misguided, reform.

Within the modern city's boundaries, traces of a few pre-Reformation castles or houses survive: Crookston, standing above the junction of the River Levern and the White Cart; Cathcart

Castle; and Provan Hall, now joined to an eighteenth-century house, but once the manor of the Lords of Provan whose prebendary occupied Provand's Lordship.

Although the physical violence associated with the Reformation erupted mostly in the east of Scotland, such a national holocaust was bound to be felt severely in a place which had for so long been an ecclesiastical centre. The cathedral was badly damaged, but was repaired by voluntary public subscription after 1574. Not only the fabric of Glasgow was affected by the triumph of Protestantism in Scotland in 1560; the whole social orientation of St. Mungo's Glasgow was deprived of its purpose.

In times such as these, Glasgow could not entirely escape disturbances to its peace. There was, for instance, the Battle of the Butts in 1544, when during Queen Mary's minority the heir-presumptive, James Hamilton, Earl of Arran, was appointed Regent, an appointment which the Queen's Regent the Earl of Lennox could not abide. So Lennox garrisoned the Bishop's Palace in Glasgow, and retired to Dumbarton Castle. The Regent besieged the palace with an army equipped with cannon, and after ten days accepted the capitulation of the garrison on honourable terms. No sooner did the besieged men emerge, however, than all but two, who somehow escaped, were massacred.

To avenge this murder, Lennox and the Earl of Glencairn decided to march through Clydesdale and devastate the Hamilton lands. Hamilton got word of their intention, and decided to occupy Glasgow. Glencairn's troops forestalled him. A fierce, if small-scale, battle took place at the Butts, or scene of the holiday of the 'wappenschaw' exercises. Glencairn's side might well have won the day had not Robert Boyd of Kilmarnock arrived with a detachment of horse to aid Hamilton, misleading Glencairn's men into believing that a whole new army had taken the field against them. As they fled, the Regent entered Glasgow, his troops plundering so extensively that, according to one contemporary, they even removed the doors and window-frames from the houses.

Just over two decades later, there was the affray which resulted in the urgent flight into France in 1560 of the last Catholic archbishop, James Beaton, taking with him the cathedral's treasures and relics and the records of the see from the earliest times. On that occasion "James duke of Chatelherault, erle of Arran, Lord Hamiltoune" had gone back on his undertaking of 1550 to defend the archbishop, the cathedral and its possessions against anyone who might attack them. Indeed, Hamilton went over to the Protestants, attacked the cathedral and destroyed the altars and relics therein, and took possession of the palace, from which he was with some difficulty expelled by a detachment of the Queen Regent, Mary of Guise's troops. What the archbishop took with him went partly to the Scots College in Rome and partly to the Charteuse in Paris, from which they were rescued and returned to Scotland by the patriotic Abbé Macpherson, a member of the Scots College, when the French Revolution again threatened them.

There was also the final episode which, in three-quarters of an hour on 13th May 1568, for ever lost Mary, Queen of Scots her throne. News was brought to the Regent Moray that his half-sister had escaped from Lochleven Castle, and was making with her forces for Dumbarton Castle, then still a Marian stronghold, where she could perhaps have held out until events moved more in her favour. Gathering round him the Earls of Glencairn, Montrose, Mar and Monteith, the Lords Semple, Home and Lindsay and Kirkcaldy of Grange, the Regent took up his position at the head of an army of about four thousand, many of them Glaswegians. He had set up camp on the Burgh Muir—which ran from Glasgow Green, through Borrowfield, to the cathedral—when news reached him that the Queen's forces were moving towards Renfrew, intending to cross the Clyde there. The importance of the hill of Langside then became considerable. The Regent's troops were able to move to it quickly, before Mary's forces, hampered by the illness of the Earl of Argyll, could reach it.

When the Queen's forces reached the top of the hill, they were too exhausted to be able to deal with the Regent's pikesmen. Even so, the fighting was severe, and Sir James Melvil of Halhill, who was present with Mary and who described the battle in his *Memoirs*, tells us that the long pikes were "so closely crossed and interlaced, that when the soldiers behind discharged their pistols, and threw them or the staves of their shattered weapons in the faces of their enemies, they never reached the ground but remained lying on the spears".

At the moment when the battle was wavering, Kirkcaldy brought up the Regent's reserves. Under pressure from their attack the Queen's forces gave way and a general flight followed.

Bothwell parted from his wife for a future which was to include his incredibly unlucky capture by a Norwegian sea captain whose daughter he had seduced many years before; imprisonment in Malmo Castle, Sweden; and, when it became clear that he was no longer a political pawn of any value, final degradation and death in chains in a cell of Dragsholm Castle, Denmark.

His wife the Queen, who had been watching the battle from a hill near Cathcart House, just over a mile to the rear, fled in such terror, it was said, that she never slackened rein till she reached Sanquhar, 60 miles away. She rested at Terregles, Dumfriesshire, before crossing the Solway into England, to throw herself on the mercy of English Elizabeth—mercy that was to mean eighteen years of imprisonment ending with death on the block at Fotheringay.

By this time, the changes to which these various troubles gave rise were beginning to affect the civil governance of Glasgow. When Archbishop Beaton left for France of his own accord, neither he nor his bishops had been legally divested of their temporalities. There therefore followed the appointment by the King of a series of 'Tulchan' bishops, so called because they represented calves, the milk of their benefices being drawn off not by them but by lay favourites of the court or officers of state.

Some of the 'Tulchans', like the gentle Archbishop Leighton and the historian Archbishop Spottiswoode—he who, before he was translated to St. Andrews, did his best to restore both cathedral and palace—were distinguished men. Others were not. None were viewed with great favour by the citizens. One of them, Robert Montgomery, was appointed Protestant Archbishop of Glasgow in 1581, on the understanding that in his case the milk-pail was to be the Lennox family. This arrangement so annoyed Glaswegians that prior occupation of the cathedral pulpit by a Presbyterian preacher, Robert Howie, was arranged, so that Montgomery's induction could not take place. The Provost of Glasgow, Sir Matthew Stewart of Minto, thereupon forced his way into the cathedral with a band of men, to carry out the royal wishes. During the ensuing struggle, Howie was pulled from the pulpit and lost part of his beard and several teeth. The preacher thereupon brought down a curse upon the head of Sir Matthew and his family. One Victorian historian traced the efficacy of this curse to the eventual impoverished extinction of Sir Matthew's descendants, though doubtless other factors played a part. In any case, Montgomery had to resign—he ended his days as parish minister at Stewarton in Ayrshire—though another 'Tulchan' was appointed in his place. The system continued until Scots exasperation with episcopacy as a system of Church government finally erupted in 1638.

Direct Church rule over Glasgow had ended in 1450, when the city became a Burgh of Regality, Bishop Turnbull and his successors then holding their authority on behalf of the King. In 1636, Glasgow became a Royal Burgh, responsible directly to King and Parliament. The growth of the traders and merchants of the middle class throughout the seventeenth century brought about a new social balance.

In 1605, the Trades House and the Merchants' House both received recognition. The traders were mostly shopkeepers and craftsmen, there being already a dozen crafts by 1600. The merchants were the wealthier exporters and importers. These two legal corporations took over the running of the city from the heads of the Church, and for more than two hundred years effectively controlled the town council.

Just before the Cathedral was demoted, it was visited by the future successful Parliamentary general in the English Civil War, Sir William Brereton. Thirty years old and with the politico-religious problems of the day not yet his concern, he arrived in Glasgow on 1st July 1634. He thought the cathedral "a brave and ancient place", and commented on the medieval lay-out of the city's streets: "two streets like a cross, in the middle of which the Cross is placed, which looks four ways into four streets". The second "Cross" in Brereton's word-play was the mercat cross, which stood at the junction of Rottenrow, Drygate and High Street, Glasgow's heart. Brereton was still able to admire "the Archbishop of Glasgow's Palace", and the university's Faculty of Arts, one side of which had been newly built. He was also able to get a good view of the changing city from the top of the nine-year-old Tolbooth. Although he could hardly have known it, he was surveying a Glasgow embarked upon one of these massive shifts of energy which were to occur and recur over succeeding centuries.

III

TRADE AND MERCHANTS

Though the sight which greeted Brereton's gaze from the top of the Tolbooth tower included both medieval ecclesiastical Glasgow before it was too seriously affected by decay and destruction, and the foundations of the new trading Glasgow which was to grow from small beginnings throughout most of the seventeenth century and flourish in the eighteenth, the city had not yet experienced the end of its trade-hampering troubles over religion.

While the National Covenant which defied the King's intention to perpetuate episcopacy in Scotland was signed on 28th February 1638 in Greyfriars Kirk, Edinburgh, the Assembly of November that year which gave practical implementation to its proposed reforms took place in Glasgow Cathedral.

Laud's liturgy had already provoked a certain amount of trouble when it had been introduced the previous year. On that occasion, the Reverend William Annan, who had preached a sermon defending the liturgy, was set upon in the dark by "some hundreds of enraged women of all qualities . . . with staves and peats". They beat him sore until "his cloak ruff and hat were rent". One or two of "the meanest" of his attackers were arrested and imprisoned, but it was not possible to deal in this way with so large a body of dissidents. Consequently, there was some anxiety in the official mind as the day for the meeting of the Assembly approached. The magistrates bought a special supply of "muskets, staffs and bandelieris", to say nothing of powder and pikes, with which they equipped "ane gaird of men" to preserve the peace while the town was full of strangers come to the Assembly.

The aristocracy was well represented, Rothes, Wemyss, Balmerino, Lindsay, Yester, Eglinton and Loudon among them. Each of the four Scottish universities sent three representatives. In all, there were present 14 ministers, two professors and ninety-eight elders from presbyteries and burghs.

The elders themselves represented a social cross-section, there being among them seventeen noblemen, nine knights, twenty-five lairds and forty-seven burgesses. But, as one contemporary historian aptly put it, in the midst of this company there were "ane, twa or thrie of ablest convenanting ministeris with ane twa or thrie reulling elders who sould voice as they voiced".

To preside over these people, the King had appointed the heir to the Scottish crown through the Stewarts, the Marquis of Hamilton, great-grandson of that James Hamilton, Duke of Chatelherault and Earl of Arran, who had so sharply let down Archbishop Beaton at the time of the Reformation by switching his allegiance to the Reformers. It was the most impressive gathering of its kind that Glasgow had ever witnessed, although the marquis, no doubt aware of the academic quality of so many of them, was distressed to observe that "not a gown was among them all, but many had swords and daggers about them".

After some fairly typical Scots quarrelling about procedure, Alexander Henderson, a minister from Leuchars, was appointed Moderator—he who once proclaimed that "the visible Church only demanded the destruction of the flesh for the saving of the soul", a doctrine, as Cyril Pearl has remarked, "which Torquemada would have recognized".

It quickly became clear that the intention of the Assembly was to alter the whole system of church government in defiance of the King. Therefore on Wednesday 28th March, after seven sittings, the Marquis of Hamilton formally left the cathedral and, under warrant from the King, declared the Assembly dissolved. In fact the Assembly refused to be dissolved, and under the Earl of Argyll, who threw in his lot with the Covenanters, declared null and void most of the previous Assemblies of the century on account of kingly interference, condemned the Prayer Book, the Book of Canons, the Court of High Commission and the Five Articles of Perth, excommunicated the bishops, refused to allow ministers to take any civil office or to sit in Parliament and declared episcopacy to be unlawful.

King Charles raised an army but, confronted with the Covenanting army on the Borders, decided that he could not fight it. The resulting negotiations, though not directly concerned with Glasgow, meant that by 1641, as J. M. Reid puts it in *Kirk and Nation*, the Covenanters had "all that they had ever hoped for. The

David Dale;

Alexander Speirs;

Robert Napier;

Hugh Tennent

Four famous Glaswegians:

Scottish Kirk and states could rule themselves in their own way. Scotland was free to make her own future".

Having achieved this success, the Scots unfortunately made the mistake of trying to foist their Presbyterian form of Church government on England, which was the real purpose of the Solemn League and Covenant passed by the General Assembly and the Scots Parliament in August, 1643, and by the English Parliament a few weeks later. It soon became apparent that the English and Scottish interpretations of reformation "according to the Word of God and the example of the best Reformed Churches" differed. The decision of the Presbyterian Scots to fight with the English Parliament against their king produced a rising in Scotland itself, under the Marquis of Montrose, who had some successes against his rival Argyll, now also a marquis.

As every schoolboy knows, Cromwell's New Model Army got hold of Charles. The Scots tried to rescue him, but were defeated at Preston. Cromwell thereupon had the King tried and executed. The Scots could not forget that the King was, after all, a Stewart, and proclaimed his son Charles II. Cromwell thereupon invaded Scotland, and by August 1651 had the country powerless before him.

So it came about that one Sunday in 1650 Cromwell made a formal procession to the cathedral to hear a sermon by the minister of the nearby Barony Church, the Reverend Zachary Boyd. Boyd preached a lengthy sermon, during which he vigorously attacked Cromwell and the English Independents. The Protector listened stolidly, but Thurloe, Cromwell's secretary, whispered to his master, "Shall I pistol the scoundrel?" "No, no," Cromwell replied, "We will manage him another way." The Protector thereupon invited Boyd to a supper which ended with a prayer of several hours duration, lasting till three o'clock in the morning.

Boyd, incidentally, left his not inconsiderable fortune to Glasgow University on condition that they should publish a collected edition of his verse. Several of the more banal of the Scottish metrical paraphrases are Boyd's work. His most ambitious effort, "Zion's Flowers", contains a dialogue in which Potiphar's Wife tempts Joseph, of which this is the dramatic climax:

3

A view of the Trongate from the east, circa *1770*
George Square, circa *1840*

Potiphar's Wife.
Now time is come. My heart it springs for haste,
About his neck my milk-white arms to cast.
I'll hold him, hug him, saying Welcome mine!
Dear mine thou art, and I am also thine!
Here's fair occasion; why desire we thus
To sport in love? None is to hinder us.
While we have time now let us do with speed.
Lovers must dare, and for no dangers dread.
Why burn we daylight? We have time and place—
My dearest Heart, now let me thee embrace!

Joseph
Madam, madam! How far misled ye are!
Think that ye are the wife of Potiphar,
My noble lord, who doth us all command.
He would not look to get this from your hand.
Sith as ye hear the matters so and so,
Now loose your grips, and quickly let me go.
If from you I this favour cannot find,
I'll rather choose to leave my cloak behind.

Potiphar's Wife
O dule! O dule! Help, help! O dule, O dule!
I am abused by a slave—a fool!

The university took Boyd's money, but put off publishing his
verses for so long that in the end they were able to get away with
erecting a small bust of him instead.

The ordinary folk of Glasgow had plenty to put up with,
apart from Cromwell. There are even grounds for supposing that
they did not too much dislike his dour enforced calm. Between
the Reformation in 1560 and 1786, when Burns so mercilessly
flayed in verse the retreating ministerial tyrants, the Kirk imposed
a joyless regime sometimes featuring plain masochistic cruelty.
There was scarcely any aspect of life into which the Church did
not peer and pry, punishing with vicious energy such 'crimes' as
absenting oneself from service, or 'gaming' on the Sabbath. The
use of informers was actively encouraged, not only to seek out
parties guilty of 'fornication' so that they could be humiliated
upon the stool of repentance week after week, according to the
supposed enormity of their crime, but also in less heinous cases.
Thus, as late as 1690, the town council of Glasgow, at the request

of the Church, adjured "the inhabitants and others residing within this burgh, that they, nor nane of thame drink in any tavern after ten o'clock at night on the week days under paine of forty shillings Scots to be payed by the furnisher of the drink, and twentie shillings Scots by the drinker". One half of this was to be used for the relief of the poor and the other half to pay the informer. This disagreeable 'nebby' (interferingly curious) aspect of the Scots character was assiduously developed, surviving in all its prurient obnoxiousness well into the nineteenth century.

The Kirk's worst penalties were naturally reserved for sexual offences. St. Paul of Tarsus had much to answer for in having established these guilt complexes associated with sex which the Calvinists used to torture themselves and those who fell under their influence. Fear, even hatred of sexual pleasure succeeded the trials and torture of witches as a favourite church-approved pastime. It is therefore hardly surprising that when Glasgow's God-fearing town councillors bought the Prebendary manse of Cambuslang from the Earl of Glencairn to be a "house of correction" for "dissolute women", the Kirk Session saw to it that those confined there should be "whipped every day during pleasure".

Religious inflictions apart, Glaswegians had also temporal tribulations to bear. There had been an outbreak of plague in 1647 so serious that the professors and the students from the university betook themselves off to Irvine. A fire had destroyed many of Glasgow's thatched-roof houses in 1600. Over a thousand families were made homeless in June 1652, when the 'great fire' of Glasgow destroyed one third of the town's housing-stock. It is therefore not surprising that in May 1657, Glasgow acquired its first "ingyne for casting water on land that is on fyre".

The restoration of Charles II in 1660 was not greeted in Scotland with as much enthusiasm as it aroused in England, because true Scots feared that before long he would once again try to force episcopacy upon them.

No one has ever satisfactorily explained whether the Scots themselves masochistically created the early excesses of Presbyterianism, or whether the system was foisted upon them by chance historical circumstance and they simply grew used to such absurdities as the alleged existence of a chosen body, 'the Elect', who could do no wrong, and the preordained damnation of the majority, who had no possible means of escaping the torments of hell—"ten thousand times ten millions of dayes" of it, according to one mathematically inclined seventeenth-century divine and so a member of 'the Elect'. Whatever the reason, the defence of the system became a matter of life or death concern for many Scots.

In 1662 the King appointed the Minister of Duns, Andrew Fairfoul, Archbishop of Glasgow, arming him with strong civil powers. Few of the Church's ministers would acknowledge his authority, and so, on 1st November, an edict was pronounced which banished the dissenting clergy from their churches and manses.

The 'killing time', when the Covenanters were a kind of human game, followed. They won a victory at Drumclog and marched to Glasgow, where Graham of Claverhouse and the royal forces had retired. Thereby the Covenanters attack was repulsed. The city narrowly escaped an organized burning* after the battle of Bothwell Brig, when the Duke of Monmouth's officers did their best to persuade him to destroy Glasgow.

A number of Covenanters were executed in Glasgow in 1666. Others suffered the same fate in 1684, having their heads cut off and publicly exhibited, while the Tolbooth was so crowded with prisoners that, according to tradition, they had to sleep in turns.

The citizens thus at first welcomed the arrival of James II and VII to the throne, although when he needed their help in 1688, 1,200 men raised for the purpose refused to obey the magistrates and would not leave the city. By then the hopes of Glaswegians were centred on William of Orange, hopes that were also to be frustrated, though in a strictly secular manner.

In 1695 the Scottish Parliament passed an Act giving powers to a company trading to Africa and the Indies. On advice from the economist William Paterson, who later became the founder of the Bank of England, the company decided to establish a colony at Darien, in Panama. On 26th July 1698, the first pioneer ships sailed from Leith, reaching Darien on 4th November with the loss of only fifteen men. Although their fort of New Caledonia was set up successfully, lack of provisions, sickness and some indiscipline amongst the settlers, together with the fever-laden Panama climate (which was later to wreak similar havoc among the workers engaged on the construction of the Panama Canal) decimated the colony, who re-embarked in three ships in June, 1699.

The hostility of the English traders and colonizers who operated

*Accidental burnings had done great damage in 1652, and again in 1677.

from more salubrious bases in the Americas, very much irked the
Scots. From the Scots point of view, the Darien Scheme had to
succeed. So the second expedition began to sail in the middle of
1699, four frigates leaving Rothesay Bay on 14th September,
carrying 1,200 emigrants (including the last of the Stewarts of
Minto) and £3,000 sterling invested by the city council on behalf
of Glasgow's citizens, to say nothing of much of the fortunes and
personal savings of private individuals.

When the final company of this second force arrived, under
Captain Alexander Campbell of Forrest, it was to find that a
Spanish force of about 1,600 men was encamped nearby at
Tubacanti, waiting only the arrival of a Spanish squadron to
attack the fort. Campbell decided to attack first, and inflicted a
surprise defeat on the soldiers. But the Scots forces could not
stand up to the Spanish squadron when it did arrive, and New
Caledonia had to capitulate.

Less than fifty emigrants managed to make their way back to
Scotland. By then, about the middle of 1700, news of the disaster
had reached Glasgow. Whole families were ruined, and when it
was learned that the English West India colonists, with the
connivance of the English government, had been forbidden to
trade with the Scots, there was anger as well as despair in Glasgow
hearts. It was beginning to look as if the English design, on both
the secular and the religious fronts, was to bring Scotland to her
knees.

Throughout this century of religious and economic upheaval,
the physical shape of Glasgow had been changing. The increasing
population—4,500 in 1560, about 7,000 by 1600 and 9,994 in
1701*—crowded into houses built on the long riggs or gardens
of the houses that fronted the main streets. The street plan
remained more or less unaltered. New merchants' houses were
built or rebuilt (all of them have since disappeared). Some of them,
like the mansion of the Campbells of Blythswood in Bridgegait,
and Silvercraigs Land, in the Saltmarket, were undoubtedly
imposing.

The university, probably the work of John Mylne, consisted of
"two roughly square courts, arranged like those of a Cambridge
college, with a tall steeple placed asymmetrically over the range
which separated the two. One court was partly arcaded on the

*The peak population of Glasgow in the seventeenth century was reached
in 1660, when the figure was 14,678.

ground floor..."* Except for a gate, transplanted in the nineteenth century to the New University on Gilmorehill, and a largely rebuilt and internal staircase, also transferred, nothing else survives the sad decision of those city fathers of the 1860s, who, for the best possible sociological reasons, destroyed so much that could have been saved and would have left Glasgow a more gracious physical character than it has since been able to construct for itself.

Three seventeenth-century towers of other public buildings have survived. The square-fronted five-storeyed Tolbooth or Town House, put up in the 1620s, was partly rebuilt and gothicized in 1814 by David Hamilton, but pulled down, except for the elegant seven-storey steeple, in 1921. The steeple, islanded by traffic as it now is, has more than once been threatened by those who think the smooth passage of vehicles more important than the visual satisfaction of people. However, perhaps the improved attitude to environmental quality of the late twentieth century means that it will never again be in real danger.

The Merchants' Hall in Bridgegait, built in 1629 by Campbell of Blythswood, a member of one of Glasgow's oldest trading families, was arranged round a courtyard, and included a hospital and guildhall, all of which were pulled down in 1817, again excepting the steeple which now surmounts the Fishmarket. Its attribution to the great Sir William Bruce is no longer thought to be probable.

The third survival has a medieval link, since the Tron Kirk was a rebuilding (1592) of the collegiate church of St. Mary and St. Anne, the spire being added in the 1630s. The main body of the church was accidentally set on fire by members of the Hell Fire Club, who had taken refuge in it after a debauch, and rebuilt by James Adam in 1793. At one time, the Tron, or weight-beam, was housed in the tower, although it was taken out in 1853 when the present arches were put up. Tower and building survive, a plumbers' store for the Corporation of Glasgow.

While Hutcheson's Hospital founded by George and Thomas Hutcheson of Lambhill survives, only the two statues of the founders are older than 1805, the date of the present building. The original building of 1641 stood in the Trongate, but was removed so that Hutcheson Street could be connected with the Trongate.

Much of the growing trade in the earlier part of the seven-

*Architecture of Glasgow.

teenth century came up the river in small boats, Glasgow's harbour at Newark (later Port Glasgow) intended to meet the needs of expanding foreign trades, not being built until 1688.

When Cromwell had the idea of incorporating Scotland "into ane Commonwealth with England" in 1652, he appointed Commissioners to go to Scotland and enforce such a union, and at the same time "by all possible waies and meanes to inform themselves of the state of that countrie, and consider of the readiest and best way for settling and continuing the peace and good government of the same". On 17th August 1655 Thomas Tucker, Registrar to the Commissionaires for the Excise in England, was instructed to proceed to Scotland to "give his assistance in settling the excise and customs there". Thus it came about that we have an impartial record of the kind of foreign trading in which Glasgow was already engaged in the middle of the century.

Of Glasgow, Tucker recorded that all but the students of the College were "traders and dealers: some from Ireland with small smiddy coales, in open boats from four to ten tonnes, from whence they bring hoopes, ringes, barrell staves"—all things needed for the craft of coopering—"meale, oates and butter; some [for] France with pladding, coales and herring, for which they return salt, paper, rosins [raisins] and prunes—some to Norway for timber and every ane theyr neighbours the Highlanders, who come hither from the isles and western parts."

Tucker, not unnaturally, was a great believer in the beneficent effects of trade. He was impressed by the situation of Glasgow, in spite of the fact that "no vessels of any burden could come nearer than 14 miles", and by "the mercantile genius of the people". He also inspected the ports on the Clyde which came under the Glasgow Collector, and thus saw Newark, not yet reconstructed as Glasgow's official port but already the place "where all vessels doe ride, unlode, and send theyr goods up river to Glasgow in small boates"; Greenock, where "small open boats trade in fish with the Western Isles and with Ireland"; Fairlie, Kelburn and Saltcoats, "from which fish and cattell were carried into Ireland"; Bute, where the inhabitants were all "countreymen and cowherds, who feede cattell and spinne, and make some woollen clothe which [they carry] to be dyed and dressed at Glasgowe, where they bring . . . whatever they have occasion of for theyr expence and provision"; and Irvine, then a small port "clogged and choaked up with sand, which the Western Sea beats into it, soe as it wrestles for life to maintaine a small trade to France, Norway and Ireland, with herring and other goods brought on horseback from Glasgow, for the purchasing [of] timber, wine, and other comodityes to supply theyr occasions with".

Tucker's fellow Cromwellian, Richard Franck, a trooper in the Protector's army, had found himself in Glasgow on his professional duties about the same period. He recorded his impressions in his *Northern Memoirs* "writ in the year 1658". In the matter of trade he was, of course, a layman: even so, he commented on "the merchants and trades . . . whose store-houses and ware-houses are stuft with merchandize, as their shops swell big with foreign commodities and returns from France, and other remote parts. . . . Nor is this all, for the staple of their country consists of linens, friezes, furs, tartans, pelts. . . . They generally exceed in good French wines, as they naturally superabound with fish and fowl". Incidentally, Franck also commented on "the splendour and gaiety of this city of Glasgow, which surpasseth most, if not all the corporations of Scotland". He admired Glasgow's "four large fair streets, modell'd, as it were, into a spacious quadrant; in the centre whereof their market-place is fixed: near unto which stands a stately tolbooth, a very sumptuous, regulated, uniform fabrick, large and lofty, most industriously and artificially carved from the very foundation to the superstructure . . . infinitely excelling the model and usual build of town halls . . . without exception, the paragon of beauty in the west".

In spite of Glasgow's religious troubles following the Restoration, the physical appearance of the city continued to impress travellers. John Ray, the Essex-born minister naturalist who prepared and published in Cambridge in 1660 the first catalogue of the plants of a district ever to be issued in England, but who was deprived of his minor fellowship at his *alma mater* by the Act of Uniformity, rode into Glasgow in 1662. No doubt he would have sympathies with the independence of mind being shown by this rebellious town. At any rate he thought it "fair, large, and well built, crosswise, somewhat like unto Oxford, the streets very broad and pleasant". The college itself struck him as being "a pretty stone building, and not inferior to Waltham and All Soul's in 'Oxon' ". Of the cathedral, he merely noted that "they call it now the High Kirk", and that they had divided it.

The most lyrical of all the recorded approval of late-seven-teenth-century Glasgow, however, comes from the English clergyman John Browne, who saw the city in 1669. "Tis situated upon the River Glotta, or cluyd, over which is paved a very fair bridge, supported with eight arches, and for pleasantness of sight, sweetness of air and delightfulness of its gardens and orchards enriched with most delicious fruits, surpasseth all other places in this tract."

The circumstance which enabled the children of these enter-prising citizens of Glasgow who had produced this prosperous and pleasant place to take the next step forward was the Act of Union of 1707.

There was opposition to it in Glasgow while it was being negotiated. Indeed, as a result of a sermon preached in the Tron Kirk by the Reverend James Clark on 7th November 1706, a mob assembled, overthrew the attempts of the magistrates to restore law and order and attacked the council chambers and the home of the Provost of the city, forcing him to flee to Edinburgh. A Jacobite publican by the name of Finlay persuaded some of the rioters to march with him to Edinburgh, with the intention of overthrowing Parliament. When they heard that a body of soldiers was on its way from Edinburgh to put down the riot, Finlay's men returned to Glasgow and separated. He and some others were arrested, but pardoned after the Act had become law.

It is perhaps difficult for us to imagine the feelings of those more educated Scots who saw nothing but advantage in the Union. They had endured a century of religious upheaval in which they were frequently at odds with England, culminating in the defeat, with English connivance, of their economically vital Darien trading venture. With the hindsight of two and a half centuries, it is easier for us to see that the advantages of federal union as recommended by that statesman and patriot Andrew Fletcher of Saltoun, rather than the incorporating union which in fact took place, would probably have been equally beneficial to the growth of the Scottish economy, and might have prevented that sapping of Scottish initiative which, throughout the twentieth century, has robbed Scotland of control of her industries to such an extent that to try to name half a dozen major Scottish-owned firms located in or near Glasgow in the year 1970 is a difficult task.

However, we cannot take refuge in history. Daniel Defoe, who had spent some time among the Scots as an English spy with the task of furthering the Union by all possible means, declared of the Scots just after the "auld sang" had ended:

If nothing else were the consequence of the Union, this must be allowed, that they are thereby disarmed from the power of doing themselves right against us, in a parliamentary manner, which strongly implies that they are more particularly in the parliamentary justice that remains, and that we ought to esteem everything that touches the honour of Scotland nationally as equally affecting all Britain. Nay, we should be nicer in an affront to the nation and nobility of Scotland, by how much the more frankly they have by the Union given themselves, as it were, into our hands.

England has not normally regarded the nations she has swallowed with such open generosity; nor did she always remember so to regard Scotland.

There were, of course, discouragements to the continuation of such amiability in that, self-interest apart, it was from Scotland that the two Jacobite risings of 1715 and 1745 erupted.

Glasgow was not directly affected by the Earl of Mar's attempts in 1715 on behalf of the Old Pretender, James VII and II's son (incidentally the year in which Glasgow's first newspaper appeared, the thrice-weekly *Glasgow Courant*, twelve pages at one penny to subscribers). The city raised a force of between five and six hundred volunteers, paid at the rate of 8d. a day, to aid the Government. It was used mainly for guarding Stirling Castle and the approaches to that town while the Duke of Argyll marched to Sheriffmuir. There, in a skirmish rather than a battle, Mar's Highlanders were put to flight. Glasgow's own defences were thus never tested, though the city's patience was, when, in 1710, the magistrates were protesting about having to maintain 353 of the Duke of Argyll's prisoners in the former Bishop's Castle, a guard of 100 being needed, rather surprisingly, to ensure their security. In 1718, however, the Government reimbursed the city just over £735 to meet their expenses.

The Glasgow forces were under Colonel William Maxwell of Cardonald, who, for his loyal pains, and as a mark of the city's gratitude for services rendered, was presented with "a silver tankard, weighting forty-eight unce, thirteen drop, at 7s. sterling per unce; and a sett of sugar boxes, weighting nineteen unce, fourteen drop, at 8s. per unce; and a server wing, weighting thirty-one unce and twelve drop, at 6s 4d per unce". The record of such precise particulars is perhaps a minor indication of Glasgow's growing commercial awareness.

Ten years later Glasgow had to contend with another riot, this time over the imposition of a malt tax, 3d. on every barrel of beer. On 23rd June 1725, the day upon which this tax on beer came into operation, a mob attacked Shawfield (where Glassford Street now is), the home of Daniel Campbell, Glasgow's Member of Parliament, who had voted for the tax. A detachment of soldiers commanded by a Captain Bushnell failed to suppress the rioters. Eventually, under the provocation of a shower of stones, the soldiers fired on the mob, killing two people. Fearful of the consequences of a further clash, Provost Miller ordered Captain Bushnell to withdraw his men. As they made their way to Dumbarton Castle, a further nine citizens were shot and killed.

General Wade then arrived to occupy the city, accompanied by the Lord Advocate, Duncan Forbes of Culloden, who caused nineteen people to be arrested and taken by Captain Bushnell to the Tolbooth in Edinburgh. Forbes, for good measure, also ordered the arrest of the Provost and all the magistrates, including some who had not been in Glasgow when the trouble arose. After a day's imprisonment, the city fathers were freed, and received back by welcoming crowds. Of the others arrested, two were forbidden to return to the city, nine were whipped through the city streets, and eight were given prison sentences. The magistrates thereupon did their best to bring Bushnell to trial for murder, but were prevented from doing so by the Government. Campbell petitioned Parliament for indemnification of his losses, and Glasgow was ordered to pay him over £6,000, which he used to buy land in Islay. Since there were additional mandatory expenses of more than a further £3,000, the Shawfield affair rankled long in the memories of Glaswegians. The deficit was met, ironically enough, by a special tax imposed by the corporation on ale and beer sold in the city.

Twenty years later they had more serious troubles to occupy their attentions. In September 1745 the magistrates received from Edinburgh a letter which today is preserved in the People's Palace, Glasgow Green. Its author was Prince Charles Edward Stewart, and its contents made the Shawfield losses seem trivial. The sum of £15,000 sterling was demanded by the prince, together with all arms then in the city and any arrears of taxes due to the Government.

At first the magistrates delayed paying up, having hopes that the troops of Sir John Cope would come to their assistance. Even before the Battle of Prestonpans put paid to that general's military usefulness, the Highland army's quartermaster, John Hay, an Edinburgh writer to the Signet, backed by members of the Clan MacGregor, turned up in person to collect their levy. Hay was persuaded to accept £5,000 in money and £500 in goods, as interim payment.

The volunteers raised by Glasgow to oppose the Jacobites took part in the Battle of Falkirk on 17th January 1746, the final Jacobite 'victory', if such it could be called, in which General Hawley was defeated and soon after which Linlithgow Palace was accidently set on fire by his shivering soldiers. Dugald Graham, a chapman versifier who later became bellman of Glasgow, was out with the Jacobite forces. In his usual atrocious verse he commemorated the Highland attitude to the Glasgow soldiers:

> The south side being fairly won,
> They faced north as had been done,
> Where next stood to bide the brush
> The Volunteers, who zealous
> Kept firing close till near surrounded,
> And by the flying horse confounded,
> They suffered sair into this place;
> No Highlander pity'd their case:
> 'Ye curs'd milita' they did swear,
> 'What a devil did bring you here?'

On the way north from Derby, the Prince and his army again entered Glasgow on 26th December 1745. Angry that the Glasgow Volunteers should have fought against him, the Prince this time demanded—and quickly got—6,000 coats, 12,000 linen shirts, 6,000 pairs of hose, a similar quantity of shoes and 6,000 blue bonnets. The Prince himself occupied Shawfield House, at the foot of Glassford Street, still the most elegant mansion in the city and then owned by John Glassford.

To instil some heart into his tired troops, the Prince held a review on Glasgow Green, on the Fleshers' Haugh. Robert Reid, who wrote *Glasgow Past and Present* under the pseudonym of 'Senex', no doubt heard from his own father that the Prince's 'newly-clad ragamuffins . . . marched to the Green by way of Saltmarket in splendid military array, with colours flying, drums beating, and the skirling notes of the Highland piobaireachd★ resounding from the pipes of every clan".

Another commentator recorded that the inhabitants of Glasgow "looked coldly" on the review, and indeed closed most of their shops by way of protest. The prince felt so bitter about his treatment while in Glasgow that he is supposed to have contemplated sacking the city before his troops evacuated it on 3rd January 1746, but was persuaded from such violent action by Cameron of Lochiel. Even so, Bailies Cameron and Coats made an enforced journey north as hostages for the balance of the goods demanded by the prince's quartermaster.

After the victory of the Duke of Cumberland at Culloden, Whiggish Glasgow hearts rejoiced, and Provost Andrew Cochrane (1693–1777), a merchant from Ayr who had settled in Glasgow in 1722 and prospered, set about trying to recover from the Government the £14,000 exacted from the city by the Jacobites. The 'hostage' bailies each received £13 15s. 8d. 'expenses' to cover the cost of their own enforced stay with the prince. In 1749 Parliament made a grant of £10,000 in part indemnification, and with that the Provost and his magistrates had to be content.

During the uncertain years after the Union, Scotland was still finding that English merchants from Bristol, Liverpool and Whitehaven were doing their best to obstruct their Glasgow counterparts through lawsuits charging them with, among other things, evading the duty on their importations of tobacco. However, in 1735, the wars of the French had the effect of closing many of the Atlantic ports of the south-west, and the trade came north. Sugar from the West Indies and tobacco from America came in in ever increasing quantities, and were then exported to England, France and the Low Countries. By 1775, more than half the tobacco imported to these islands was coming in through Glasgow.

In his later years Andrew Cochrane—himself a pioneer of the tobacco trade, a shipowner and a partner of the Glasgow Arms Bank—expressed the view that the spectacular rise of Glasgow was due to the business acumen of four men: Alexander Speirs of Elderslie, James Ritchie of Busby, William Cunninghame of

★Reid senior's knowledge of pipe-music must have been weak. While the Jacobites had doubtless much to lament, the pibroch is neither used for marching nor for collective performance.

Lainshaw, and John Glassford of Dougalston—who had started out in business without £10,000 between them.

Alexander Spiers (1714–82) was the biggest importer, owning a seventh of all that came into the Clyde, and a twelfth of what Europe imported. He used his immense fortune to buy Elderslie, the Renfrewshire lands associated with the memory of Sir William Wallace. In his lifetime a prudent speculator, after his death his fortune continued to help Glasgow, for his wife and daughter were generous in giving money for charities to be administered by the Merchants House, where Speirs's portrait hangs today.

Ritchie somehow managed to combine a dour business mien with a more relaxed *alter ego* when attending the meetings of the Hodge-Podge Club.

John Glassford (1715–83), Prince Charlie's unwilling host, though at one time owner of the largest number of ships and the second most important tobacco owner—according to Tobias Smollett in *Humphrey Clinker* (1771) he was known to have had "five-and-twenty ships with their cargoes his own property, and to have traded for above half-a-million sterling a year"—proved to be deficient in Glaswegian canniness, in that his speculations turned out in the end to be unsound. He was also such an enthusiastic gambler that he had a private gaming house built on his estate. He must nevertheless have been an interesting character. When the American War of Independence broke out, unlike his colleagues in the trade, he supported the revolutionaries.

The only one of the four tobacco 'lords' to live through the crash which followed the American upheaval was William Cunninghame (d. 1789), and he turned it to advantage by buying up all the existing stocks of tobacco on which he could lay his hands. With the fortune thus made through the profitable sale of what quickly became a very scarce commodity, he was able to buy his estate of Lainshaw in Ayrshire.

All four men are remembered in Glasgow, and the mansion of one of them, Cunninghame's house, still stands in what is now Royal Exchange Square. Built in 1788, it was enlarged between 1827 and 1832 by David Hamilton, when it became Glasgow's Royal Exchange. Indeed, it was held in so much affection that when there was a proposal to pull it down in the 1840s to join Ingram Street and Gordon Street, public outcry forced the planners to think again. It was further added to by David Thomson in

1880, and, with its Corinthian pillars to remind us of its second life, it now enjoys a third usefulness as Stirling's Library.

The Shawfield Mansion was demolished in 1795, but Glassford Street, which runs through what were its grounds, commemorates its most famous former owner.

There are a few humbler survivals of those years when the 'tobacco lords' walked the crown of the road dressed in scarlet cloaks and cocked hats and carrying gold-mounted canes, lesser persons making way for them as they swept past. The east side of Candleriggs, with its plain four-storey commercial buildings on top of warehouses, gives some idea of the sort of buildings in which tobacco fortunes were made. In spite of their names, Virginia Street and the Tobacco Exchange (later, Crown Arcade) both date from the second decade of the next century. In the Trongate itself, the best of these survivors of the tobacco days is number 182, formerly Spreull's Land; the street as a whole has suffered a sorry decline from the grace and dignity it must once have possessed. Daniel Defoe, who knew Glasgow both as 'Alexander Goldsmith', a spy amongst us sending back secret reports to Queen Anne's Minister, Robert Harley, and later, when he came openly on four short journeys made between 1724 and 1726 to enable him revise impressions for his *Travels Through Great Britain*, recorded that it made a vigorous impression on him.

He found the university, "a very spacious building, contains two large squares or courts, and the lodgings for the scholars and for the professors" which he pronounced "very handsome", adding "the whole building is of stone, very high and very august". Of the city itself, he wrote: "The four principal streets are the fairest for breadth and the finest built that I have ever seen in one city together. The houses are all of stone and generally equal and uniform in height, as well as in front; the lower story generally stands on vast square Dorrick columns, not round pillars and arches, which gives passage to the shops, adding to the strength as well as the beauty of the building. In a word, 'tis the cleanest and beautifullest and best built city in Britain, London excepted."

The most famous and probably the most distinguished building in eighteenth-century Glasgow was the town hall, put up eleven years after the third edition of Defoe's book had appeared. It was erected by Allan Dreghorn between 1737 and 1748, its style influenced by the piazzas of Covent Garden, designed by Inigo

Jones and Isaac de Caux after 1630. Added to at the end of the 1750s, its real fame, however, only came to it after 1780, when it was bought by the Tontine Society, whose chairman was Pat Colquhoun, a future provost of Glasgow. It was then remodelled inside by William Hamilton to include a coffee room, well stocked with newspaper and periodicals and "universally allowed" to be the most elegant of its kind in Britain, perhaps in Europe", and renamed the Tontine Hotel. The breadth and spaciousness of the street it dignified has, fortunately, been preserved for us in a picture painted by John Knox early in the nineteenth century, just before the long decline towards slumdom had begun.

Dreghorn, who was primarily an iron and lead merchant, is also credited with the beautiful St. Andrew's Church—he probably depended heavily upon his technical advisers—which went up in 1739 to form the eventual centre-piece of St. Andrews Square, laid out in 1768 but from which the original houses have now all gone or been so drastically altered as to be unrecognizable. Incidentally, Dreghorn is said to have had his own workmen build for him in 1752 the first four-wheeled carriage to be seen on Glasgow streets.

St. Enoch Square, begun in 1782, is also now unrecognizable in its original lay-out. The North British Hotel, though with an added storey and a new extension to the west, will soon be the sole reminder of the once-gracious George Square, which was laid out in 1787, but now, dwarfed by looming towers, has become the far from homogeneous modern heart of the city.

By the time the American War of Independence ended in 1783, the residents of these new squares, and of the more prosperous older parts of the city, had other forms of financial support than the revenues from the sale of tobacco on which to rely. Once ships began regularly to arrive with cargoes of tobacco, it was not long before Glaswegians realized that these same ships could carry on their outward journey articles manufactured in the city which would meet the growing day-to-day needs of those who, until the outbreak of war in 1775, were colonists.

John Gibson, whose *History of Glasgow* was published in 1777, listed the industries which had grown up in his own lifetime as including the manufacture of hardware, nails, shovels, threads and tapes, leathercraft, glass-making and—most important of them all—cotton textiles.

The 1780s marked the real impact of the Industrial Revolution

Claremont Terrace, circa 1852
The Royal Exchange, circa 1830

on Glasgow. From 1780 the pace of change quickened, and the old Scots way of life altered, both in the country and in the town. Before we allow ourselves to move forward with these changes, let us take a look at the social customs and enjoyments of those who lived in this still countrified city.

Alexander ('Jupiter') Carlyle, later Minister of Inveresk, and the man who successfully defied the Kirk's post-Reformation ban on theatre-going by attending a performance in Edinburgh of the verse tragedy of *Douglas* by his friend and neighbour, the Reverend John Home of Athelstaneford, recalled in his *Autobiography* his student days in the Glasgow of the 1740s. He considered that learning was then thought to be "an object of more importance" in Glasgow than in Edinburgh, but that Edinburgh had the advantage when it came to "manner of living, and in those accomplishments, and that taste that belong to people of opulence and persons of education". Glasgow had few 'gentry', and, according to Carlyle, the manner of living was "coarse and vulgar". In contrast with Edinburgh, less than half a dozen families had manservants, some of whom were kept by professors who took in boarders.

What was a typical middle-class day like in the tobacco era?

The merchants would have been up early to collect their mail, after which they returned home for a porridge and herring or egg breakfast, washed down by beer of their own brewing. Morning was the time for commercial bargaining. There followed a long lunch hour as afterwards the shops stayed open until eight. Then there was perhaps a final tavern hour, before supper was taken at home, followed by family prayers and a ten o'clock bedtime.

Some, however, varied this order of things, for Carlyle goes on: "The principal merchants took an early dinner with their families, and then resorted to the coffee-house or tavern to read the newspapers, which they generally did in companies of four or five in separate rooms, over a bottle of claret or a bowl of punch". Carlyle thought that the young ladies of his youth had ungainly manners (which he attributed in practical terms to the absence of a teacher of French or music in the city) and little otherwise to commend them but "good looks and fine clothes". Carlyle also tells us that living was cheap, it being possible to dine on roast beef, potatoes—turnips and potatoes had been introduced into Scotland in 1723—and small beer for 4d.

4

The College of Glasgow, circa 1690
The College of Glasgow as opened in 1870

Captain Thomas Hamilton, the son of Professor Hamilton, who occupied the Chair of Anatomy and Botany from 1781 to 1790, had been brought up in the Glasgow of the tobacco lords, along with his brother Sir William Hamilton, the philosopher. After fighting through the Peninsular Campaign, in which he was wounded, Captain Hamilton "commenced author" (to use Burns's phrase) by producing a novel, *Cyril Thornton*,* which Blackwood published in 1827. It is a racy tale in the Galtian manner, much of it set in Glasgow, where young Cyril Thornton comes to be educated, and where his uncle was David Spreull, whose "country-house in the Trongate formed part of a large tenement which he had originally built, and which, from this circumstance, was generally known by the patronymic of 'Spreull's Land'".

Because of his important family connection, young Cyril found himself invited to dinner at the home of the Provost of Glasgow. The description, if perhaps less than fair to the ways of the tobacco lords, nevertheless was doubtless inspired by Hamilton's own early recollections of Glasgow society: "The dinner, if not elegant, was plentiful. Corned beef and greens at the top; roast sirloin at the bottom; ham and boiled mutton, *vis a vis*, at the sides; the goose and turkey at the opposing corners."

After ten minutes silent food-stuffing, and then some animated conversation when the jaws of the guests were occupied in a manner less concentrated, the ladies rose from the table and withdrew from the company.

The ladies were no sooner gone than Bell Geordie made his appearance bearing a bowl of extraordinary dimensions, which he deposited on the table. Lemons, sugar, limes, rum from Jamaica and the Leeward Islands soon followed, and expectation sat on every brow. It was not a matter of easy arrangement by whom the ingredients were to be mingled. The Lord Provost called on Mr. Walkinshaw, but Mr. Walkinshaw could not think of officiating in presence of so superior an artist as Mr. Mucklewham. Mr. Mucklewham modestly yielded the palm to Major Macguffin: Mr. Macguffin begged to decline the honour in favour of Mr. Pollock; Mr. Pollock in favour of Dr. Struthers; and Dr. Struthers once more pushed the bowl to Mr. Mucklewham, who after many bashful excuses, was at lengths prevailed on to "handle the china".

*Which could well be re-issued today.

I have already noticed the solemnity and entire absorption of mind with which this portion of the Bacchanalian rites is uniformly celebrated in Glasgow, but it was now for the first time that I became witness of the fact. When the beverage had been duly concocted, at least half an hour passed, during which the merits of the punch formed the sole topic of conversation in the party. On this subject, even the most taciturn and obtuse members of the company waxed eloquent. Whether the liquor was too strong or too sweet, whether it would be improved by another "squeeze of yellow", or an additional lump of sugar, became topics of animated and interesting debate, in which all but myself took part.

Every improvement which human ingenuity could devise with regard to punch, having been at length suggested, the business of drinking commenced in good earnest, each replenishing of the glasses being prefaced by a loyal or patriotic toast by the Lord Provost. "The King, the Queen, the Prince of Wales", "the Trade of Clyde" having been drunk in bumpers, the current of conversation was gradually diverted into other channels. They were channels, however, in which the lack of any understanding was little calculated to swim. The state of the markets, the demand for ginghams, brown sugar, cotton, logwood and tobacco, were matters on which my interest was precisely equal to my knowledge.

There were jokes, it is true, and, judging from their effect, good ones; but they were so entirely local, and bore a reference so exclusive to people of whom I knew nothing, and manners of which I really desired to know nothing more, that I found some difficulty in contributing the expected quota of laughter to the general chorus of my more hilarious companions.

Standards of living varied according to where one had one's home. Since virtually everything had to be transported by sea, people living near seaports had an easier life than those who lived out of range of the delicacies and up-to-date household goods imported from London. As the century went on, food began to be served on pottery, sometimes even on china dishes, rather than on pewter plates or on still older wooden platters. Sunday observance was strict. On the Sabbath day, some people "did not sweep or dust the house, nor make the beds, nor allow any food to be cooked or dressed", while others "opened only as much of the shutters of their windows as would serve to enable the inmates to move up and down, or an individual to sit at the opening to read".

The first self-contained house, as opposed to a flat entered from a common stair, went up, Carlyle tells us, in 1735. Spinets and harpsichords could be found in the homes of the wealthy, and after 1780 pianos, some of them manufactured by John Broadwood, a Scots carpenter who had gone to London and who played a leading part in the founding of the piano-making industry there. The attempts by Robert Foulis to found an academy of arts in 1754 unfortunately foundered in 1775 because of lack of public support, but the press* which he ran with his brother Andrew made Glasgow-printed books widely "esteemed on the Continent no less than at home".

Furniture was mostly made by local craftsmen. Wealthier people who wanted upholstered mahogany furniture had to send to London for it until 1760 when an upholsterer found it worth his while to set up shop in Edinburgh. Water had to be fetched by carriers from wells. Hygiene was non-existent, all refuse being left on the street in stinking heaps. Those who could not afford wax candles had to make do with the smelly, flickering light of a cruse. Coal was available in Glasgow and in coastal towns. Club life developed. Among the more famous were the Hodge-Podge, a literary club which met fortnightly in Cruickshank's Tavern and had Dr. John Moore for a member; the Anderston, which met on Saturday afternoons in John Sharpe's inn at Anderston with Professor Robert Simson, the mathematician, as its leading light; and the Morning and Evening Club, which met twice daily at Currie's Close, on the east side of the High Street, for discussions over punch. The Merchants' Hall, rebuilt in 1659, was the scene of the winter assemblies of Glasgow society. For humbler folk, there were inns and taverns, like the 'Saracens Head', opened in 1755 by the brewer Robert Tennant, and the 'Black Boys', both in the Gallowgate; Jane Hunter's in Trongate; Lamont's at the head of Stockwell Street; and Mrs. McAlpine's oyster shop, the 'Iron Ravel Cross', on the north side of Trongate.

In good weather golf could be played on Glasgow Green. A student attending the university in 1721, left us an amusing account of the game, couched in exalted heroic couplets:

*The first printer to settle in Glasgow, George Anderson, had to be bribed with £100 Scots to move from Edinburgh with his goods and chattels in 1638. On Anderson's death, his son received a similar 'subsidy' to take over his father's business. Robert Sanders succeeded Anderson junior in 1661. In 1713 Thomas Harvie became printer to the university. In 1718 James Duncan introduced type-making in his Saltmarket shop. Robert Urie set up as a printer in the Gallowgate in 1740, printed the first issue of the *Glasgow Journal* in 1741, and was responsible for several of Robert Foulis's fine books.

In Winter, too, when hoary frosts o'er spread
The verdant turf, and naked lay the mead,
The vig'rous youth commence the sportive war,
And, arm'd with lead, their jointed clubs prepare;
The timber curve to leathern orbs apply,
Compact, elastic, to pervade the sky;
These to the distant hole direct they drive;
They claim the stakes who hither first arrive.

Intent his ball the eager gamester eyes,
His muscles strains, and various postures tries
Th' impelling blow to strike with greater force,
And shape the motive orb's projective course.
If with due strength the weighty engine fall,
Discharged obliquely, and impinge the ball,
It winding mounts alofts, and sings in air;
And wondering crowds the gamester's skill declare.

But when some luckless wayward stroke descends,
Whose force the ball in running quickly spends,
The foes triumph, the club is cursed in vain;
Spectators scoff, and e'en allies complain.

Thus still success is followed with applause;
But ah! how few espouse a vanquished cause.

Golf has always been regarded by its Scottish devotees as an adjunct to good health. Provided one retained one's health—and woe betide the eighteenth-century Glaswegian unlucky enough to fall into the hands of doctor or surgeon!—then Glasgow must have offered its better-off citizens a life of cheerful bustle, country-side diversions and the steadily expanding promise of developing opportunity. For many generations to come, Glasgow was to produce plenty of men who knew how to turn opportunity to good purpose, both for themselves and for their city.

IV

KING COTTON

In 1777, John Gibson had proclaimed: "Let but a spirit for manufacturing be diffused among the people, and we will never want manufacturers; for, should a change of fashion, which operates powerfully upon manufacturers, banish at once any particular branch, the people possessed of this spirit will immediately turn their attention to others."

In 1765, the population of Glasgow was 28,000. By 1780, it had jumped to 43,000, by 1791 to around 67,000, and by 1830 to 200,000. This rise in population reflects the growing employment opportunities which the city was able to offer. The growth of industry and commerce is well illustrated by David Macpherson, writing in 1805, in his *Annals of Commerce*.

Before America became independent of Great Britain, the foreign commerce of Glasgow was chiefly with that country; and consequently it was deranged by that event. But the enterprising spirit of the merchants has found new channels of commerce, sufficient to employ their capitals and industry. They have also turned their attention more than formerly to manufactures, whereby the city has become the centre and fostering parent of a prodigious number of manufacturing establishments. There are thirty printfields within the influence of this hive of industry. The towns and villagers in a circuit of many miles around, and some at considerable distances, are filled with spinners, weavers, and many other classes of work-people, depending upon the fabrics of the loom and the stocking frame; and there are in the neighbourhood several ironworks for making cannon and all other articles of cast iron, which, taken collectively, are perhaps scarcely inferior to the Carron Works.* The works for window glass, bottle glass, and orna-

*The Carron Ironworks, some 3 miles south of Falkirk, had been founded by Dr. Roebuck of Sheffield in 1760. Burns turned up to visit them on Sunday 26th April 1787. On being refused admission, he scratched some harsh lines on the window of a Falkirk inn:

mental glass are extensive and thriving. Sugar baking, malting and brewing are all established concerns. But it would be almost as difficult to particularise all the manufactures of Glasgow as those of London, and it may suffice to say that manufactures of almost every kind are carried on with spirit and activity, and generally in joint stocks by companies, or, as they generally are called here, *concerns*, under the management of one or more of the partners; and that the manufactures requiring fire have the vast advantage of coals close to the city.

The machinery which ran the mid-eighteenth-century factories had to be imported from England, Holland or France. The man who was to make it possible for Scotland to manufacture the machines she needed, and to export others, was James Watt (1736–1819), the son of a Greenock ship chandler.

As a young man, Watt got a job as an instrument-maker in the physics department of Glasgow University. In 1764, while repairing a model of a Newcomen steam engine owned by the university, he realized that if the steam was condensed in a separate vessel which could be kept cold, the efficiency of the engine would be greatly increased and fuel consumption reduced. His own laconic description of how the idea came to him is worth quoting, if only for its splendidly Scots matter-of-factness:

I had gone to take a walk on a fine Sabbath afternoon. I had entered the Green by the gate at the foot of Charlotte Street, and had passed the old washing-house. I was thinking upon the engine at the time, and had gone as far as the herd's house, when the idea came into my mind that as steam was an elastic body, it would rush into a vacuum, and if a communication were made between the cylinder and an exhausted vessel, it would rush into it, and might there be condensed without cooling the cylinder. . . . I had not walked further than the golf-house when the whole thing was arranged in my mind.

Thus, while he did not invent the atmospheric steam engine—

We cam na here to view your works,
  In hopes to be mair wise,
But only, lest we gang to hell,
  It may be nae surprise:
But when we tirl'd at your door,
  Your porter dought na hear us;
Sae may, shou'd we to hell's yetts
                              come,
  Your billy Satan sair us!

Thomas Newcomen did that in 1712, though the steam engine goes back at least to Hero of Alexandria—Watt produced the first expansion steam engine, which he later made double-acting, fitting it with a centrifugal governor. Because his engines worked under what was termed technically 'low pressure', they were also safer than their uneconomic predecessors. In 1769 and 1773, he took out with Matthew Boulton of Birmingham patents which incorporated the basic features of the steam engine which was to dominate Victorian transportation and industrial life.

Their first engines were used to pump water out of the tin and copper mines of Cornwall, and elsewhere. Before long, cotton mills using water-power had converted themselves to steam. The first Watt steam engine is said to have been put into a Scottish cotton mill at Springfield, on the Clyde, in 1792. Lancashire mills had Watt engines earlier and Newcomen engines were functioning at Leadhills and elsewhere well before 1792.

Cloth-making had, of course, been carried on in Glasgow, at least domestically, since medieval times, though the quantities produced must have been small. The plaids which Thomas Tucker saw worn both in Edinburgh and Glasgow represented an advance for the industries. Defoe described the material of which they were made as "a stuff crossed-striped with yellow, red and other mixtures". He also tells us that at the time of his visit, muslins were manufactured and "sent into England and to the British plantations, where they sell at a good price".

In 1727 Parliament appointed a commission, later known as the Board of Trustees for Manufacturers, to administer a fund for the encouragement of industry, particularly the linen industry. (The board became the corner stone of the future British Linen Bank.) This gave encouragement to housewives to grow lint (flax) and hemp, and led to the development of linen-making, particularly in the east.

Linen seems to have been introduced to Glasgow in 1725, as a result of the enlistment of a certain William Wilson of East Kilbride to the Scots Guards. When he returned to Glasgow from service on the Continent in 1700, he brought back from Germany a blue and white chequered handkerchief, and proceeded to experiment in copying it, eventually with success. Wilson himself had not the capital to exploit his discovery, and died in poverty, his last contribution to society being his occupancy of the post of town drummer. But others profited. The first Cambric and Printfield was erected in Pollokshaws in 1742, and soon legislation against the importation of French cambrics provided encouragement for the expansion of the linen industry. Furthermore, a Glaswegian named Harvey in 1732 managed to import from Holland not only two inkle looms but also a skilled Dutch workman, thus breaking the Dutch monopoly in the making of tapes.

The invention by Hargreaves of the spinning jenny, and by Arkwright of the spinning frame, further stimulated production of cotton yarn. An English firm set up the first cotton mill at Rothesay in 1778. In 1780, James Monteith, a Glasgow linen-weaver who had been experimenting in the mixing of a fine hard-spun cotton yarn with linen yarn in the making of cheap fabrics at his Anderston factory, discovered how to weave an imitation Indian muslin entirely out of cotton. So successful was he, in fact, that he caused a dress of it to be woven and em-broidered with jewels for presentation to Queen Charlotte. Such success provoked imitations. By 1787, many new mills were set up beside Scottish rivers. His own six sons all became cotton manufacturers. In the west, cotton began to oust linen. By the end of the century, Glasgow had gone over wholeheartedly to cotton-making, leaving Forfarshire and Fife the centres of Scotland's linen industry.

One of James's six sons, also James, an ambitious man, is often referred to by early historians of Glasgow as the father of the Glasgow cotton industry, principally because during the troubles of the 1790s, when many Glasgow banks failed, causing a trade paralysis, he opened an auction room in London which enabled him make a profit of £80,000 in a very few years, and thus keep the industry he led prosperous. But another son, Henry (1765–1848), who took over his father's factory in Anderston, was the more prominent citizen. He triumphantly defied the tobacco lords' privilege of exclusively attending the more select assemblies and twice became Provost of Glasgow—in 1814 for a year, and again in 1818—a position to which no weaver's son would have dared to aspire in his father's hey-day. He represented Lanark district of burghs in Parliament in 1821.

Another pioneering contemporary of James Monteith senior was David Dale (1739–1806). Dale was the son of an Ayrshire shopkeeper and the prototype of Sir Walter Scott's Bailie Nicol Jarvie in *Rob Roy* (at whose hands, incidentally James Monteith's ancestors, who came from Aberfoyle, had suffered, thus driving them to Glasgow to earn a living). Dale began as an importer of Dutch and French linen yarns, but soon came to realize that there was more profit to be made in the manufacturing side. Along with James Monteith and some others, David Dale invited Arkwright to visit Glasgow in 1783. Dale showed Arkwright a site by the Falls of Clyde at Lanark, and persuaded the inventor to enter what proved to be a short-lived partnership in a cotton-spinning mill set up at the town of New Lanark which Dale founded. Not all Arkwright's English friends were pleased at the help thus briefly given to the Scot, and Arkwright, who had begun life as a barber, was frequently teased for having "put a razor in the hands of a Scotsman who would one day shave us all".

By 1793 Dale had the largest mill of its kind in the United Kingdom, employing some thirteen hundred men and women, many of whom had formerly been destitute. Dale fed, clothed and housed these workers, ruling them with a kind of benevolent paternalism.

Three years after Dale's death, the Poet Laureate Robert Southey, in company with the great Scots civil engineer Thomas Telford, visited New Lanark, and commented on the establishment. He thought the mills

perfect of their kind, according to the present state of mechanical science, and that they appeared to be under admirable management; they are thoroughly clean and so carefully ventilated, that there was no unpleasant smell in any of the apartments. Everything required for the machinery is made upon the spot, and the expence of wear and tear is estimated at 800£ annually. There are stores also from which the people are supplied with all the necessaries of life. They have a credit there to the amount of sixteen shillings a week each, but may elsewhere deal if they chuse. The expences of what he calls the moral part of the establishment, he stated at 700£ a year. But a large building is just completed, with ball and concert and lecture rooms, all for "the formation of character", and this must have required a considerable sum, which I think must surely be down to Owen's private account, rather than to the cost of the concern.

Owen's stores were, in fact, the first stirrings of the Co-operative Movement in Scotland.

Southey, however, had doubts about the long-term practicability of this Utopia by the Clyde. By this time, it was being run by Dale's son-in-law, Robert Owen, who took over new Lanark by purchase in 1799, and came to manage it on 1st January 1800. Southey went on:

> Owen in reality deceives himself. He is part-owner and sole Director of a large establishment, differing more in accidents than in essence from a plantation; the persons under him happen to be white, and are at liberty by law to quit his service, but while they remain in it they are as much under his absolute management, as so many negro-slaves. His humour, his vanity, his kindliness of nature (all these have their share) lead him to make these *human machines* as he calls them (and too literally believes them to be) as happy as he can, and to make a display of their happiness. And he jumps at once to the monstrous conclusion that because he can do this with 2210 persons who are totally dependent on him—all mankind might be governed with the same facility. . . . He keeps out of sight from others, and perhaps from himself, that his system, instead of aiming at perfect freedom, can only be kept in play by absolute power. Indeed, he never looks beyond one of his own ideal square villages, to the rules and proportions of which he would squeeze the whole human race. The formation of character! Why, the end of his institutions would be, as far as possible, the destruction of all character. They tend directly to destroy individuality of character and domesticity—in the one of which the strength of man consists, and in the other his happiness. The power of human society and the grace, would both be annihilated.

Whatever may have been the situation at New Lanark, it is doubtful if, in 1819, the year of Southey's visit, much grace was to be found in Glasgow's "eighteen steam weaving factories, containing 2,800 looms, and producing 8,400 pieces of cloth weekly"; doubtful, too, if those who laboured long hours in the city's fifty-two cotton mills, with their 511,200 spindles, weaving over a million yards valued at £5 million, found much time or opportunity to develop their character.

In 1804 James Graham (1765–1811), the son of a Glasgow lawyer and himself an advocate, produced anonymously a poem called "The Sabbath", which, in spite of being savaged both by the *Edinburgh Review* and later by Lord Byron, achieved a broad measure of popularity; so much so that Graham's wife, reading the poem in ignorance of the identity of the author, is said to have remarked to her husband, "Ah, James, if you could only write like this!" While today we would hardly share Mrs. Graham's

literary enthusiasm, the social comment her husband's lines contain
is probably a more knowledgeable reflection than Southey's.

> With dovelike wings peace o'er yon village★ broods
> The dizzying millwheel rests; the anvil's din
> Hath ceased; all, all around is quietness.
> Less fearful on this day, the limping hare
> Stops and looks back, and stops, and looks on man,
> Her deadliest foe. The toil-worn horse, set free,
> Unheedful of the pasture, roams at large,
> And, as his stiff, unwielding bulk he rolls,
> His iron-armed hoofs gleam in the morning ray.
>
> But chiefly man the day of rest enjoys.
> Hail, Sabbath! thee I hail the poor man's day!
> On other days the man of toil is doomed
> To eat his joyless bread, lonely, the ground
> Both seat and board, screened from the winter's cold
> And summer's heat by neighbouring hedge or tree.
> But on this day, embosomed in his home,
> He shares the frugal meal with those he loves . . .
>
> Hail, Sabbath! thee I hail, the poor man's day!
> The pale mechanic now has leave to breathe
> The morning air pure from the city's smoke,
> While wandering slowly up the riverside
> He meditates on Him whose power he marks
> In each green tree. . . .

The wretchedness of these "pale mechanics"—to say nothing
of their children labouring twelve or thirteen hours a day—who
toiled for six weekdays at looms and in factories, was aggravated
by a number of outside factors. There was a failure of the harvest
in 1799, when it was the poorest and largest section of the community that starved. On 15th February 1800—the year in which
the first Glasgow police force came into being, an earlier attempt
by the magistrates to appoint one of their own number 'Intendant
of Police' having been defeated in Parliament in 1788—bread
riots occurred. There was another, equally basic cause of unrest:
growing unemployment, chiefly among the hand-loom weavers.

The earliest power-mills in Glasgow had spun cotton yarn for
the hand-loom weavers to make into cloth. When, in the early

★There were mills at 'villages', like Partick and Govan, on the outskirts of
Glasgow, which have long since been engulfed by the city.

decades of the nineteenth century, the factories began manufacturing their own cloth, the economic pressures on the
hand-loom weavers operating from their own cottages became
considerable. There had been the Calton weavers' riot in 1787, as
a result of their employers' refusal to grant a wage increase. The
56th regiment arrived from Ayr to assist the 39th regiment in
preserving the peace, though in the doing of this three weavers
had been shot. Providence, it seems, was on the side of law and
order on this occasion, for on a September night "the Captain of
patrole" ordered a roll of his men to be called. While they were
mustered for this purpose, the hanging stairs leading to the
Assembly Room of the Tontine buildings collapsed on the spot
where the men would normally have been sheltering. (A reporter,
writing in the contemporary *Glasgow Mercury*, provided the
classic text-book comment on the craft of non-reporting by commenting: "had they been on the stair they could not have escaped
being crushed to death".)

About 1800, when for a second year a crop failure resulted in a
grain shortage and widespread distress among the pool, a hand-
loom weaver could earn the then good wage of £2 10s. a week.
But thereafter wages fell to as little as 10s. as the factories gradually
took over. Rum, cheaply available through Glasgow's West
Indies trading connections at the close of the eighteenth century,
had become unobtainable because of the Napoleonic War. Its
place was being taken by whisky and gin. In these spirits, available
at all hours in numerous drinking-shops, the poor sought a solace
which also inflamed their grievances.

The war with Napoleon which broke out in 1797 had at first
found some support amongst liberal-minded people who still
drew some inspiration from the ideals of *liberté, égalité, fraternité*.
But when it became clear that 'Boney' posed a practical threat of
invasion with no such high-minded beliefs attached to it, Glasgow
responded to the patriotic call to arms both with men and with
money. There was a review of the troops on Glasgow Green in
1804. Although Glasgow's nine regiments were never called out
on anything more serious than rumours of invasions, the citizens
took much pride in the fact that the victor of Corunna, Sir John
Moore (1761-1809), the son of Burns's friend Dr. John Moore,
was a Glasgow man commemorated to this day by a statue in
George Square. The British sea victory at Cape St. Vincent
resulted in St. Vincent Street receiving its name.

For Glaswegians, one of the worst features of the Napoleonic
War was the easy spread of rumour, news from abroad taking so
long to travel. Fortunately most of the alarming rumours eventually turned out to be false. 'Senex' remembered that:

> During the time of the French war, it was quite exhilarating to
> observe the arrival of the London mail-coach in Glasgow, when
> carrying the first intelligence of a great victory, like the Battle of
> the Nile, or the Battle of Waterloo. The mail-coach horses were
> then decorated with laurels, and a red flag floated on the roof of
> the coach. The guard, dressed in his best scarlet coat and gold
> ornamented hat, came galloping at a thundering pace along the
> stones of the Gallowgate, sounding his bugles amidst the echoings
> of the street; and when he arrived at the foot of Nelson Street . . .
> he there discharged his blunderbus in the air. On these occasions a
> general run was made to the Tontine Coffee-room to learn the
> great news, and long before the newspapers were delivered, the
> public were advised by the guard of the particulars of the glorious
> victory, which flew from mouth to mouth like wild-fire. The
> Coffee-room soon became densely crowded, the subscribers
> anxiously waiting the delivery of the newspapers, and every one
> repeating the information scattered abroad by the guard. When
> the papers were delivered, all was bustle and confusion to learn
> what the *Courier* said, or what the *Star* said.

It was after the victory of 1815 at Waterloo that men who had
been in the fighting service came back in numbers to a Glasgow
very different from the city they had left, perhaps as long as
twenty years before. Returning soldiers swell unemployment. In
1815, a mob attacked Kirkman Finlay's house in Queen Street,
and had to be dispersed by soldiers. As a Member of Parliament,
he had voted for 'Prosperity' Robinson's Corn Law, which had
the effect of prohibiting the import of corn until the price of
home-grown corn reached 80s. per quarter, a protective measure
favouring the landowning interest which caused the price of
bread to shoot up and forced the poorer people to rely upon
potatoes. In 1816, some 40,000 people came together in Thrush-
grove demanding action to redress their grievances. By 1817,
indeed, the foundations of Glasgow's 'radical', later 'red', reputation had already been laid, for a secret parliamentary committee
referred to the city in a report as being "one of the places where
treasonable practices prevail to the greatest degree".

By 1819 the police and troops were daily to be seen in the
streets dispersing people who looked as if they might be about to

riot. On Sunday 1st April of that year, real trouble broke. There was desultory rioting, mostly by weavers in the outlying districts affected by the shortage of work. Eighteen men were arrested and tried for high treason. Andrew Hardie, an ancestor of Keir Hardie, and John Baird, both from Bonnymuir where they had been demonstrating in favour of Parliamentary reform and the extention of the franchise, were publicly hanged and then beheaded at Stirling, the executioner holding up Hardie's mangled, illiterate head by the hair and crying: "This is the head of a traitor." James Wilson, another of the eighteen, suffered a similar fate in front of 20,000 spectators on Glasgow Green. The remaining fifteen were transported for life.

In 1822, another hungry weaver, Richard Campbell, was scourged through the streets by the public hangman, being given twenty lashes with "a formidable cat o' nine tails at four separate stopping places", the last man to be publicly whipped in Glasgow. Later in the same year John Provan's factory in Great Clyde Street was wrecked, a mob having erroneously got the notion that he was a resurrectionist or digger up of the dead to provide university anatomists with cadavers. Five men received sentences of transportation for their share in this affair.

In 1825, the right to strike was recognized. The Catholic Emancipation Act was passed in 1829. When the Reform Bill, against which the dying Sir Walter Scott had so disastrously campaigned in Jedburgh, received its majority in the House in 1832, there was a joyous demonstration on Glasgow Green attended by more than 70,000 people, Lord Provost Dalglish's house in West George Street being illuminated with 3,000 new gas jets highlighting the city's motto, "Let Glasgow flourish". Since 1817, the town council and the Glasgow Gas Light Company, whose chairman was Lord Provost Henry Monteith, had jointly brought gas to the city, so it has to be admitted that the Provost had a vested interest in letting the attractions of the new illuminant be seen.

There was to be another near-mutinous decade before the threat of riot receded from Glasgow. In any case, neither the weavers nor the textile industry had much cause to rejoice. The spinning and weaving of cotton soon ceased to be Glasgow's major job-opportunity provider, although for a time the factories went on growing in number.

By 1860 the peak of the cotton industry was reached. In that year chimneys of some sixty cotton mills lacquered the sky with soot, employing nearly 20,000 people, about three-quarters of them women, working on 20,000 looms. Two things happened to cut down this apparently flourishing industry to the point where, a century after its peak, it had all but disappeared from the city. One was the failure of the Western Bank in 1857. Although the Western Bank had an authorised capital of £4 million, four of the largest textile firms found themselves unable to pay their debts because of a commercial crisis in America. Soon after came a cotton famine, the American Civil War cutting off supplies from the Southern States between 1861 and 1865.

There were other less immediately obvious causes too, not least the fact that some of the countries which had hitherto been among Glasgow's best customers for the high-quality textiles the city produced, had begun to set up their own industries, which they protected by tariffs. Another cause was Glasgow's excessive concentration on high-quality muslins, which ceased to sell well after the bankruptcy following the Western Bank failure. To get rid of their high surplus stocks, the manufacturers sold them at so low a price that even the workers were able to buy them. Consequently the ladies of fashion were no longer very keen to buy the material when normal production could be resumed. In any case, for reasons that have never been wholly examined, Lancashire, specializing in coarser but very cheap cotton cloths, was able to capture the market in Africa, India and the Far East, where there were no tariff barriers. Lancashire's cheap trade thrived as Glasgow's quality trade shrank.

Not many buildings erected during the earlier years of Glasgow's cotton period survive. The Assembly Rooms in Ingram Street, the centre portion of which was put up by Robert and James Adam in 1792, but the wings of which were added by Henry Holland in 1807, stood on the corner of George Square until it made way for an extension to the Post Office in 1890. Soon after, the centrepiece was rebuilt, with alterations, as the triumphal McLennan Arch on Glasgow Green. During the Assembly Rooms' century of useful life, the building housed many of the city's most glittering Victorian social functions, attracting them away from the Tontine.

Another vanished work by the Adams was the old Royal Infirmary, begun in 1792 upon the site of the ruined Bishop's Palace. Adam's Infirmary survived until the early years of this

'Greek' Thomson's Great Western Terrace, 1894
Rochead's Grosvenor Terrace

century, when the present overbearing successor was put up, itself now under sentence of replacement.

The house which the brothers built for David Dale survived until the 1950s, when, in spite of protests, it was needlessly pulled down by the City's Education Department during a period when officially-sanctioned vandalism was almost the order of the civic day. Two houses by James Adam, dating from 1793, and originally intended to accommodate university professors, survive at the time of writing in the High Street, on the corners of College Street, their impressive columns rising above singularly tasteless modern shop fronts; and the pleasing remains of a house by both brothers at number 60 Wilson Street can still be seen, though its open arcade has gone and a mansard roof has been added.

The finest urban survivor of this renewal stage of Glasgow's prosperity is undoubtedly Robert Adam's Trades House in Glassford Street, built in 1791 and still serving its original purposes, though it now looks somewhat crushed in by what J. M. Reid calls the "tall insignificance of its southern neighbours", and it has to carry an incongruous and tasteless shop sign on the ground floor of its northern wing. James Sellars reconstructed the interior in 1887.

Since the loss of Garscadden House, only the remarkable Pollok House survives among former great country houses now engulfed by Glasgow. Begun by William Adam about 1737, it was finished by his son John in 1752, but it suggests a backward look towards the style of Sir William Bruce rather than the classicism which the other members of the Adam family were so successfully evoking. Sir William Rowand Anderson added sympathetic wings and a terrace in 1892.

Today, the house and its magnificent park around the White Cart, which is spanned by a delightful eighteenth-century bridge, are managed by the City of Glasgow and the National Trust for Scotland for the benefit of Glaswegians and those who visit their city. The fine collection of pictures includes an El Greco portrait, "Lady with Fur Wrap". Chamber-music concerts are held regularly during the winter months in the elegant drawing-room. A gallery to house the art collection bequeathed by the shipowner Sir William Burrell is to be built in the grounds of Pollok House.

During the period when cotton spinning and the manufacture of cotton textiles together formed Glasgow's staple industry—from 1780 to about 1830—the population rose from 40,000 to

5

Old Vennel in the High Street, 1888

200,000. This rapid increase led to the expansion of the city through the creation of several 'new towns'.

George Square, which has already been mentioned, was 'West End' in relation to the old town around the cathedral, and when first put up housed such leaders in industry as the brothers W. and J. Coats, who had already a monopoly in the manufacture of cotton thread; Patrick Colquhoun, future Provost, founder of Glasgow's Chamber of Commerce, promoter of the Tontine Society, and with Cooksons of Newcastle the introducer of the first "crystal manufactory" to Scotland, that at Verreville; and Thomas Dunmore, a founder partner of the Arms Bank.

During the reign of 'King Cotton', the city moved farther west still, as the lands of the Campbells of Blythswood began to be built upon. The Campbells of Blythswood, a family tracing their origins to Colin Campbell, merchant and trader in Glasgow in 1615, several of whose sons became Provost of the city in turn, possessed a splendid mansion in the Saltmarket which, according to 'Senex' in *Glasgow Past and Present*, had been built during the seventeenth century. Oliver Cromwell occupied it in 1650, and it survived until about 1829, though by then long since abandoned by the Campbells. They next occupied a mansion distinguished by "five tympanny windows to the front with tappietouries", the front elevation of the property looking out on Bridgegait, the large garden rambling down to the Clyde. About the middle of the eighteenth century, the house was divided and let out, Provost Colin Campbell having by then acquired the lands of Blythswood for "a mere wanworth" (approximately one farthing an acre, according to 'Senex').

In 1804 a large feu was taken by a Glasgow merchant, William Harley, who had made money by laying pipes from his property at Willowbank, where there was a spring, to the intersection of Bath and West Nile Streets, from where four-wheeled carts carrying tanks distributed the water for sale. In 1810 Harley built dairies, a 'Cowhouse' accommodating 100 cows which were fed by "the operation of a wheel and pinion, placed on the outside portion at the transverse passage", baths,* and some houses in

---

*According to James Clelland's *Annals of Glasgow* (1816), cold baths for gentlemen, ladies, boys and girls, and hot baths including "five stretching Baths for Gentlemen". Similar arrangements were made for the ladies, "the avenues to which are formed with shrubberies, and are quite distinct from those leading to the Gentlemen's Baths".

what became Bath Street. On the top of Blythswood hill, Harley laid out an enclosed garden with a fountain, admission to which was open to anyone who bought a ticket. Harley thus founded one of Glasgow's cotton era 'new towns', though to no advantage to himself, for he overreached himself financially in doing so, and by 1816 was bankrupt (as soon afterwards, incidentally, were the trustees who took over his responsibilities). However, his pioneering development had suggested to others what could be done, and soon there was no lack of persons anxious to build upon the salubrious hilly site on the right side of the city to avoid most of the smoke from the growing number of factory chimneys. Among the most prominent of these speculative builders were Dugald Bannatyne, a Dr. Cleland, William Jack and Alexander Garden.

Cleland and Jack put up houses in Bath Street, Alexander Garden in St. Vincent Street. From 1820 a descendant of Alexander Hamilton, William Garden, extended the family enterprise further up the hillside, though he too went bankrupt, his trustees continuing the work for a decade or so, until Garden hastily emigrated to America. To this series of financial failures, Thomas Burns added his name in 1827, though not before he had managed to build a substantial part of West Regent Street.

With this development, which J. R. Kellett has calculated increased the Campbells' income from (in modern figures) £6,000 per annum to £300,000, a Glasgow style of house emerged, all the Blythswood buildings being erected originally as elegant homes. In their definitive book *Architecture of Glasgow*, Andor Gomme and David Walker describe the basic unit of the Blythswood 'new town' as being:

a fairly short terrace two or three storeys high, generally with centrepiece and end pavilions given considerable emphasis. . . . Pediments are rarely used, though pilasters appear at times where houses were individually designed. There is a fair number of porches of various orders regularly punctuating the smooth facades; cornices are generally heavy and emphatic; those on the windows and window surrounds especially so. The facing is of course all ashlar . . . now a darkish silver grey, but recent cleaning has revealed a lovely soft biscuity colour underneath.

They rightly deplore the recent widespread but misdirected custom of painting such stone, as a substitute for its proper maintenance and repair. They also comment on the solid, upstanding dignity of these well-proportioned buildings abounding in detailing that is often beautiful.

All the streets of this 'new town', which was built on the gridiron plan later adopted by many American cities, still have examples of houses in this Blythswood Glasgow Style. Commercial pressures began to be exerted against them as long ago as the 1840s, when the first of them suffered the change to commercial use. Since then there have been many intrusions, some of the Victorian replacement buildings being distinguished, but only the Norwich Union building from our own age having distinction, albeit of a totally alien order to the quality of its original neighbours. Gaps are being torn in the old fabric so constantly that before long the 'feel' of the streets built in the Blythswood Glasgow style will have been destroyed, taller newcomers outscaling the remaining houses with the dreary cosmopolitan anonymity currently fashionable.

It is therefore fortunate that Blythswood Square, on the summit of what was once known as Harley's Hill, has been designated a conservation area under the Civic Amenities Act of 1967. John Brash was the architect for H. W. Garden in 1823. Unfortunately, the sense of unity of the square depended upon the sympathetic corner buildings of the streets leading into it from each of its four corners. One of these has been replaced by the glaringly hostile and thoroughly commonplace building which houses the offices of British Rail.

The show-piece of the square is the Royal Scottish Automobile Club, which occupies the whole of the east side. Here the unity of the window groupings, the balancing pavilions and the window astragals have been preserved. All the properties on the south side have recently been rebuilt behind the original facade. Many of the windows have been replaced with plate glass, or with more modern swivel devices. Without astragals, most buildings built before 1850 seem somehow to gape disconcertingly. Charles Rennie Mackintosh put a characteristic *Art Nouveau* door on number 5, which houses an art gallery where some internal reworking is reputedly by his disciple James Salmon junior, grandson of Brash's pupil James Salmon senior.

The Blythswood development spilled northwards up Garnethill, on the other side of the dividing valley of Sauchiehall Street. Many of the buildings here were originally flats, intended for humbler people. Unlike the square on the crest of its prouder neighbour, Garnethill has fallen on hard times, and, with the exception of the Glasgow School of Art, itself a magnificent cuckoo in an otherwise shabby nest, is likely to be totally redeveloped before the end of the century.

Another direction in which development took place during Glasgow's cotton days was southwards, across the Clyde. In 1780 the village of Bridge-End or Gorbals lay just across the river. Beyond and around it was agricultural land divided into crofts with names like Trades Croft, Kirk Croft, Wellcroft, Windmill Croft, Stirlingfauld and Gushet Fauld—land which was owned, for the most part, jointly by Glasgow Corporation, the Trades House and Hutcheson's Hospital.

When Glasgow officially extended its boundaries to take in Gorbals, James and David Laurie got possession of some 47 acres of the old croft lands, and on a speculative basis proceeded to plan a development "according to one plan or design, whereby it was in a manner set apart for houses of a superior description". David, who seems to have been the leader of the partnership, in 1802 engaged Peter Nicholson to design the two terraces of Carlton Place (so-named to honour the Prince Regent), and Italian craftsmen were brought to Glasgow to carry out the work of embellishment and decoration, all at a cost of just under £10,000.

These dignified three-storey terraces with basements, each of forty bays, have pavilions with Ionic porches and coupled columns, with a double porch for the centrepiece. There has been some damage to the group as a whole—the loss of two pavilions and the addition of a mansard roof—but a post-Second World War restoration has given some indication of the kind of dignified waterfront Glasgow could and should one day possess, if commercial pressures do not tempt the city to throw away the environmental opportunities which necessary redevelopment on the north bank of the river offers. Laurieston House, Nicholson's showpiece, was intended by David for his own use. Indeed, the lavish Italian plasterwork, now happily restored, was intended to impress the Prince Regent, the future George IV, during a proposed visit to the city. Because of rioting, however, the prince's advisers decided to leave Glasgow out of his itinerary.

The two terraces are divided by the entrance to South Portland Street, which John Laurie lined up with Buchanan Street, across the river. Abbotsford Place, its continuation, was for some time a favourite street with Glasgow's doctors. Those four-storey terraces with their Ionic and Corinthian porches, fronting on to broad streets, are a forlorn reminder of the imposing scale of the development which the Lauries had hoped to establish.

But their plans went awry. Buchanan Street and Abbotsford Place were not to be linked by a bridge. Then there were the tolls to be paid by residents from the south side using the other bridges, until a suspension bridge was put up especially for their use in 1853, a toll of one halfpenny being charged during the first few years it was in use. But what really overthrew the Lauries' ambitions for the area was the unplanned building which went on behind the north side of the central axis. The tenements put up by master builders like James Ballantine and John Binnie (whose relative, Thomas, built Monteith Row, which looks on to Glasgow Green, and features in Guy MacCrone's novels of Glasgow life, *Wax Fruit*) were sold as shells, to be completed to the customer's requirements. This was symptomatic of the unplanned approach which soon began to affect even land uses. What was intended to be a residential district became a jumble of housing and small industries, closely mixed. This was in large measure due to the fact that until almost the middle of the nineteenth century, Glasgow Corporation had no jurisdiction south of the river. Consequently, it could not prevent William Dixon, who since 1837 had owned the famous 'Dixon's Blazes' (which in time were to cast an orange glare over the surrounding district at night) building a trackway right across Laurieston's principal streets to the quay at Windmillcroft. Neither could the corporation stop the setting up of brickworks and coalfields on the outskirts of the district, nor the gradual proliferation of all sorts of small backyard industries. Gradually the wealthier residents moved out, the big houses were divided and sub-divided. After 1830 tenements were built subdivided from the start, and the course was set for Gorbals to become within half a century perhaps the worst, and certainly the most notorious, slum in Europe!

While the Lauries were ambitiously busy on the south side, new public buildings were appearing in and around the old town —William Stark's St. George's Church went up in 1807 in what is now St. George's Place, a Wren-influenced building which is today one of the main adornments of Buchanan Street. We have lost most of Stark's other public buildings, including his Bell's Park Lunatic Asylum of 1809 (which survived for more than a century), and the original Hunterian Museum of 1804, famous for its Doric portico with Tuscan columns, was sacrificed with the rest of the old university, although it survived into the twentieth century. The Justiciary Court House facing Glasgow Green, and also dating from 1807, was remodelled by J. H. Craigie in 1910, and is now a building of no particular interest.

Fortunately, more of the work of Stark's contemporary David Hamilton (1768–1843) has survived. Numbers 151 to 157 Queen Street give some idea of his earlier solid classical manner. Hutcheson's Hospital in Ingram Street, built in 1805 to replace the seventeenth-century original in the Trongate, also has obvious classical overtones, in spite of its slightly mannered detail. To most Glaswegians, however, Hamilton is best known for the work he did in 1827-9 on the Cunningehame mansion of 1778, to fit it out for its existence as Glasgow's Royal Exchange. The old house seems to have been cased in, while a powerful Corinthian portico was added to the east end, topped by a surprising but effective cupola. To the west stands Archibald Elliott the second's Royal Bank, put up in 1827, recently totally rebuilt within its shell in accordance with Glasgow Corporation's intention to conserve the original character of Buchanan Street. Royal Exchange Place, another of the corporation's Conservation Areas, which flanks the bank and the Royal Exchange (now Stirling's Library), is also Elliott's work.

Hamilton also rebuilt the Tolbooth behind the old steeple (now only the steeple itself survives); St. Enoch's Church, now demolished; and in 1841 the ornate Western Club in Buchanan Street, also recently given a totally rebuilt interior. For the remarkable Kirkman Finlay, the textile manufacturer who successfully ran Napoleon's blockade to get his cotton goods into Europe, who sent Glasgow's first ships to open up both the India and China trades, and who became one of Glasgow's most distinguished early nineteenth-century Lord Provosts, a Member of Parliament and Lord Rector of her university, Hamilton built the spacious Castle Toward, on the Cowal shore.

During the cotton phase of Glasgow's expansion, though it never had the kind of overall plan which gives Edinburgh's New Town its unique grand design, Glasgow must still have been a very fair city. Several observant travellers visited it.

William and Dorothy Wordsworth arrived in Glasgow on Monday 22nd August 1803, in their Irish jaunting car. They were

on their way to the Trossachs and the Highlands. They put up
at the 'Saracen's Head', then "quiet and tolerably cheap, a new
building", according to Dorothy. Both brother and sister were
tired, and glad to have a place of rest. But the observant Dorothy
soon had out her diary and her critical pen.

> I shall never forget how glad I was to be landed in a little quiet
> back parlour, for my head was beating with the noise of carts which
> we had left. . . . But with my first pleasant sensations also came the
> feeling that we were not in an English inn—partly from its half-
> unfurnished appearance, which is common in Scotland, for in
> general the deal wainscots and doors are unpainted, and partly from
> the dirtiness of the floors. Having dined, Wm. and I walked to the
> post-office, and after much seeking found out a quiet timber-yard
> wherein to sit down and read our letter. We then walked a con-
> siderable time in the streets, which are perhaps as handsome as
> streets can be, which derive no particular effect from their situation
> in connexion with natural advantages such as rivers, sea or hills.
> The Trongate, an old street, is very picturesque—high houses with
> an intermixture of gable fronts towards the street. The New Town
> is built of fine stone, in the best style of the very best London streets,
> at the west end of the town, but not being brick they are greatly
> superior.

Dorothy Wordsworth then went on to record some lively
general impressions. "One thing must strike every stranger in
his first walk through Glasgow—an appearance of business and
bustle, but no coaches or gentlemen's carriages. During all the
time we walked in the streets, I saw only three carriages, but these
were travelling chaises. I also could not but observe a want of
cleanliness in the appearance of the lower orders of the people,
and a dullness in the dress and outside of the whole mass, as
they moved along."

Traditionally the Scots were never very good innkeepers, and
the dirt and disorder of Scottish inns and hotels was commented
upon by travellers far into the nineteenth century. Temperament
and a foolish sense of pride were—and to some extent, still are—
responsible for a certain traditional lack of welcoming gracious-
ness. More practical reasons were responsible for the dirty state
of the Glaswegians seen by Dorothy Wordsworth. Cleanliness
necessitates a plentiful supply of cheap water.

Glasgow's water at the turn of the century came from thirty
public wells from which it was fetched by the water-bearers of

those who could afford such help, and thirty other wells or pumps in the gardens of mansions in Buchanan, Queen and Miller Streets. Water was also drawn from various rivers and streams around the city. Cleanliness and hygiene, especially amongst the poorer people who had to fetch their own bucket-loads of water, cost a great deal of effort, since they could hardly afford to buy from the pony-carts at a halfpenny a stoup.

In 1806, however, the Glasgow Water Works Company was formed. It pumped water from the Clyde at Dalmarnock to reservoirs from which, after filtration, the water was then pumped to the city centre and to the new suburbs. In 1808, the Cranston Hill Company set up a similar operation at Anderston, but soon moved alongside its rival at Dalmarnock. These companies competed with each other until 1858, when they amalgamated. Even so, many Glasgow houses were to be without piped water for another three-quarters of a century!

In spite of the fact that piped water was at least available by the time Robert Southey, the Poet Laureate, arrived in Glasgow in the autumn of 1819, on his way back from a tour of the Highlands made in company with the Scots engineer Thomas Telford, inn conditions had improved very little. The hotel at which Southey stayed had been built in 1757 as the residence of Provost John Murdoch, though by 1790 it was an inn. It, and a neighbouring mansion of matching Georgian character and dignity, survived in Argyle Street until replaced by a 'Greek' Thompson building in 1863. Wrote Southey, under an entry dated 27th September:

> We drove to the Buck's Head in Argyle Street. Large as this house is, they had no room with a fire, when we arrived cold and hungry, at ten o'clock on a wet morning.
>
> The inns in large cities are generally detestable, and this does not appear to form an exception from the common rule. But it afforded what I cannot but notice as a curiosity in its kind unique, as far as my knowledge extends. In the *Commoditié*, which is certainly not more than six feet by four, there was a small stone, which as I learned from certain inscriptions in pencil on the wall, is regularly heated in the winter.

Southey, like the Wordsworths before him, set out to explore on foot.

> A City like Glasgow is a hateful place for a stranger, unless he is reconciled to it by the comforts of hospitality and society. In any

other case the best way is to reconnoitre it, so as to know the outline and outside, and to be contented with such other information as books can supply.

Argyle Street is the finest part; it has a mixture of old and new buildings, but is long enough and lofty enough to be one of the best streets in G. Britain. The Cathedral is the only edifice of its kind in Scotland which received no external injury at the Reformation.*

Southey found two faults with the cathedral. One related to the "smeary appearance" of the painted-glass windows, which have long since been removed. The other belonged to "the unclean part of the national character; for the seats are so closely packed that any person who could remain there during the time of service in warm weather, must have an invincible nose. I doubt even whether any incense could overcome so strong and concentrated an odour of humanity".

The university, however, struck him as having "an ancient and respectable appearance".

Southey had come into Glasgow from Dunbarton, commenting that as he drove "packed in a coach . . . several steamboats were plying on the Clyde", and that "yesterday morning when we rose, there was one smoking before the window at Arrochar on Loch Long".

There had been experiment with steam-ships as far back as 1788, when, on 19th October, Robert Burns, among others, either saw or even sailed on a paddle steamer which crossed Dalswinton Loch at approximately 5 miles an hour. It had been built for Patrick Miller, an enterprising Dumfriesshire laird, by William Symington. A year later, Symington built a larger 7-miles-an-hour boat for Miller, which sailed on the Forth and Clyde Canal, a waterway constructed between 1768 and 1790, and on which passenger boats ran, latterly purely for pleasure, until the outbreak of the Second World War. In 1802, the *Charlotte Dundas* was built by Symington for towing purposes on the canal. The adjacent proprietors, however, complained of the damage caused by its wash to the banks, and it had soon to be beached and abandoned.

At the turn of the century, a still youthful engineer, Henry Bell, settled in the new town of Helensburgh, on the Clyde,

*Not quite true. St. Magnus Cathedral, in Kirkwall, Orkney, sustained no damage at the Reformers' hands.

becoming its first Provost. He had begun as a millwright, working with his uncle. Later, he worked as a shipmodeller at Bo'ness, from where he emigrated to London, where he served under Rennie, the engineer. In 1790, he was back in Glasgow, running his own carpenter's business, and in 1807 he moved downriver to Helensburgh. The problems and possibilities of steam navigation had been occupying his mind since 1786, but lack of money prevented him from developing his ideas in practice. In 1809, he built "hot and cold Baths" at Helensburgh, and an adjacent hotel (which survives, with an added storey, as the Queens, although the baths have disappeared).

An American, Robert Fulton, came to England in 1804, and ordered a steam engine from the Soho works of Messrs Boulton and Watts. In 1807 that engine was driving a little paddle steamer the *Clermont*, between New York and Albany. Bell is known to have examined the unfortunate *Charlotte Dundas* and to have corresponded with Fulton. In August 1815 Bell advertised the first sailings of his own "steam passage-boat *Comet*, between Glasgow, Greenock and Helensburgh, for passengers only". The *Comet*, which took five hours to get from Glasgow to Greenock, had "handsome carpeting . . . a sofa clothed with marone . . . twelve small windows, each finished with marone, curtains, with tassels, fringe and velvet cornices, ornamented with gilt ornaments, having altogether a very rich effect. Above the sofa there is a large mirror suspended and at each side bookshelves are placed, containing a collection of the best authors, for the amusement and edification of those who may avail themselves of them during the passage."

The *Comet* was not herself a success, but by the time Southey saw the steamers on the Clyde, more than forty of these long-chimneyed wooden paddlers were sailing on regular services at a profit. One of these, the *Marjory*, built by William Denny of Dumbarton in 1814, was the first steamboat to sail on the Thames. Another, and one that presumably paid, was the *Waterloo*, built at Port Glasgow in 1816, a wooden steamship of 72 tons owned by a certain G. Brown. It had the honour of featuring in a book by John Galt called *The Steamboat*, a collection of tales told while in passage down the Clyde by a certain Thomas Duffle, lodger of Mrs. MacLecket, Boyle's Land, Saltmarket.

The *Waterloo* had brought Mr. Duffle and his garrulous story-telling acquaintances from Glasgow to Greenock.

After landing . . . our cargo of Greenockians, the steam was again set to work, and the vessel, with all that orderliness and activity which belongs to the enginery, moved round, and, turning her latter end to Greenock, walked over the waters straight to Helensburgh. This is not a long voyage naturally, being no more than four miles, if so much, but it is not without its dangers; and we had a lively taste and type of the perils of shipwreck in crossing the bank, a great shoal that lies midway in the sea. For it happened that we were later for the tide than the Captain had thought; so that, when we were in what the jac-tars call the mid-channel, the gallant "Waterloo" that had come all the way from Glasgow like a swan before the wind, stuck fast in the mud. Never shall I forget the dunt that dirled on my heart when she stopped, and the engines would go no further. Fortunately, as I was told, this came to pass just at the turn of the tide, or otherwise there is no saying what the consequences might have been.

A fellow-passenger from the West Indies distracted Mr. Duffle's anxieties from the potentialities of the Clyde winds with a rumbustious tale about a Jamaican hurricane, talking "until the steam-boat began to move, and in the course of a minute or two . . . was paddling her way towards Helensburgh". There, at Henry Bell's Baths Hotel, Mr. Duffle got "a chack of dinner . . . and a comfortable tumbler of old double-rum toddy", after which he felt fortified enough to inspect the "hot and cold baths for invalid persons, and others afflicted with the rheumatism and such like incomes".

David Napier adapted the steamship for deep-sea routes, and in 1818 put the *Rob Roy* on to the Greenock–Belfast route, though later she was sold to serve between Dover and Calais. Napier's cousin, Robert, played an important part in the development of river paddlers, mostly built by John Ward and Company at Greenock, and engined at the Vulcan Foundry, though the first of all iron ships, the *Fairy Queen*, came from the Garscube Road Foundry of John Neilson and Company in 1831.

With the development of the steamships, water, where available, became for a time the fastest, safest and most comfortable means of travel, a distinction it was to enjoy throughout Glasgow's cotton era, until the development of the railways.

Robert Reid (1773–1865), who used the pseudonym 'Senex' and from whose recollections of old Glasgow I have already quoted, has left an account of three holidays to the coast made by wherry in pre-steamship days when he was a boy, between

1778–82. A voyage to Dunoon was undertaken in a hired wherry in 1779, the family having first made arrangements to keep themselves in food throughout the summer, since they could "put no dependence on getting provisions, not even fish, in such an out of the way place".

When the day of departure came, the Reid family had "a pretty fair passage down the river till the tide met us at Dunglass; our progress now became slow, and a little below Dumbarton Castle, we fairly stuck fast upon a sandbank. Here we remained for several hours till the tide flower, when we again got under sail."

The Reids were at least luckier than another Glasgow gentleman who, in 1817, mistrusting the new-fangled steamboats, hired a fast, shallow-draught sailing-wherry, known as a 'fly', to take himself and his family to Gourock for summer quarters. In their case, "all the first day was occupied in making the passage to Bowling Bay, where we cast anchor for the night. Weighing anchor next morning, we proceeded down the Clyde, but were so buffeted by wind and waves that, after spending the whole day at sea, we were compelled to return to Bowling Bay. The third day we succeeded in making Port Glasgow in the afternoon." Here, they abandoned the fly, hired post-horses, and so reached Gourock, the whole affair having cost the "wet sick and exhausted" gentleman £7 14s. 3d. Had he trusted one of the new steamers, the *Marion* for instance, the journey would have taken about four hours, and cost him only a few shillings.

It would even have been possible for him to travel by stage coach virtually all the way, for the first regular stage coach service between Glasgow and Greenock began to operate in 1763, taking nine hours. By 1789, the journey time had been cut, and the service was twice daily every weekday.

Throughout the cotton era, there was a steady improvement in stage-coach services, both as regards speed and frequency. The first stage coach to Edinburgh, owned by one William Hume, had begun running as long ago as 1678. Not until 1749, when grants and subsidies were provided by Glasgow magistrates to ensure that the burgesses were given preferential treatment, was a regular service inaugurated, taking twelve hours. After 1758 there was a four-horse coach carrying the mail. By 1789 five stage coaches were running daily between Glasgow and Edinburgh.

The first regular London service, via Newcastle, began in 1758 and took seven days. In 1790, a link through Carlisle was formed, reducing the time to four days. The time for the London mail coach eventually came down to sixty-six hours, and by the year of Southey's visit, 1819, eight coaches drawn by four horses and seven drawn by two left Glasgow daily—one to London, three to Paisley, and one each to Hamilton, Kilmarnock, Ayr and Perth, in addition to the Greenock and Edinburgh services already mentioned. It cost a passenger travelling by four-in-hand stage coach from Glasgow to London—a journey which involved forty-five changes of horse—the sum of £40, a lot of money in those days.

In a private coach such as befitted the daughter of General Graham, Governor of Stirling Castle, under whose care the Bonnymuir martyrs had been held awaiting trial, 19-year-old Helen Graham travelled from Stirling to Glasgow, *en route* for Largs, on Monday 24th July 1826.

The day was beautiful, but very hot. . . . We changed horses at Cumbernauld, which retains its pristine bleak appearance. . . . We wended our way over moorland ground presenting no other aspect but green crops, reeds and rushes, till coming to the vicinity of Glasgow rich wood and cultivation rewarded appear. The harvest was completely begun; many fields were cut down, others filled with merry bands of reapers hard at work. The scene changes from this to clouds of smoke proclaiming the entrance to the western metropolis, and distilleries, manufactories, long ranges of buildings in succession, conducted to the George Hotel, where we had an early dinner.

We then went out and surveyed the new buildings, Blythswood Place, Garden Square, etc., which are very handsome, but rather a steep ascent, for which one is to be sure rewarded by pure airs, comparatively speaking, and a fine view. From the heights above, we decended to the regions below, which presented a more bustling appearance, and here the Glasgow *belles* and *beaux* were parading. We saw our old servant, Anderson, in his shop and his little wife, buried in crockery ware and embosomed in hard fish and bacon hams. The town was rather dull, owing I suppose to the present state of the trade, and there were scarcely any equipages to be seen.

We took our departure from The George when the evening breeze began to blow. The streets on the bank of the Clyde I like better than the situation of Garden Square, being more gay and cheerful. After passing through the towns, the environs and country are very pretty, very rich, finely wooded and a pleasing variety of hill, and dale, numbers of very pretty villas extend a long way.

It was perhaps a pity that Helen Graham, who inherited something of her aunt, the novelist Susan Ferrier's, gift for racey character-drawing (as her *Parties and Pleasures*, covering the years 1823 to 1826 show), did not spend a night in Glasgow, for she was a keen theatregoer, and it would have been interesting to have had her comments upon whatever dramatic or operatic fare was being offered.

She could have had the opportunity of visiting the Theatre Royal, built by public subscription on 1804, and regarded as the most luxurious playhouse north of London, within a few yards of the Assembly Rooms in Ingram Street, and accessible both to Argyle Street and the Blythswood New Town. It was accidentally burned down in 1829. Glasgow's other theatre, the 'Caledonian' in Dunlop Street, had been built in 1782, after prolonged clerical opposition. It survived until destroyed by fire in 1863. The fate of these theatres, and of some of their successors, differed only from what happened to their primitive predecessors by the uncontrived nature of the conflagrations.*

Earlier efforts at establishing theatres had met with burnings 'inspired' by that religious mania which was so strong a feature of Scottish life from the triumph of the Reformers in 1560, to the 1770s, when the tyrannical arrogance of the pre-destined 'Elect' became so ridiculous that the prying domination of every aspect of life by the Kirk eventually produced a revolt against its authority. By the time Burns was writing "The Holy Fair", "Holy Willie's Prayer", "The Kirk's Alarm" and other satirical hammer blows, the "black craws" were already on the run. True, they made something of a come-back among the middle and upper classes in high Victorian times, three-quarters of a century later: but never again was their hold over ordinary folk to be what it had been in the seventeenth and early eighteenth centuries.

Most of the famous actors and actresses, from Mrs. Siddons and Mrs. Jordan to Kemble and Kean, appeared on Glasgow's stages during the cotton era, plays by Shakespeare, Dryden, Goldsmith and Sheridan rubbing shoulders with pieces like *Raising the Wind*, *Love Laughs at Locksmiths*, and *The Honeymoon*. There were also

---

*A timber shed adjoining the Bishop's Palace had housed performances in which the famous Digges and Mrs. Ward, among others, had appeared from 1752. Two years later a sermon by George Whitefield caused the 'congregation' to set it on fire. Glasgow's first real theatre, built in 1762 and opened by Mrs. Bellamy, was burned in 1780. It stood outside the city boundary, at Grahamston, where the Central Station now is.

the operas of Mozart and Weber, keeping company with Sir Henry Bishop's musical versions of dramatized Scott novels, *Guy Mannering* and *Rob Roy* being the most popular.

The principal Glasgow newspaper was the *Advertiser*, published thrice weekly from 1783 to 1801, after which it became *The Glasgow Herald* (a daily only since 1859). Between 1791 and 1865 there was also the thrice weekly *Courier*. The first Glasgow daily paper, the *North British Daily Mail*, did not begin publishing until 1847.

For those who preferred to read at home, newspapers apart, there were the libraries. John Smith senior, founder of Glasgow's best and longest surviving bookshop, founded a circulating Library at the 'George Buchanan's Head', facing the Laigh Kirk, Trongate, in 1783. Five thousand volumes were available to the public for a yearly subscription of 10s. A rival Archibald Colbrough soon afterwards offered 4,500 volumes on similar terms at his shop in the High Street.

In 1791 Walter Stirling, merchant and magistrate, left his library of 804 books, £1,000 and some heritable property for the setting up of Glasgow's first public library, the books being kept at first in a room in the Surgeons' Hall, St. Enoch Square, then in the Hall of Hutcheson's Hospital, and latterly in 48 Miller Street.★

There were also periodicals like *The Glasgow Magazine*, where in 1783 part of the Dumfries-shire poet John Mayne's poem "Glasgow" first appeared. After serving his apprenticeship as a printer with the Foulis Brothers, Mayne spent his adult life in London as a printer and part proprietor of *The Star* newspaper. In 1803, he was induced to complete his Glasgow poem. In its final form it provides a vital picture of life in the city at the turn of the century, as even a few stanzas show:

> In ilka house, frae man to boy,
> A' hands in Glasgow find employ;
> Even little maids, wi' meikle joy,
> Flower lawn and gauze,
> Or clip wi' care the silken soy
> For ladies' braws.

★The Stirling's Library is now housed in the former Royal Exchange Building in Royal Exchange Square. It seems that so strong was Stirling's aversion to novels, he directed that the books to be bought after his death "should be rather rare and curious than those of the common and ordinary kinds". The Stirling Library has remained largely a 'technical' library.

Their fathers weave, their mothers spin
The muslin robe, so fine and thin
That, frae the ankles to the chin,
    It aft discloses
The beauteous symmetry within—
    Limbs, necks and bosies. . . .

Look through the town! The houses here
Like noble palaces appear;
A' things the face o' gladness wear—
    The market's thrang,
Business is brisk, and a's asteer
    The streets along.

Clean-keepit streets! so lang and braid,
The distant objects seem to fade;
And then, for shelter or for shade
    Frae sun or shower,
Piazzas lend their friendly aid
    At any hour. . . .

Wond'ring, we see new streets extending,
New squares wi' public buildings blending,
Brigs, stately brigs, in arches bending
    Across the Clyde,
And turrets, kirks and spires ascending
    In lofty pride. . . .

Wow, sirs! It's wonderfu' to trace
How commerce has improved the place.
Changing bare house-room's narrow space,
    And want o' money,
To seats of elegance and grace,
    And milk and honey. . . .

Glasgow Fair apart, in the years between Mayne's first draft of his "Glasgow" poem and the publication of it in its final form, there were other public pleasures and diversions: more than a dozen public executions, always a popular spectacle; a great frost in 1780, and an even more severe frost which lasted for four months in 1785, when the Clyde froze and carnivals were held on the ice; a flood in March 1782, when the Clyde rose 20 feet, forcing householders in Saltmarket to evacuate their houses by boat and drowning a woman in the Gorbals; a fire which burned nine houses in Gorbals in 1786, followed in the same year by what was thought to be an earth tremor; the introduction to Glasgow from Paris by the surgeon John Jamieson of the first umbrella in 1782; and in 1795 the balloon ascents of Vincent Lunardi from St. Andrew's Square to Hawick, and from the Merchants' House Garden in the Bridgegait to Campsie. As Burns enthusiasts will remember Lunardi lent his name to a certain style of lady's bonnet. But his ascents did not always inspire such charming flights of fancy. Away up in Shetland, John Mill, a parish minister who kept a diary, remarked sourly of Lunardi's first ascent from Edinburgh a decade earlier: "Oh! how much are the thoughtless multitude set on these and like foolish vanities to the neglect of the one thing needful!"

The obvious influence on Mayne is Burns, who himself visited Glasgow in 1787, and again in 1788,* when he stayed in the Black Bull Hotel, built for the Highland Society in 1758 (not to be confused with Old Black Bull Inn, on the other side of the road). But Glasgow cannot lay any real claim to Burns's loyalties in the sense that Edinburgh can. However, the novelist Tobias Smollett served his apprenticeship as a surgeon in the city, and both James Boswell and John Wilson ('Christopher North') studied at the university. Scott's friend Joanna Baillie—remembered now not for her unreadable and unactable verse dramas but for her little song "Saw ye Johnie comin'?"—went to school in Glasgow. C. A. Oakley thinks that she probably played some part in influencing her distant relatives and fellow natives of Lanarkshire, William and John Hunter, anatomist and surgeon respectively, to bequeath to the university their valuable scientific collection, still preserved in the Hunterian Museum at Gilmorehill.

Scott himself was often in Glasgow. He spent some days at Ross Priory, on Loch Lomond, where his friend the Principal Clerk of Session, Hector MacDonald Buchanan, lived. Scott's son-in-law, John Gibson Lockhart, also a Glasgow graduate, has left us a brightly painted verse-portrait of one of Glasgow's 'characters', Captain Archibald Paton, a retired military man renowned for his remarkable precision and dapper dress:

> His waistcoat, coat and breeches,
>   Were all cut of the same web,
> Of a beautiful snuff-colour,
>   Of a modest, genty drab.

*Probably more frequently, the shorter visits not being recorded.

The blue strip in his stocking
  Round his neat slim leg did go,
And his ruffles of the cambric fine,
  They were whiter than the snow.
Oh! we ne'er shall see the like of Captain Paton no mo'e!

In dirty days he picked well
  His footsteps with his rattan
Oh! You ne'er could see the least speck
  On the shoes of Captain Paton.
And on entering the coffee-room,
  About two, all men did know
They would see him with his *Courier*
  In the middle of the row.
Oh! we ne'er shall see the like of Captain Paton no mo'e!

Undoubtedly the most famous of Glasgow's men-of-letters, at least in his own day, was Thomas Campbell (1777–1844), the youngest of the eleven children of a Virginia tobacco merchant. After graduating at Glasgow, and leading a strenuous and varied literary life the main ornament of which in the esteem of his contemporaries was his long poem "The Pleasures of Hope", Campbell was elected Lord Rector of his *alma mater* in 1826, Scott being among the defeated candidates.

"Hohenlinden", "Ye Mariners of England" and "The Battle of the Baltic" have kept his fame alive among English school-children, though the Scots may prefer "Lord Ullin's Daughter". I remember best his little poem, "Florine", set to music by Francis George Scott; a poem not affected by nationalities.

Could I bring back lost youth again
  And be what I have been,
I'd court you in a gallant strain,
  My young and fair Florine.

But mine's the chilling age that chides
  Devoted rapture's glow,
And love—that conquers all besides—
  Finds Time a conquering foe.

Farewell! we're severed from our fate
  As far as night from noon;
You came into the world too late,
  And I depart so soon.

In a city which relied on the classical teaching of its grammar school for over 200 years, continuing these traditions in the new school put up in 1787 on the north side of George Square, and where education was inevitably only available to the privileged few, the pleasures enjoyed by the ordinary more or less illiterate citizen were not exactly literary. Brutal sports like cock-fighting had their secret following. But many of the delights of Glasgow Fair were innocent enough, as recorded by the handloom weaver John Breckenridge (1790–1840).

> The carles, fu' cadgie, sat cocking
>   Upon their white nags and their brown,
> Wi' snuffing and laughing and joking
>   They soon cantered into the town.
> 'Twas there was the funning and sporting;
>   Eh, lord! what a swarm o' braw folk—
> Rowly-powly, wild beasts, wheels o' fortune,
>   Sweetie stan's, Maister Punch, and Black Jock.
>
> Now Willock and Tam, geyan bouzie,
>   By this time had met wi' their joes;
> Consented wi' Gibbie and Susie
>   To gang awa' doun to the shows.
> 'Twas there was the fiddling and drumming;
>   Sic a crowd they could scarcely get through—
> Fiddles, trumpets, and organs a-bumming;
>   O sirs! what a hully-baloo.
>
> Then hie to the tents at the paling,
>   Weel theekit wi' blankets and mats,
> And deals seated round like a tap-room,
>   Supported on stanes and on pats.
> The whisky like water they're selling,
>   And porter as sma' as their yill,
> And aye as you're pouring they're telling,
>   "Troth, dear, it's just sixpence a gill!"
>
> Says Meg, "See yon beast wi' the claes on't,
>   Wi' the face o't as black as the soot!
> Preserve's! it has fingers and taes on't—
>   Eh sirs! it's an unco like brute!"
> "O woman, but ye are a gomeral
>   To mak' sic a won'er at that!
> D'ye na ken, ye daft gowk, that's a mongrel
>   That's bred 'twixt a dog and a cat.

"See yon souple jaud, how she's dancing,
  Wi' the white ruffled breeks and red shoon!
Frae the tap to the tae she's a glancing
  Wi' gowd, and a feather abune
My troth, she's a brae decent kimmer
  As I have yet seen in the Fair!"
"Her decent!" quo' Meg, "She's a limmer,
  Or, faith, she would never be there."

" 'She's a limmer', quo' Meg"; in other words, a comely performer. Good Meg, if she but knew it, was merely echoing that
anti-pleasure principle firmly inculcated into the Scots temperament by the Reformers, a principle the sterile resonancing of
which sounded down into the twentieth century. To be able to
perform on the stage with professional skill may have indicated
involvement with 'sinfulness' to the douce Glaswegians of the
cotton era; strangely, however, to overeat, drink too much, and
dance themselves into exhaustion was hampered by no such
kirkly stigma.

Now they ate and they drank till their bellies
  Were bent like the head o' a drum;
Syne they rase, and they capered like fillies,
  Whene'er that the fiddle played bum.
Wi' dancing they now were grown weary,
  And scarcely were able to stan',
So they took to the road a' fu' cheerie
  As day was beginning to dawn.

V

THE YEARS OF IRON

Cotton and textiles continued to be manufactured in Glasgow in considerable quantity until the 1860s, after which the industry went into decline, partly, as we have mentioned, because of other investment opportunities, partly because of the cotton famine which resulted from the American Civil War, but more probably because the Lancashire mills had gone over to producing cheaper materials increasingly in demand while Glasgow stuck to quality production. This decline continued into the twentieth century, accelerating during the depression of the 20s, when 'rationalization'—the buying by an English firm of a Scots firm in order to close it down—all but finished off the textile industry in the west of Scotland.

The textile industry in its hey-day did, however, encourage the development of a number of ancillary industries. Charles Tennant (1768–1838)—Burns's 'Wabster Charlie'—founded the St. Rollox chemical works in 1800. Tennant manufactured a bleaching agent the success of which resulted in his becoming the largest firm of its kind in Europe, its 436-feet-high chimney—known as 'Tennant's Stalk', the tallest in Europe—depositing smoke over the city and greyish waste around the factory, neither of them by-products which improved the quality of the environment.

Another industrialist, Charles Mackintosh (1766–1843), a manufacturer of dyestuffs, discovered how to dissolve rubber and use it to waterproof fabrics. He set up a factory in Glasgow to produce mackintoshes in 1834, though later the business was transferred to Manchester, where it is now owned by the Dunlop Rubber Company. There was also a growing demand for machinery for mills, collieries and the new steamships. But the industry, which, from about 1830 to 1870, occupied the dominant position in Glasgow's economic life, was the manufacture of cheap iron.

Iron smelted with charcoal had been manufactured in Scotland at the Lorn Furnaces, built on Loch Etive by the Argyll Furnace Company, since 1754, but the ore was shipped from England, and the iron was sent back there. Roebuck, Cadell and Company's Carron Works, founded in 1760, smelted with coke a mixture of Scots and English ores, but had to import bar iron from Sweden and Russia.

Thomas Edington, who had been a traveller with the Carron Company and later manager of the slitting-mill at Cramond, near Edinburgh, went into partnership with William Cadell in 1786 to promote the Clyde Ironworks, and with John Gillies of the Dalnotter Ironworks and William Robertson of the Smithfield Iron works to promote the Muirkirk Ironworks in 1789. The Clyde works aimed at providing Carron with bar iron to remove the need, sometimes difficult to meet, to import it, while Muirkirk produced bar iron for general use. Other less successful ironworks came into being, notably at Cleland (Omoa) in 1789, and at Glenbuck, Calder, Shotts, and Markinch around the turn of the century. The trouble with the produce of all the early Scottish ironworks was that it was too expensive, priced out of every market except that of Scotland.

As long ago as 1801 David Mushet had discovered the rich fields of blackband ironstone which lay more or less totally unworked in the west of Scotland—'wild coal' it had been called when it was thought to be useless. The ironworks at Calder and Clyde did use a little, mixed with other ores, but found that its advantages were offset by the difficulty of smelting it in the small cold-blast furnaces then commonly in use.

In 1828, however, the manager of the Glasgow Gas Works, J. B. Neilson, while carrying out experiments at the Clyde Ironworks, discovered how to use hot instead of cold air in the blasting furnace. The combination of hot-blast furnace and blackband ironstone produced the recipe for cheap pig-iron which cut coal consumption by at least 50 per cent and enabled iron to be sent to England and sold there 15 to 20 per cent cheaper than the English product. Low mineral royalties, cheap coal and cheap labour, with a plentiful supply of jobless Highlanders or Irish always available to break strikes, were further factors which gave the Glasgow ironmasters their keenly competitive edge, especially after 1840, when a method of heating the blast with waste gases from the furnaces was discovered.

Between 1830 and 1843 the expansion of the iron industry was as startling as had been the rise of the cotton industry between 1780 and 1790. At Gartsherrie the Bairds built their first furnace in 1830. Within a decade they had seven furnaces going and were the leading Scottish producers, responsible for about 25 per cent of Scotland's total output. Whereas in 1830 there had been twenty-five furnaces enabling Glasgow to produce about 40,000 tons, by 1843 sixty-two furnaces were producing upwards of 250,000 tons annually. In the peak year, 1870, approximately 120 furnaces were producing nearly a million and a quarter tons.

At the beginning of the 'railway mania', Scotland was thus well placed to supply railway iron throughout the United Kingdom; which was fortunate because, before 1830, with the notable exception of the Carron Works whose finished goods were internationally famous, Scotland was slow to develop the manufacture of malleable iron, in spite of the ready supply of cheap fuel to hand which might have encouraged its ironworks masters to try to do so. The fact was, however, that even Henry Bessemer, whose Bessemer Converter eventually led to the establishment of the steel industry, tried and failed to produce high-quality metal from Scottish ores during a visit to 'Dixon's Blazes'. By the 1850s several ironmasters who insisted on using local materials were finding it difficult to produce the better grades of malleable iron needed for the propeller shafts of the bigger ocean-going steamships. By the 1870s, the ores found near Middlesbrough were enabling northern England to produce better iron so cheaply that it began to oust the Scottish product, even in Scotland.

Until the arrival of the railways, or at least their immediate predecessor the waggon-ways, heavy cargoes such as coal had to be shipped by water, if any quantity was to be transported. Canals like Telford's Caledonian Canal, and to some extent the Forth and Clyde Canal in which both Smeaton and Watt had a hand, were national in purpose. The Forth and Clyde Canal shared with smaller connecting canals like the Monkland and the Union the primary purpose of exploiting more economically the natural resources of Central Scotland. By 1822, when the canal network was completed, coal could be sent from the Monkland coalfields to Port Dundas in Glasgow or to Port Hopetoun in Edinburgh. A canal intended to link Glasgow, Paisley and Ardrossan, however, never got beyond Johnstone.

Although a passenger use was developed for some of these

canals, and a tourist industry use survived until 1939, they came upon the scene too late to be profitable for long. During the Forth and Clyde canal's first fifty years of operation it is reckoned to have carried up to 3,000 ships annually and to have been paying its shareholders a dividend of 30 per cent as late as 1837.

Shareholders gifted with foresight, or aware of what had been happening since 1824 at the Monkland coalfield, should have begun to think about getting rid of their canal shares by this time. A waggon-way had been constructed from Monkland to Kirkintilloch, leading from the Old Monkton collieries to the Forth and Clyde Canal. In 1826, locomotives supplanted horses on this line, and there is some evidence that passengers may also have been carried over the 10-mile stretch of the main track. In 1828 the Ballochney Railway added three branches to the Monkland to Kirkintilloch line, the result being a dramatic fall in coal prices, first in Edinburgh and later in Glasgow.

The real beginning of railroad travel in Scotland was on 27th September 1831, when the Glasgow and Garnkirk railway, which had opened for mineral traffic in 1827, first carried passenger at 7 miles an hour along its 8-mile length from St. Rollox Station. It used steam locomotives from the beginning. Most of those early railways—though, curiously, not the Glasgow and Garnkirk—were phenomenally successful, the benefits they conferred leading not only to an upsurge in the mineral values of the areas they served but naturally also to a substantial rise in the value of the owning company's shares.

In 1830, the Pollok and Govan Railway Company and the Rutherglen Railway Company were formed, the former with capital of £66,000, the latter with £20,000. These were small enterprises.

The second major Glasgow railway was also originally associated with coalfields. In 1837, the line to Paisley, Kilmarnock and Ayr was authorized, designed to serve the Ayrshire coalfields. (In 1869, the Glasgow and South Western Railway Company secured the unfinished Ardrossan canal and later built their link from Port Eglinton to Paisley along its bed.)

Thereafter, railway development was not tied so closely to coalfields. The Glasgow to Greenock line was authorized in 1837 and was opened for passenger traffic in 1841. The Edinburgh and Glasgow Railway Company, with a capital of £900,000 and a loan of £300,000, linked Glasgow to Edinburgh in 1842, the tunnel between Queen Street and Cowlairs, where a locomotive works was established, costing £40,000.

Since 1832, a railway line to connect Scotland and England had been talked of and some survey work had been carried through; but throughout the 1830s a dispute raged about the route to be followed. The route to connect Edinburgh with London through Berwick-upon-Tweed and Newcastle was obvious enough. The row which developed was over the Glasgow to London link. Should the line go over Beattock Summit, with all the engineering and subsequent operating difficulties this would entail? Or should the line traverse the flatter Ayrshire coalfields further to the west? A Royal Commission formed to investigate the proposals during the years of railway mania, which came to a peak about 1845, had actually favoured the Nithsdale route in preference to that via Beattock; yet in 1845, a Parliamentary decision was given in favour of the Caledonian Railway Company's Beattock route. It opened in February 1848, two years after the North British Railway Company's east-coast route had first crossed the border at Berwick.

Construction of the rival Nithsdale route was authorized in 1846, and the Glasgow, Paisley, Kilmarnock and Ayr Railway was, after an amalgamation, soon to become the Glasgow and South Western Railway Company, the third of the three big companies which dominated railway operation out of Glasgow throughout the nineteenth century.

To the north, the Scottish Central Railway ran up to Perth in 1840, its owners amalgamating eventually with the Caledonian Railway. Travel from Glasgow was further extended to Inverness and Nairn in 1855—eventually to Thurso—along the track of the Highland Railway, and from 1852, to Elgin and Lossiemouth along the track of the Great North of Scotland Railway.

C. A. Oakley has pointed out that Glasgow had become the second city of the British Empire some forty years before the direct rail link with London was established. Even so, Glasgow Corporation was at first reluctant to allow the new means of travel to penetrate to the heart of the city. Both the Glasgow, Paisley, Kilmarnock and Ayr and the Glasgow, Paisley and Greenock companies had to be content with a station on the south side of the river; yet the owners of the Glasgow and Edinburgh line were able to build their terminal at Queen Street in the 1840s (reconstructed in the 1880s), and Buchanan Street station, the terminal for the companies running to the north, went up in 1849. Although in passenger-carrying terms the London link was by far the most important, the Glasgow and South Western Railway Company's station was kept out at Bridge Street. The St. Enoch Station and hotel were not completed until 1880. It was 1879 before the Caledonian Company could bring their trains into Central Station, having previously used Buchanan Street Station or an inconvenient station at the junction of Cathcart Street and Pollokshaws Road. Both new stations necessitated the construction of separate railway bridges over the Clyde.

Buchanan Street Station has totally disappeared in our own day, while St. Enoch, its platform tracks filled up with concrete, does much-needed temporary duty as one of the city's largest and most convenient car parks, before finally making way for new development. Queen Street Station, the work of James Carswell, though modernised internally, still carries its two great fanes, one of which is likely to be obscured by the redevelopment of the northern side of George Square.

It was from Queen Street Station that the first Sunday train ran from Glasgow, setting out for Edinburgh on 13th March 1842, "filled with peaceful and respectable persons, gliding quietly away on its mission," as a contemporary journalist gracefully put it. Such a smooth departure must have disappointed the Presbytery of Glasgow, who had denounced the running of Sunday trains as "a flagrant violation of the law of God as expressed in the Fourth Commandment, a grievous outrage on the religious feelings of the people of Scotland, a powerful temptation to the careless and indifferent to abandon the public ordinances of Grace, and most disastrous to the quiet of the rural parishes along the line of the railway, by the introduction into them every Sabbath, of many of the profligate and dissipated who inhabit the cities of Glasgow and Edinburgh".

In Edinburgh a threatening battery of ministers, presumably unaware of the inclusion of their city in their Glasgow brethren's condemnation, lined the platforms and informed the detraining passengers that they had bought tickets to hell, a claim which does not seem to have deterred many of them from making their way towards Princes Street.

Janet Hamilton, a remarkable Lanarkshire woman (married in Glasgow by John Gibson Lockhart's father), fifth in descent from John Whitelaw, a Covenanter executed at the Old Tolbooth of

Edinburgh for his part in the battle of Bothwell Brig, herself
unable to write until she was 50 and the mother of ten children,
celebrated the occasion in "The Sunday Rail", which rises to this
indignant smoke-plume of a climax:

> Now range up the carriages, feed up the fires!
> To the rail, to the rail, now the pent-up desires
> Of the pale toiling million find gracious reply,
> On the pinions of steam they shall fly, they shall fly,
> To beauties of nature and art to explore,
> To ramble the woodlands and roam by the shore,
> The city spark here with his smart smirking lass,
> All peg-topped and crinolined, squat on the grass,
> While with quips and with cranks and soft-wreathed smiles,
> Each nymph with her swain the dull Sabbath beguiles.
>
> Here mater and paterfamilias will come
> With their rollicking brood from their close city home,
> How they scramble and scream, how they scamper and run,
> While pa and mamma are enjoying the fun!
> And the urchins bawl out, "Oh, how funny and jolly,
> Dear ma, it is thus to keep Sabbath-day holy."
>
> Now for pipe and cigar and the snug pocket-flask,
> What's the rail on a Sunday without them, we ask?
> What the sweet-scented heather and rich clover-blooms,
> To the breath of the weed as it smoulders and fumes?
> So in courting and sporting, in drinking and smoking,
> Walking and talking, in laughter and joking,
> They while the dull hours of the Sabbath away.
> What a Sabbath it is! Who is Lord of the day!

Mrs. Hamilton, who wielded a powerful pen on behalf of the
temperance movement (which sought to remove the palliative of
the poor man's despair without doing anything to alleviate the
social causes of his distress), was not, of course, on the side of the
Sunday travellers; but irony wielded in a losing cause is apt to end
up wearing a somewhat ambiguous edge.

The effect of the arrival of the railways upon the fabric of
central Glasgow must have been somewhat similar to that which
the construction of urban motorways is having upon the city
today. For one thing, it settled the already declining fortunes of
Laurieston, the Laurie brothers' housing development south of the
river; for another, it cut broad swatches through medieval and

pre-Industrial Revolution Glasgow. Much of what went had become an overcrowded health hazard. Unfortunately—and this is not simply the hindsight of a later generation with different values—much that could have been conserved, using other means to solve the social problems, was thoughtlessly swept away. Up to a point it is fair to compare the way mid-nineteenth-century Glaswegians treated the heart of our city with what, say, contemporary Copenhageners or Hamburgians did to theirs. Our Glasgow forebears do not emerge with much credit on the environmental side, however admirable their social promptings.

Their most disastrous decision was to demolish the medieval university in order to make way for High Street Goods Station. This had first been mooted in 1845, when a move to Woodside had been proposed, but a powerful faction of magistrates and professors at that time took the view that a university should remain at the heart of a place and, by its influence, try to revivify it. In Glasgow, however, money has always talked loudly, and short-term economic gains have usually seemed more attractive than long-term environmental advantages. By the 1860s, when a second railway bid came in, the idealists had lost the battle.

There were other implications connected with the coming of the railways: physical implications such as the need for engine building and repair works, like those established at St. Rollox and Springburn; and social implications arising from increasing opportunities for quicker and cheaper travel. Only the middle classes were able to make full use of this latter benefit, for the wages and holidays of the working classes did not allow more than an occasional day trip on the Clyde—or 'Doon the watter', to give this now-vanished pleasure its traditional local nomenclature.

The increasing number of paddle-steamers sailing from the Broomielaw was making the frequently-deepened upper river almost overcrowded. During the 1850s, the issue between the private owners of these Clyde steamers became one of speed versus comfort. For a time, speed won. The Clyde steamers of the mid-century years were mostly lean, rakish affairs, designed to paddle themselves up and down the Firth with the minimum water resistance, their decks as free as possible of luxury structures which might act as impediments against the wind.

An account of the days of cut-price steamer competition, of dangerous racing in order to snatch away a rival's potential passengers, of steamers banging each other at piers, of captains insulting their rivals through advertisements printed in local papers, and of the sturdy individuality which characterized many of the owner/skippers who operated throughout the Iron Years, has been written by Captain James Williamson, founder of the Williamson Line. Captain Williamson, in his later years a dandy with a white goatee beard, inherited the business created by his father, one of the earliest steamer operators on Loch Lomond who moved over to the Clyde. Captain Williamson himself served his apprenticeship as an engineer and then as a ships master, qualifications not regarded as essential in the early days of steamboat operation. His book *Clyde Passenger Steamers* (1904) deals, as might be expected, with engineering and other technical developments, but also preserves for us fascinating social glimpses, in the writing of which he was able to draw on his own memories and those of his family.

Some of the fast but primitive steamers which took the workers away for a few hours from the forges and the foundries and the grime of Glasgow to the mountainy loveliness of the Firth of Clyde, at a cost of as little as a shilling for a day's outing, came to an untimely end. Huge prices were paid for the acquisition of vessels to run the Federal blockade in the American Civil War. Many of these frail paddlers were battered to pieces in mid-Atlantic before they could reach their new owners. Those that survived made large profits for their unscrupulous operators.

The railway companies were slow to appreciate the profitability of the steamboat business, and at first left the private operators to vie among themselves for the privilege of running to train connections.

Attempts in 1844 and again in the 1850s by the proprietors of the Greenock Railway (later amalgamated with the Caledonian) and in 1848 by the Wemyss Bay Steamboat Company Limited (an associate of the Greenock and Wemyss Bay Railway Company, also eventually amalgamated with the Caledonian) to run their own steamers failed. To travel by a privately owned steamer connecting with the train meant a more expensive journey than a sail 'all the way'. Even so, the obvious eventual threat of railway competition during these peak years of the private owner was clearly one which could not be wisely disregarded, especially after the North British Railway built a railhead pier at Craigendoran in 1883, and the Caledonian Company opened at Gourock in 1889.

One of the reasons for the provision of these increasing travel facilities between Glasgow and the Clyde Coast was the tendency for more and more wealthy Glaswegians to follow the example of Kirkman Finlay, for whom David Hamilton had built Toward Castle in 1821, and build holiday houses for themselves along the northern fringes of the estuary, turning little villages like Strone, Kirn and Innellan into water-front clusters of ornate Italianate villas with large gardens. When transporting the owners of these summer villas from their places of leisure to their city offices in the morning, and bringing them home again at night, the shorter the travelling time the better was likely to be the pressure of customers. One of the forms which competition took was steamer racing.

The practice of steamer racing came to a climax on 27th May 1861, when two new paddle-steamers, the *Ruby* and the *Rothesay Castle*, owned by rival companies, were both scheduled to leave Glasgow at 4 p.m. bound for Greenock and Rothesay.

Andrew MacQueen, another historian of the Clyde Fleet, has left us an account of this contest in his book, *Echoes of Old Clyde Paddle-Wheels* (1924).

It had been arranged that the steamers were to change berths at the Broomielaw on alternate days. On Monday 27th May the advantage fell to the *Rothesay Castle*.

Right well she availed herself of it, for, having the lead, she kept it, travelling as never steamer had travelled on the river before. At twenty past five, the spectators on the Custom House Quay at Greenock saw her race past, with the *Ruby* in close attendance. Keeping up the pace, the *Rothesay Castle* finished at Rothesay Quay two and a half minutes ahead of her rival, having covered the distance in two hours twenty-eight minutes. The feat was suitably recognised, the awards being made the following Monday by Bailie Raeburn at the River-Bailie Court, where Captain Brown of the *Rothesay Castle* was fined a guinea for reckless navigation and Captain Price of the *Ruby*, in view of the reputation he had acquired for similar exploits, double the amount.

But Price, who had no doubt provoked Brown, was not to be cured by a mere 2-guinea fine. A few months later, he ran a neck-and-neck race with the *Neptune*, colliding with her twice and missing out Gourock, where he should have called, in order to maintain his lead.

"What right has this man, Price," thundered *The Glasgow*

Herald, "to entrap people into his vessel for a safe summer-day sail and then subject them to the terror of a violent death by explosion or collision?"

This time the River-Bailie Court provided the answer. Price lost his command, and reckless racing came to an end.

While rail and steamer travel were mostly the concern of the well-to-do, in the city itself the horse-drawn omnibuses, which first appeared on the streets in 1834, carried a broader cross-section of the public. Working men of the poorer sort still preferred to walk to factory or foundry, for low-cost 'workers' tickets were not introduced until about 1894. The well-to-do relied for transport upon their own carriages throughout Victorian times, a status-symbol provoking the same sort of snobbery as the motor car was to inspire a hundred years later.

Robert Frame began running buses at 2d. the single journey between Barrowfield Toll, Bridgeton and Gusset-House, Anderston on 1st January 1845, and before long the magistrates had to lay down safety regulations to curb dangerous speeding by no less than four rivals. The famine of 1846 which raised the price of corn from 16s. to 35s. a boll (six bushels), bankrupted Frame and his rivals. After eighteen busless months, Forsyth, Braig and Mitchell tried running services. The 'father' of Glasgow's street transport system, however, was Andrew Menzies (1822–73), who took over many of the city's omnibus services early in the 1850s. His buses were painted in the Menzies tartan, those of his rival, Duncan MacGregor, in the tartan of Rob Roy. Gentlemen travelled on the exposed top deck, leaving the ladies the shelter of the straw-floored lower deck. Journeys in these vehicles can hardly have been pleasant experiences, especially in wet or steamy weather.

Menzies lived long enough to pioneer the introduction of the railway principle, thereby lowering wheel friction and giving faster and smoother running. After much opposition, his Glasgow Tramway and Omnibus Company was allowed by Parliament to run tramcars in 1870. The corporation laid the tracks, and in 1872 the first horse-drawn tartan tramcar ran from St. George's Cross to Eglinton Toll. Menzies died soon after, but his pioneer plans were developed by John Duncan, a Glasgow lawyer. Tramcars eventually ran over eleven routes under private enterprise, the longest being from St. Vincent Street to Dennistoun, before the corporation took them over in 1894.

The entrance to Glasgow School of Art

In 1871 the Vale of Clyde Tramways received Parliamentary sanction to run steam cars from Paisley Road Toll to Govan, but these were not very successful. Paisleyites may still have remembered tales of the explosion of the boiler of a prototype steam omnibus in 1830.

Changes were also taking place on the roads leading into Glasgow. While the Statute Labour Act of 1772 laid an obligation upon residents to maintain streets within the city, the roads outside were developed by turnpike companies who charged tolls to those who used them. The growth of the city gradually engulfed some of these toll bars, so that some of the new suburbs found themselves immediately on the wrong side of them. This meant that suburban residents had to pay in order to get past the toll bars to reach their offices in the city centre, and pay again when they wanted to go home at night. Squabbles constantly arose at the toll bars themselves. Forceful, though perhaps less violent, arguments were constantly being put up by aggrieved industrialists to the Provost of Glasgow and the turnpike trustees. Although it was not until 1878 that an Act of Parliament abolished toll rights on Glasgow's roads and bridges, an intermediate arrangement was reached whereby the Statute Labour Trust, later the Police Board, took over the cost of maintaining any road if two-thirds of the area through which it ran had been built over. The toll bar was then shifted out beyond the new suburb.

One of the advantages of the railways was that they cut out the need to pay these irksome tolls. In a short time they drove the lumbering stage-coaches off the roads and on to Christmas cards and calendars. Until the development of the internal combustion engine gave travel by road supremacy of convenience over all other forms of surface transport, roads had to take third place against the coastal shipping services and the railways. Even trunk roads like that built by Telford from Glasgow to Carlisle were intended only for light carriage traffic, and for the driving of cattle to market centres. Incidentally, the building of the Glasgow-Carlisle road resulted in the construction of some fine Telford bridges, notably at Hamilton and Elvanfoot, although neither was as impressive as his bridge over the Dee at Tongueland, in Kirkcudbrightshire, or his Cartlands Crags bridge near Lanark, over the gorge of the Mouse Water.

During the Years of Iron, Glasgow's population multiplied

7

Glasgow School of Art—the Library

dramatically and the city continued to spread. In 1830 the population had been 200,000. By the 1870s, it had multiplied to half a million. There was a tremendous influx of Irishmen during the 1840s reaching its climax in 1846 as a result of the disastrous potato famine of that year. Many of the immigrants crossed the Irish Sea on a deck passage costing only 6d. and were virtually paupers when they arrived. They found quick employment in the dirtier jobs which Glasgow's expanding economy was creating; but most of these jobs produced less than the mid-century average wage of about a pound for a sixty-nine-hour week. Irish immigrants were therefore forced to crowd into the cheapest accommodation available, old sub-divided narrowly spaced houses in the wynds and vennels of central Glasgow.

Being Catholics, they usually had large families. Infant mortality was high among them, and the problems of hygiene and health created by so dense a concentration of people in inadequate housing soon became considerable. The Irish also brought with them celebratory habits which did not exactly endear them to the dourer native Scots with the chill of Calvin sobered through several blood-generations. With what money they had, these new Glaswegians drank heavily and roistered heartily among themselves, wakes for the dead involving not only the usual disturbances associated with communal drunkenness but a risk of fire to close-packed properties and the spread of infectious diseases like cholera and typhus. Thus the basis of such antipathy as there is between Scots and Irish (who, after all, derive from one stock!), Scots-speaker and Gaelic-speaker, Catholic and Protestant, goes back to the inability of Glasgow to house adequately the influx of much-needed Irish labourers and their families in the 1840s.

The Irish influx also spread outwards from the old town, causing David Laurie to exclaim in the 1830s: "We have been submerged by an inundation of Irish poor. They seldom have any furniture which the landlord can seize, and what they have they remove at night." Under conditions such as Laurie describes the 'moonlight flittin'' was introduced to Glasgow, and there were sown the first seeds of the curious Scots belief that housing is a gift from God, who needs no rent—a belief which was eventually to result for many years in the acceptance of lower standards of council housing in Glasgow than in comparable English towns, and which latterly helped place on the city's metaphorical back a staggering burden of debt.

In spite of this overcrowding of the older areas, building for those who could pay at least some rent was going on at an unprecedented rate. Tenements of a new style designed to house the working classes were being put up from about 1830 onwards. These were sub-divided from the start, and had no bathrooms. In later years, brick towers were run up the back of these tenements providing one 'stair-heid' water-closet between two floors of dwellings, to serve six to ten families. The inadequacy of such meagre sanitary provision resulted in conditions of degradation and squalor which no one who ever inspected them would readily forget.

Within two decades, even these tenements were becoming so overcrowded that a system was devised whereby a metal label or 'ticket' was affixed to the side of a house indicating the number of adults and children (half-adults) permitted to sleep there. Nightmen were employed to carry out spot checks that the number was not being exceeded, a practice which had to be continued until after the First World War.

Until the Second World War the middle classes believed in the adage "safe as houses". Most of these working-class tenements were owned by people who had never seen them, and were managed by a middleman or factor. They provided their owners with a reasonable income until after 1920, when mandatory rent restriction kept that income static, although the cost of repairs went on mounting. As a result, not only the old, overcrowded and insanitary tenements, worn out and overdue for demolition by the end of the Second World War, but also adequately appointed 'twilight' tenements capable of modernization for a further useful lease of life in a city which is chronically short of houses were, of necessity, simply allowed to deteriorate beyond hope of economical recovery, the owners of the title-deeds in many cases being elderly great-great-granddaughters of the original investors and living frugally on fixed incomes.

The four- and five-storey tenement became the characteristic architectural unit of Victorian Glasgow. Until about the middle of the century, it was primarily a form of dwelling for the working classes, but after 1850 it was developed as a kind of extension of the middle-class terrace idea. Basically, both tenement and terrace derive from the medieval Edinburgh 'land'.

In order to try to overcome the various problems of balance and monotony which long lines of towering tenements create, certain stylistic characteristics became fairly generally adopted. Because each flat was to be self-contained, and each family would consider itself entitled to rooms having the accepted 12- or 14-feet-high ceilings, the Georgian practice of lowering the ceilings of the upper floors of a buildings and reducing the size of the windows accordingly, could not be applied. In an attempt to evolve a different kind of variety, the architects of the early tenement blocks usually marked off the first floor either with a heavy cornice or a series of pediments, sometimes with both. The top-floor windows carried no decoration, but a sense of graduation was achieved by putting rather less heavy pediments above the windows of the middle floors.

Avoiding horizontal monotony was a more difficult problem, and the architects of the earlier working-class tenements rarely achieved it. Pavilions were occasionally added, or advantage taken of turned corners to add pillared decorative work, as on the corner of Minerva Street and Argyle Street, a block built in 1853 by Alexander Kirkland (the architect responsible in 1850 for the huge sweep of St. Vincent Crescent). Later, especially in tenements intended to be occupied by what Sir W. S. Gilbert described as "the lower middle classes", the tenements had often only three storeys. Experiments were also made with window spacing. The establishment in popularity of the bay window during the 1880s did more than anything else to solve the problem of horizontal monotony.

Today many of these early tenements stand in one or other of the city's twenty-seven Comprehensive Development Areas, where virtually total rebuilding, and a shedding of 60 per cent of the present population, is envisaged. It is natural for us to think of Glasgow's cliff-like sootened tenements as the hemmers-in of much of the poverty, squalor and violence popularly associated with the city. Yet when these tenements were new and honey-coloured, they must have been spacious, dry and weather-proof compared to the cramped-up though picturesque thatch-roofed old houses in the centre of Glasgow.

There is perhaps little point now in trying to analyse in detail what went wrong. Many of the broad causes of decline are obvious. But the decline might have been less severe over the middle period of our own century had not political prejudice deflected any practical possibility of help being given to landlords to maintain acceptable housing standards. Many Glaswegians have yet to accept the fact that environmental quality has to be paid for by someone. Neither the now all-but-non-existent rich nor the central government can be expected to meet bills a larger share of which could, without hardship, be met by those who enjoy the benefits.

While the first spread of tenement building filled in the immediate environs of eighteenth-century Glasgow, building was going on further out for those in a position to pay for a fine new terrace house set among gardens. There were three areas in particular splendidly developed in this way. During the 1830s Sauchiehall Road, as it was then called, had "for its sylvan charms . . . long been the favourite promenade of the beauty and fashion of the city". There was also Woodlands, the hill to the north overlooking Sauchiehall Street. And there was the long, straight Great Western Road, leading from the end of the Cowcaddens straight out towards the West Highland hills.

An Aberdeen architect, George Smith (1793–1877), was one of the earliest to have a hand in the laying-out of the first two of these areas, which together now make up Glasgow Corporation's Park Conservation Area. In doing so, he helped to evolve another characteristic Glasgow style—that of the long terrace which contrives to achieve a clearly defined satisfying sense of entity.

Smith, whose practice was in Edinburgh, began in 1831 with Woodside Crescent, which once started at right angles from Sauchiehall Street at Charing Cross and curved round up the hill to become Woodside Terrace. Woodside Crescent has now been shorn of its first six houses to accommodate the western flank of the motorway which bisects Charing Cross. Some think it a rather severe terrace of identical three-bay two-storeyed houses, each with a Doric porch; but enough is left of the original curve to give it a graceful binding role at its lower eastern edge of the Park Conservation Area. Woodside Terrace was built by 1842, straight along the hillside, looking south, and facing Woodside Place, put up by Smith in 1838. Facing Sauchiehall Street, and back-to-back with Woodside Place, Smith's Newton Place is the simplest and most severe of all these terraces. Smith was also responsible for Lynedoch Crescent (1845), which makes clever use of the westward slope up which it is built. To the west of Woodside Terrace, John Baird built a great mansion about 1842. Wings were added in 1847 to make it into the present Claremont Terrace. These houses have large porches with Ionic columns, and the end-pieces of this terrace are pleasingly emphasized. In the same year, John Burnet senior (1814–1901) added Fitzroy Place, while Alexander Taylor, in Royal Crescent, provided what must surely be the most eclectic contribution to the splendid Sauchiehall Street series of terraces.

In 1854 Sir Joseph Paxton, the designer of London's Crystal Palace, was given a new commission in Glasgow. Already he had laid out Queen's Park, in the south side of the city, and the Botanic Gardens, run by a private company in the West End. Now, along with the architect Charles Wilson (1810–1863), he was invited to lay out a new park which would serve the Sauchiehall Street and Woodlands Hill terraces. Originally called the West End Park, its name has been changed for many years to Kelvingrove, after the river that flows through it. Wilson was also given the task of laying out the still unbuilt sections of Woodlands Hill.

Wilson (who, incidentally, had begun his career as Hamilton's chief draughtsman) was one of Glasgow's finest architects, though he was, and is, scarcely known at all outside Glasgow. The highly original building he put up in St. George's Place in 1854 for the Royal Faculty of Procurators, a kind of Venetian palace rich in ornate decorative work, particularly in the lavishly magnificent library, has no equal of its kind and scale in Glasgow, and few anywhere in the United Kingdom.

The crowning glory of his Woodlands Hill scheme was Park Circus, not wholly circular in spite of its name but a flat centre-piece with curving wings and two quadrants separated by roads. The whole conception has proportions of Georgian quality, though heavier in detail. The decorative work on the ground-floor masonry, part vermiculated, helps to give it its special character. The convex Park Terrace, with every third house a pavilion, almost French-like in character with steep mansard roofs, as if crowning the hilltop, creates distinction of another order. This terrace, which looks out across Kelvingrove Park, provides an impressive spectacle from Sauchiehall Street or Kelvin Way.

Wilson's final contribution to Woodlands Hill was La Belle Place, with the Queen's Rooms (1857), a classical temple carrying an inventive frieze. Once a recital hall, it is now a Christian Science church. Unfortunately it has had its fenestration altered and its stonework painted. The craze for painting stonework in areas such as this, though the outcome of a laudable urge towards improvement, is much to be deplored, since the paint cannot easily be removed and neighbouring buildings may have to be similarly treated in the interests of terrace conformity if practical conservation is to restore a sense of unity.

The Woodlands Hill scheme was not completed. Some tenements continued Park Terrace round towards the north, but the north face itself was never built upon. At present utilised as playing fields for the Park School for Girls, it has for more than a century offered a challenge which no architect has thought fit to take up. Perhaps the time has passed when any kind of sympathetic completion could be evolved.

To Glasgow people, the Park Conservation Area is recognized as a landmark by its towers. Three of them belong to Wilson's Free Church College, now Trinity College and part of the university, a brilliantly original building. The forward tower looks like an Italian campanile; the twin towers have been described as Lombardic. The building as a whole has certainly an Italian 'feel'. The fourth tower once belonged to Park Church, but is now attached to a contemporary office block.

Wilson built the first of the magnificent terraces which line Great Western Road between the Botanic Gardens and Hyndland. His Kirklee Terrace, originally called High Windsor, was begun in 1845. Standing on a raised bank above the road, it has been described as "a grand Italianate palace". Rochead's Kew Terrace —some say Decimus Burton's—(1849), which it faces, is, by comparison, severely plain, though it wears an air of quiet dignity.

Rochead, an Edinburgh man, like Wilson did his stint as chief draughtsman to David Hamilton. He practised in Glasgow for thirty years until he retired to his native city in 1870. Of his public works, the best known are the now internally reconstituted Western Club in Buchanan Street (1841) and Northpark House, originally built in 1869 for two art-loving brothers, J. and P. Bell, to accommodate their pictures and *objets d'art*. The last brother to die, a misogynist and recluse, must have birled in his grave when, in 1883, his former home was bought by a pioneer of women's education, Mrs. John Elder, and named Queen Margaret College after Malcolm Canmore's wife. Professors from the university had given "Occasional Lectures for Women" since 1868, and in 1877 a Glasgow association for furthering higher education for women had been formed with Principal Caird as chairman. At first, Queen Margaret College operated separately, though using the lecturing services of some members of the university staff. By the 1930s, however, numbers and other factors made integrated teaching at Gilmorehill imperative. In 1935 the building was sold to the British Broadcasting Corporation, whose headquarters it thereupon became. The small addition to the back of the building by Charles Rennie Mackintosh was originally used by Glasgow's first women medical students. Later additions were less happy. The need to build a bomb-proof studio for orchestral performances as the Second World War loomed, resulted in the erection of a hideous concrete box, which looks as if it is shouldering out the original buildings.

Rochead's most original achievement was undoubtedly his contribution to the Great Western Road development, Grosvenor Terrace, which went up in 1855. He had already been responsible in 1852 for the eastern section of Buckingham Terrace, where he used cantered bay windows, then an innovation. The western section was completed in 1858, the same year as the completion of his Ruskin Terrace.

Grosvenor Terrace has a Venetian appearance. Its large number of identical circular-headed windows repeated on each of its three storeys led David Walker and Andor Gomme* to observe that it "looks almost as if a design for cast iron has been adapted for stone with as much glass and as little masonry as could safely be allowed". Much of it is now given over to hotels. It was in Grosvenor Terrace that the Aunt Bel of Guy MacCrone's Glasgow saga, *Wax Fruit* and its sequels *Aunt Bel* and *The Hayburn Family*, spent her kindly, though socially exclusive, married life.

Hard by St. George's Cross John Bryce, whose brother David had been Rochead's teacher, built the charming but now somewhat dilapidated Queen's Crescent in 1840. A few years before, he had been responsible for some of the more elaborate monuments in the Necropolis Cemetery set out on the wooded area above the cathedral—notably, the Jews' Enclosure, the Catacombs and the Egyptian Vaults. This extraordinary conception, born in the mind of Provost James Ewing in 1832 and fully approved and supported by the Merchants' House, was intended to be an ornamental garden as well as a cemetery, the idea being that quiet walks among the illustrious dead would prove a source of uplift and inspiration to the living by constantly reminding them of the fleeting nature of human life. To make certain that

Architecture of Glasgow (1968).

these heady delights should be tempered with the Scots belief in the sinfulness of pleasure, a reproachful statue of John Knox by Robert Forrest had already been erected on the highest hillock.

During the Iron Years, there was also something of an outburst of church-building, though less extensive than that which broke out in later Victorian times. When Dr. Thomas Chalmers and 200 ministers walked out of the General Assembly of the Church of Scotland in May 1843 over the patronage issue to found the Free Church of Scotland, more churches became necessary so that those who felt the individuality of their sectarian approach to a common God to be the major issue of the age could satisfy their consciences through separate worship. The Ramshorn Church, around which many famous Glaswegians lie buried, Lockhart's Captain Paton among them, came down in 1824. It was replaced by St. David's, which still stands, the old name frequently applied to it. Some new churches—like Boucher's and Cousland's Renfield Free Church, put up in 1851 but demolished in 1968, or John Carrick's Renfield Street Church (1842), demolished in 1965 to make way for British Home Stores —were familiar landmarks, if not particularly distinguished ones. Rochead's Park Church also went up during this spate of church-building. With the shift of population away from the areas served by central city churches, and the slowly dwindling numbers of regular church-goers, like so many others it became redundant. Unfortunately, an adventurous scheme to floor it internally and convert it to secular use, thought up by the architect Geoffrey Jarvis, came too late for practical consideration. The nave of the church was demolished to make way for an office block, and the tower alone has been conserved.

Another surviving church of the period is Alexander 'Greek' Thomson's Caledonian Road Church, built for the United Presbyterians in 1856, but gutted by vandals, of whom Glasgow breeds a larger than fair share, in 1965. The corporation of Glasgow has conserved the splendid shell as a 'motorway monument'. Thompson's best work lies outwith the period of this chapter, and is therefore dealt with in the next.

Although many early Victorian Glasgow churches have been demolished—the population drift to suburbia began to gather momentum after the First World War—even the meritorious survivors are too numerous to mention.

The leaders of Glasgow business and social life were mostly

bound up with church work in one way or another, and provided the money from which these new churches were built. However pleasing the exteriors of many of them, the thoughts and actions generated within their shelter were often less worthy. C. A. Oakley quotes G. M. Young's summing up of the English counterpart of Victorian inter-church wrangles: "the stupid self-satisfaction of one side—the prurient self-righteousness on the other—the scolding, the melodrama, the self-martyrdom." For the second time in her history, the contentious antics of her churchmen reflected one of the least admirable aspects of Scotland's way of life. While it is undoubtedly true that the Victorian Church in Glasgow had in its ordained ranks many high-minded ministers animated with zeal for improving the welfare services and educational opportunities of the poor, even here there are ugly blotches, like the story told by one of the leaders of the reform movement in the city, Peter Mackenzie. He described the plight of an Irish family destitute in the street on a snowy January night in 1847, one child out of seven dead, the mother herself dying of consumption, victims of a Church ruling that soup kitchens for the destitute were not to be opened on the Sabbath for fear of offending the Lord.

Other sources of charity were available, however imperfect in their operation. Once the Burgh Reform Act did away with their traditional functions connected with the running of the city, the Trades House and the Merchants' House turned themselves into charitable institutions, which they still remain.

Several circumstances encouraged the rise of the Chartist movement, which had considerable support in Glasgow from 1838 until it petered out in the 1850s. The post-war slump which followed 1815 was followed by frequent 'slacknesses' of trade, years such as 1819, 1825–6, 1829, 1832, 1837 and 1840–3 bringing waves of hopeless distress to industrial towns like Glasgow. There was also the realization that the Reform Bill of 1832 had enfranchised the middle classes, but not the workers.

In 1837, the London Working Men's Association collected the six points which formed the basis of radical agitation into one document, the People's Charter. These points were: equal electoral areas, universal suffrage, payment of members, no property qualifications, vote by ballot and annual parliament. All except the last have come to pass.

'Missionaries' came up to Scotland to organize Chartism

throughout the country. By 1839 Glasgow had five large associations, mainly based on delegates from trades, factories and districts. Henry Vincent and Feargus O'Connor, the most eloquent and the fiercest of the Chartist leaders, both visited Glasgow.

The disenfranchised, through the Chartist associations, elected members to an anti-Parliament known as the Convention, which was to present to the Commons a petition signed by the masses of the working classes, for the enactment of the principals of the Charter. If the Commons refused, then there was to be a general strike (the 'Sacred Month'). The Commons did refuse, preparations were put in hand for the 'Sacred Month', and the convention then discovered that it had no organization to carry through its threat.

A petition calling for a 'National Assembly' was presented on 10th April 1848, the year of European revolution. The Government packed London with troops and police, and the procession to accompany the petition was abandoned.

The disappearance of Chartism from the United Kingdom scene was due in part to the prosperity following the repeal of the Corn Law (1846) and the enforcement of Lord Shaftesbury's factory reforms.

In Glasgow, Chartism was riven down the centre almost from the start by arguments as to whether or not physical force was justifiable, the Scots remaining, in general, firmly against any such ultimate action. There were later squabbles over the desirability of allowing middle-class interests to merge with those of the Chartists (who particularly disliked the 'shopocrats', and in a few places founded Chartist stores), and on whether or not to support Corn Law repeal without a demand for universal male suffrage. One of the most influential of the short-lived Scottish Chartist newspapers came out in Glasgow, *The Scottish Patriot* (1839–41). *The Glasgow Argus* (1833–47) was sympathetic to the Chartists' aims.

Although nothing like the Welsh insurrection led by John Frost happened in Glasgow, Chartists were suspected of having encouraged the riot of 6th March 1848. So much distress was prevalent at this time that the magistrates engaged large numbers of men to break stones until more purposeful work could be found to occupy them. A free distribution of food from soup kitchens had been promised by Bailie Stewart, the acting chief magistrate. A mob ostensibly made up of the unemployed gathered on Glasgow Green to listen to a series of speakers urging the people to demand food or money as a right, without any return in the shape of labour, and to "do a deed worthy of the name of France".

There was apparently no direct incitement to violence. As the mob dispersed, some people moved towards the City Hall to find out what further measures for their relief the magistrates proposed to take. On the way there, they broke into a gunsmith's in the Trongate and armed themselves. Rioting then broke out in Ingram Street and soon spread to many other parts of the city. Thieves made off with watches and jewellery, while hungry men and children seized food and clothes. As the soldiers moved in and the Riot Act was read, barricades made out of carts were set up in the streets. Ordinary well-fed citizens were rapidly enrolled by the magistrates as special constables. In the end it took cavalry charges and the arrival of reinforcements from Edinburgh to restore order. There was further rioting at Bridgeton the next day, when six people were shot. *The Scotsman* of 8th March thought it "unjust in itself" to call these disturbances "Chartist riots. They had nothing political about them, and it is unfair to attach their disgrace to any political party, however rash and violent." Thirty-five men thereafter received sentences ranging from eighteen years' transportation to one year's imprisonment.

Grim though conditions were for those at the lower end of the social order during the Iron Years, many people found means and opportunity for enjoyment of one kind or another. Glasgow was slow in taking to itself the visual arts. Bailie Archibald McLellan presented his collection of pictures to the city and commissioned James Smith to build his McLellan Galleries, which opened in 1854. When the city heired the collection on his death, the gift was so little valued that some of the pictures were offered for sale at absurdly low prices. Those that were left had to wait for another generation to appreciate the bequest, by which time the practice of picture-buying by individuals to adorn the walls of their own homes was becoming widespread amongst those with money to spare for luxuries.

Literature perhaps fared rather better than painting, although the serious reading public at the time of Scott's death was probably not more than four or five thousand throughout the whole of Scotland. The popularity of Scott among people in the West of Scotland, for whom *The Lady of the Lake* and *Rob Roy* had done so much, continued after his death in 1832, the young Queen Victoria being one of his most devoted readers. Thomas Hamilton (1789–1842) produced his novel *The Youth and Manhood of Cyril Thornton*, from which I have already quoted; and John Galt (1779–1839) though born in Greenock, depicted middle-class small-town life in *Annals of the Parish* and Glasgow life in parts of *The Entail*.

William Motherwell (1797–1835), born in a house at the corner of College Street and High Street, the son of an ironmonger, was once thought by some to "rank close after Sir Walter Scott and the Ettrick Shepherd". No doubt the tearful "Jeanie Morrison", which carries the Burns tradition into that slough of sentimentality where it oozed and splashed with feeble but persistent motion throughout most of the nineteenth century, was much to the taste of some Glaswegians.

> I wonder, Jeanie, aften yet,
>> When sitting on that bink   [school-bench]
> Cheek touchin' cheek, loof locked in loof,
>> What our wee heads could think!
> When baith bent doun ower ae braid page,
>> Wi' ae bruik on our knee,
> Thy lips were on thy lesson, but
>> My lesson was in thee.

Despite an interest in Nordic balladry, Motherwell was a member of the group concerned with the publication of a post-Burnsian anthology *Whistlebinkie* (1835), which brought poetry in Scots almost down to its nadir. The group met regularly at David Robertson's bookshop, 108 Trongate, and in Mrs. Anderson's Sun Tavern, in the Saltmarket. "At the head of them all," wrote James A. Kilpatrick,* "sat Motherwell, short, stout, and muscular of build, a man of fine poetic sympathies . . . a very considerable personality in Glasgow."

Among the others was William Miller (1810–72), described by Robert Buchanan as "the laureate of the nursery"; with some justice on the strength of one poem known to every Scots child:

> Wee Willie Winkie rins through the town,
> Up stairs and doon stairs in his nicht-gown,
> Tirling at the window, crying at the lock,
> "Are the weans in their bed, for it's now ten o'clock?"

Literary Landmarks of Glasgow (1898).

"Hey, Willie Winkie, are ye coming ben?
The cat's singing grey thrums to the sleeping hen,
The dog's spelder'd on the floor, and disna   [sprawled]
   gi'e a cheap,
But here's a waukrife laddie that winna fa' asleep!"

Another Whistlebinkieist, Alexander Rodger (1784-1846), neatly summed up the curiously false values generated by watered-down Calvinism, which were common among Glasgow's respectable middle-class circles, with

Behave yoursel' before folk,
Behave yoursel' before folk,
And dinna be sae rude tae me,
   As kiss me sae afore folk.

It wouldna gie me muckle pain,
Gin we were seen and heard by nane,
To take a kiss or grant you ane;
   But gudesakes! no before folk
Behave yoursel' before folk,
Behave yoursel' before folk,
Whate'er you do when out o' view,
   Be cautious aye before folk!

If further proof of such false gentility were needed, there is the story Charles Mackay (1814-89) tells of the occasion when the great actor Macready was brought to Glasgow by J. H. Alexander in 1846. The Lord Provost invited him to dine, then went to Mackay in a panic for advice when the actor suggested a Sunday meal.

"What am I to do?" inquired the Lord Provost in much perplexity, and speaking broad Scotch. "I'm no that strait-laced mysel', and wad just as soon gie him his dinner on the Sabbath as on ony other day; but then I'm Lord Provost, ye ken, and bound to set a good example. If I were to gie a dinner on the Sabbath, and to a player too, I should raise such a hullabaloo in a' the pulpits of the town against me, as I culdna stand against. If I were no' the Provost, I wadna mind; and if the man were no' a player, it wouldna look half so bad against me. What's to be done?"

Mackay offered to take over the role of host, and invite the Lord Provost as a guest.

"Ou aye!" said the Provost, "I'll come, and bring my friends. But ye maun let me pay for the dinner and the wine. I shall bring ten friends, and Macready and mysel' will just mak up the dozen. And you'll just invite as mony as your table will hold. Not a word of contributing; the dinner will be at my expense; but ye mustna' let ony body ken it."*

Mackay, who knew the Whistlebinkieists and had no doubt sunk his pint with the rest of them at the 'Sun', was a brilliant journalist of his period who spent most of his life in the South, although he edited *The Glasgow Argus*, which appeared between 1833 and 1847. In some of his own popular verse he reflected something of the then prevailing British optimism that the millennium was at hand:

> There's a good time coming, Boys, a good time coming,
>   And a poor man's family
> Shall not be his misery
>   In the good time coming.
> Every child shall be a help
>   To make his right arm stronger.
> The happiest he, the more he has,
>   Wait a little longer.

Another of his songs provides an early example of the "wider still and wider" variety of ballad, though no doubt it found a warmer reception with the wealthy Lowlanders who stayed at home than among the dispossessed Highlanders whom poverty and the Clearances were then forcing to emigrate:

> Cheer, boys, cheer! the steady breeze is blowing,†
>   To float us freely o'er the ocean's breast,
> The world shall follow in the track we're going,
>   The star of empire glitters in the west.

The poet hailed as the most promising of mid-Victorian Glasgow writers was Alexander Smith (1830–67), a native of Kilmarnock whose *Life Drama* (1853), an incredibly uneven performance, caused him to be labelled a "spasmodic" by his critics, and induced the witty W. E. Aytoun to parody it mercilessly in *Firmilliam*. But Smith achieved one good poem, "Glasgow", in which he captured vividly the sights and sounds of the city at the height of its mid-Victorian iron power:

Forty Years Recollections (1877).
†Credited by J. H. Millar in his *A Literary History of Scotland* (1903) to Mackay, but by Harold Scott in his *English Song Book* (1938) to Henry Russell.

Draw thy fierce streams of blinding ore,
Smite on a thousand anvils, roar
   Down on the harbour-bars;
Smoulder in smoky sunsets, flare
On rainy nights, with street and square
   Lie empty to the stars.
From terrace proud to alley base
I know thee as my mother's face.

When sunset bathes thee in his gold,
In wreaths of bronze thy sides are rolled,
   Thy smoke is dusky fire;
And, from the glory round thee poured,
A sunbeam like an angel's sword
   Shivers upon a spire.
Thus have I watched thee, Terror! Dream!
While the blue Night up crept the stream.

The wild train plunges in the hills,
He shrieks across the midnight rills;
   Streams through the shifting glare,
The road and flap of foundry fires,
That shake with light the sleeping shires;
   And on the moorlands bare,
He sees afar a crown of light
Hang o'er thee in the hollow night.

At midnight, when thy suburbs lie
As silent as a noonday sky,
   When larks with heat are mute,
I love to linger on thy bridge,
All lonely as a mountain ridge,
   Disturbed but by my foot;
While the black lazy stream beneath
Steals from its far-off wilds of heath.

And through thy heart, as through a dream,
Flows on that black disdainful stream;
   All scornfully it flows,
Between the huddled gloom of masts,
Silent as pines unvexed by blasts—
   'Tween lamps in streaming rows.
O wondrous sight! O stream of dread!
O long dark river of the dead! . . .

Robert Adam's Trades House

It is interesting to compare this picture of mid-Victorian Glasgow with Mayne's verse-picture* of the city seventy years before. Eighteenth-century Edinburgh had Robert Fergusson to celebrate her attractions, but otherwise the Scots tradition has never been particularly rich in urban poetry, and these two pieces by Mayne and Smith are almost the only effective poems of their kind to come out of the West until John Davidson began to prelude the arrival of the Scottish Renaissance writers.

Glasgow had one strange literary lodger between 1841 and 1843 in Thomas De Quincey (1785-1859), who lived in solitude at 110 Rottenrow, his room stuffed with papers, before returning to Edinburgh where he remained until he died.

The pursuit of music was also much more chequered in Glasgow than in Edinburgh. Andrew Thomson, who apparently organized concerts in Glasgow's College Hall during the second decade of the century, mounted a performance of a work called *The Intercession* in 1819. This, he claimed was "the first time that an entire oratorio had been attempted" in the city. A festival was held in Glasgow in 1821, and another in 1823. But the gentlemen's subscription concerts, a late eighteenth-century institution, apparently had to be wound up because of lack of support in 1822. The opening of the City Hall in 1841, and the Queen's Room in 1857, provided fashionably suitable premises.

The first complete performance of Handel's *Messiah* to be given in Scotland took place in the City Hall in 1844, when one of the soloists was the popular tenor Sims Reeves.

Two music societies—the Glasgow Musical Association, founded in 1843, and the Glasgow Harmonic Society, dating from 1853—amalgamated in 1855 to form the Glasgow Choral Union, thus encouraging and fostering a love of choral-singing applied to serious works, a tradition still happily with us. Glasgow held what is subsequently described as its First Festival (the two previous efforts not counting, since they did not include choral works) in the City Hall in 1860. During the four days for which this festival ran, *Messiah* was again given, along with Mendelssohn's *Elijah* and *Gideon*, an oratorio by one of Mendelssohn's English pupils, Charles Edward Horsley.

It would be wrong to suppose that those musical occasions were of interest to more than the cultured minority of Glasgow's prosperous middle class. A broader cross-section of the community

*See page 80.

attended the Glasgow theatres of the Iron Years, though, as with music, the drama depended on middle-class patronage. The Christmas pantomime matinee, for instance, had become an institution by about 1850.

The splendid Theatre Royal in Queen Street, at the corner of what is now Royal Exchange Square, went up in flames in 1829, nine years after a performance of Mozart's *Don Giovanni* had marked an innovation. An advertisement for this performance promised that the "Grand Crystal Lustre of the front Roof of the Theatre, the largest of any of this time in Scotland, will in place of the Wicks and the Candles and the Oil Lamps be Illuminated with Sparkling Gas". The previous illuminants were certainly a big enough fire risk, but leaking joints in the pipes carrying the "sparkling gas" were to result in further theatre conflagrations.

The old Caledonian Theatre in Dunlop Street had fallen on evil times after its Queen Street rival opened. By 1807, its boards were given over to third-rate variety artists like "Bauldy Cochran, with mouth of alarming dimensions, who would on a pasteboard horse sing 'Greenock Post', and 'Duncan McCallaghan' to the great delight of a discerning audience". Unfortunately, neither of these pieces has survived in the recorded annals of Scots song, so we are unable to judge their merits.

By 1825, the 'Caledonian' was up for sale, and the most colourful of all Glasgow's actor-managers, John Henry Alexander, described by an unappreciative contemporary as having had "a somewhat varied career as tragedian, low comedian, character actor, and heavy gent", tried to buy it, only to find that Seymour, the manager of the Queen Street theatre, had forestalled him. So Alexander bought the cellar underneath the 'Caledonian', and on the night when Seymour opened upstairs with *Macbeth*, downstairs, Alexander opened in the basement (which he advertised as "The Dominion of Fancy"), with a piece called *The Battle of Inch*. Walter Baynham, in his book *The Glasgow Stage* wrote of that opening night: "Macbeth was acted nearly throughout to the tuneful accompaniment of the shouts of the soldiery, the clanging of dish covers, the clashing of swords, the banging of drums, with the fumes of blue fire every now and then rising thro' the chinks of the planks from the stage below to the stage above. The audience laughed, and this stimulated the wrath of the combating managers."

The magistrates then allocated the contending managers different nights for their performances, but when it was the turn of "The Dominion of Fancy" to put on its production, Seymour hired a brass band to play for his private entertainment above.

A further instruction by the magistrates that "neither party was to annoy the other" led to Seymour's upstairs audience lifting floorboards and pouring water on Alexander's audience beneath, and later to both houses mounting productions of the same pieces simultaneously. There was a final flurry when the two theatres offered simultaneous productions of Weber's *Der Freischutz*. On Alexander's first night, Seymour's supporters lifted the stage planks during the incantation scene, grabbed the dragon by the tail, and prevented him extinguishing his fumes, to the great consternation of that inflamed monster. However, a piece called *Tom and Jerry* ran successfully in both houses for over a month, ending this cat and mouse rivalry.

When the Queen Street theatre went up in flames, fired off by leaky gas, Seymour opened a new Theatre Royal in York Street with *The Merchant of Venice*, billing Edmund Kean as Shylock. J. H. Alexander then acquired the Dunlop Street 'double' theatre and rebuilt it as one establishment in 1840, offering in his first season Diamond's *Royal Oak, or the Days of Charles II*. *Paul Pry*, *Cramond Brig*, *Guy Mannering* (with Mackay as Bailie Nicol Jarvie), Edmund Kean in *Othello* and Charles Kean in *Richard III* were only a few of the varied selection of plays with which Alexander regaled Glasgow audiences in the ensuing years of his theatrical reign.

Two other places of entertainment further broadened the Glaswegians' choice of theatrical fare. D. P. Miller, a former showman at Glasgow Fair, made so much money with his penny-a-time Great Gun Trick that in 1842 he was able to open a new theatre, the 'Adelphi', in the Saltmarket. He was the first to bring another famous Victorian actor, Phelps, to Glasgow in the title role of *Hamlet* in 1843. 'The Adelphi' went up in flames in 1848. In 1838 Edmund Glover, a member of a famous London theatrical family, opened 'The Prince's', a converted exhibition hall in West Nile Street, so salubrious that the Western Club booked a box permanently for the convenience of its members. Incidentally, the Prince's was said to have been the first theatre in Scotland to have the stalls separate from the pit.

In 1845, another actor-manager, Anderson, known as 'the

Wizard of the North', built the largely wooden City Theatre at the foot of Saltmarket opening with Balfe's opera *The Bohemian Girl*. It went up in spectacular flames in 1845, the embers carrying west to George Square.

Tragedy became all too real at the Dunlop Street theatre one Saturday in 1849. During the performance of *The Surrender of Calais*, flames flickered around a leaking gas joint in the lower part of the house, but were quickly put out. Panic, however, broke out in the upper gallery, and the occupants rushed for the stairs. Although the street doors were open, some of those first to reach the bottom stumbled and fell, and within seconds the whole stairway was a compressed fallen throng. As *The Glasgow Herald* put it the following Monday: "The weak were trampled down by the strong—the latter only to be trampled down by the furious crowd in the rear. The noise of the cries and groans, and the struggle for bare life, was most agonizing." Sixty-five people died, causing especial "grief among the working classes. . . . One poor lad in Dunlop Street was the picture of woe. He had taken his sweetheart to the theatre. She was carried away from him in the rush; and in his attempt to save her he had only been able to grasp her bonnet and shawl. With these still in his possession he often exclaimed to the by-standers—'How can I go home to her parents without her, and tell them of this!' "

But the Dunlop Street theatre really did go up in flames after a performance of the pantomime *Bluebeard* in 1863. We are again indebted to *The Glasgow Herald*—the leading newspaper of the time, together with, after 1847, the *North British Daily Mail* (forerunner of today's *Daily Record*)—for the information that "the appearance of the conflagration was awfully grand" and that "sixty thousand gallons of water derived from our noble Highland lochs" were poured into the flames during the course of an hour, providing a spectacle which was eagerly watched by an appreciative crowd, most of whom would probably never have been inside any theatre doors. Patched up after the fire, the Dunlop Street theatre functioned for a further five years until it was pulled down to make way for part of the approaches to St. Enoch Station.

If the working man wanted dramatic diversion, he might find his simple tastes more adequately catered for at Mumford's penny 'geggie' which was located at the foot of the Saltmarket. Mumford, a Bedfordshire man who first came to Glasgow with a travelling marionette show, from 1835 offered heavy melodrama at his roughly put-together booth. J. H. Alexander managed to get an injunction against Mumford's 'geggie', forcing it to close. But Mrs. Mumford carried on and other 'geggies' were in due course set up, flourishing at least into the 70s and for long making a regular appearance on the Green during Glasgow Fair, along with travelling circuses.

In the Iron Years, the music halls had not yet established themselves, the kind of fare they were later to provide being then offered by public houses. There were also crude and prolonged bouts of fisticuffs, ruffians like Deaf Burke killing Simon Byrne in the ninety-ninth round, Byrne having some time previously killed Sandy MacKay in the forty-seventh round. It was an age of 'characters', too, like The Juggler Malabar; Hawkie, a dwarf with a turn for four languages; and Fesa, who spat on people's backs and then exacted a tip to clean off the spittle from their clothes: the uncouth products of illiteracy and deformity.*

Drinking shops abounded, and, as there was no really effective restrictive legislation regarding the sale of drink until 1854, gutter-sprawling drunkenness abounded. Indeed, beer was commonly served by the quart until the 1840s.

Better taverns, like Jamie Begg's in Hutcheson Street, or the nearby MacArthurs, served food as well as drink. It was also the age of the club, particularly well known being the City Club, a literary-minded gathering which met in the Bank Tavern, Trongate. Its members included the journalist Hugh Mac-Donald, whose enormously popular book *Rambles Around Glasgow* makes fascinating, if somewhat wordy, period reading even today. The Garrick Club, which met in MacLaren's in Dunlop Street, had amongst its members J. H. Alexander and Carlisle-born Sam Bough, then a theatrical scene-painter but later a Glasgow water-colourist and much admired ben-and-glen painter in oils. A few years ago you could pick up a Sam Bough for the price of the frame. Today, with the renewal of interest in Victorian achievement, his reputation and the price his work fetches have risen.

Only the middle-class folk had houses spacious enough to allow them to entertain. Enormous dinners were consumed in their homes in the fine new terraces and crescents. The working classes, living in single rooms or, at best, in but-and-ben accommodation,

*Some of them commemorated in a Victorian poster, reprinted in 1970.

existed on porridge and milk washed down by pennywheep or small beer for breakfast, and on broth and cheap dishes like sheep's head, pig's trotters or salted herring for the rest of the day. They had no inducement to stay at home, and many of those who were not drinking simply stood about the streets.

The class structure was rigid. The upper class comprised the titled aristocrats, who kept very much to themselves. The middle classes divided into upper (professional men and leaders of trade and industry), middle (small merchant and shopkeepers), and lower (respectable working men).

One tenth of the city's population lived in absolute poverty—deservedly, according to the upper- and middle-class Victorian view, probably because they drank or were idle. Liberal Victorians believed strongly in the rights of the individual to dispose of his energy and his property as he saw fit. Charity, however welcome to the recipients, was often bestowed with such cold self-righteous hauteur that it has looked to later eyes like conscience salving.

While bare-footed children played their singing games, their peever and their peeries and bools, in the streets of Glasgow into the twentieth century—they have still nowhere else to play in some of the worst of the condemned districts, though since the Second World War they need no longer go without shoes—at least by 1860 most children were getting some kind of primary education, albeit in wretchedly overcrowded schools. Knox's system of education for all children, involving the provision of a school for every parish—laid down originally so that children might recognize "the Trewth" as he understood it—as maintained by the Scottish Education Acts of 1684 and 1696, would probably have broken down in Glasgow under the pressure of the Irish influx but for the work of David Stow (1793–1864). Stow had met and been influenced by Dr. Chalmers, who, with others, had been instrumental in founding Sunday schools which tried to provide basic secular education for poor children. Stow not only founded his own weekday school for 100 pupils in Drygate, but took the first steps towards overcoming the teacher shortage by founding in 1836 his Normal School for the Training of Teachers in Cowcaddens.*

*Nevertheless, in 1970, although Jordanhill Training College for Teachers is the largest establishment of its kind in Europe, there is still a teacher shortage in Glasgow of around six hundred, as a result of which some primary pupils are only receiving part-time education.

Secondary education, except through the grammar schools, was non-existent. Even so, with one out of every 205 pupils in Scotland receiving a secondary education compared to one out of 1,300 in England during the 1860s, the post-Reformation tradition of the superiority of the Scots educational system was clearly still holding its own.

Technical education was advanced with the founding in 1796 of the Andersonian University, which provided evening classes in arts, law, theology, physics and chemistry, held in the rooms of the grammar school in George Street. A brilliant but bad-tempered professor of Oriental languages and then of natural philosophy, John Anderson, had sensed the desirability of relating the teaching of scientific subjects to the needs of industry, and on his death had left his fortune for the setting up of a university for "mechanics". Unfortunately his 'fortune' proved to be much less ample than he must have imagined. However, out of one of these grammar school evening classes which his Will inspired, taught by a Dr. Ure, eventually came not only the Mechanics Institute, which was to provide technical classes in many parts of the city, but also eventually, built in Edwardian times on the site of the Andersonian University, the Royal Technical College. This in turn developed in our own day into Glasgow's second centre of learning, the University of Strathclyde. It now incorporates not only the Royal Technical College building, but also the former Scottish College of Commerce, a development of the Glasgow Commercial College which had first been set up to educate aspiring business men in 1845.

Inevitably there were public events and spectacles to provide talking points throughout the three decades of the Iron Years. The Jamaica Bridge of 1772 proved to be inadequate and was replaced by a new one in 1833. The old Glasgow Bridge at the foot of Stockwell Street came down in 1834, and was rebuilt as the Victoria Bridge in 1856. Two years later, a different kind of spectacle was the sensational trial of Madeleine Smith, daughter of the architect James Smith, designer of the McLellan Galleries. The family lived in Blythswood Square. Madeleine, by all accounts a pretty girl, too intelligent to be readily confined within the semi-literate female conventions of the age, took to herself a lover, handsome Pierre Emile L'Angelier, a clerk from the Channel Islands working in Glasgow. Three years later an eligible suitor appeared, but L'Angelier was unwilling to give Madeleine up.

He was thought to have died of arsenic poisoning after drinking a cup of cocoa prepared by Madeleine. At her trial she was deserted by all her family, except for one brother. She was shown by the prosecution to have purchased arsenic. Because of this, and because she admitted that L'Angelier had been her lover, the public at large pre-judged her guilty of murdering him. Doubtless there would be much tut-tutting in middle-class families, especially those with nubile daughters, when the jury returned the Scots verdict of "not proven".* Madeleine eventually went to America where she began a new life, surviving into her nineties. Her story has continued to exert a fascination on writers and playwrights, possibly because she was the first Victorian London-finished 'miss' to rebel, in however unorthodox a manner, against social beliefs which did not admit that women had the right to possess either intelligence or the capacity for physical passion.

Next year there was another scandal, less titillating but more serious in that it affected large numbers of small savers. This was the failure of the Western Bank, the second† of the three major failures in the history of Scottish banking. The Western Bank had been founded in 1832, seven years before the City of Glasgow Bank. Both banks sought to break the restrictive arrangements imposed on Scottish banking by the system of 'closed shop' consultation practised by the chartered banks whose head offices were in Edinburgh. In order to be able to pay a half per cent higher rate of interest than their Edinburgh rivals, the Western Bank did not invest as high a proportion of their deposits in safe low-yielding government stock as did the others. Also, unlike the older banks, the Western Bank used a large proportion of its resources in discounting ordinary trade bills. Under such working circumstances, clearly, any sudden call for funds through the failure of several clients at once could pose a threat to financial stability. The Western Bank's shareholders and directors included at various times some of the best known and wealthiest of Glasgow's industrialists, men like the Bairds of Gartsherrie, and James Dunlop of the Clyde Ironworks.

Although for a time the Western Bank prospered, achieving

---

*Which has been said to mean: "We know you did it but we can't prove you did!"

†That of the first, the Douglas, Heron and Company Bank in Ayr in 1773, does not directly concern us here, although some prominent Glaswegians suffered severely as a result of its fall.

deposits of over £5 million and having paid-up capital of £1½ million and an extensive network of branches some of which pioneered late-night opening in Glasgow, the failure in 1857 of four of the leading firms who were its clients produced exactly the kind of strain under which it was vulnerable. Even so, all might have been well had the Edinburgh banks come to its assistance as some of the other Glasgow banks did. But Edinburgh's banking community chose to risk discrediting in the public mind the whole Scottish banking system rather than rescue its non-conforming rival. The refusal of the Edinburgh banks to accept the Western Bank notes, though well secured by the personal fortunes of those behind it, was merely the most widely publicized aspect of an incident which left a stain upon the history of Scottish banking.

Many famous writers visited Glasgow in these years. Dickens came on the invitation of the Sheriff of Lanarkshire, Sir Archibald Alison, and again in the following year, when the great novelist appeared on the stage of the Dunlop Street theatre as Master Shallow in a production of *The Merry Wives of Windsor* designed to raise money to pay for a curator to look after Shakespeare's birthplace in Stratford. He also gave readings in 1858, when he noted gleefully that three evenings and one morning netted him £600, and on 25th February 1869 made his last appearance in Glasgow.

Thackeray first came in 1851, and in 1856 lectured on the humorists and on the Four Georges in the Athenaeum in Ingram Street. This was the former Assembly Rooms, rented then acquired by the Athenaeum proprietors. It was demolished in 1800 to make way for an extension to the General Post Office, by which time the new Athenaeum in St. George's Place (now part of the Royal Scottish Academy of Music and Drama) had been opened.* Trollope was a postal surveyor in the Glasgow district during the winter of 1857–8, his Glasgow experiences being reflected in *The Three Clerks*.

Several travellers set down their reactions to Glasgow during the Iron Years. At the beginning of this period, the composer Mendelssohn, on his way back from that Hebridean journey

---

*The "handsome frontage" to Buchanan Street was added in 1883. The original decision to form an Athenaeum arose out of a meeting held in Steele's Coffee-House on 10th January 1847. Having taken in the former Liberal Club, it is now the Royal Scottish Academy of Music and Drama.

which resulted in the Overture "Fingal's Cave" and the "Scotch" Symphony, reached the city in company with his friend and travelling companion Karl Klingemann, Secretary to the Hanoverian Legation in London. On 10th August 1829 Klingemann recorded their arrival from Inveraray.

In Glasgow there are seventy steam-boats, forty of which start every day, and many long chimneys are smoking. An excellent inn refreshes us; the waiters minister to us with two hands and as many feet, as steam-service in hotels has not yet been invented. . . . We have seen and admired, Glasgow. This morning we were in a stupendous cotton mill as full of maddening noise as the falls of Monass. What is the difference to the ear? One old work woman wore a wreath of cotton, another had tied up her aching tooth with it. Hundreds of little girls toil there from their earliest days and look yellow. But there will ever exist poetry about it. Systematic order becomes sublime, and the whole swallows itself up in succession, like seasons and vegetation.

Twenty years later, on 14th August 1849, Queen Victoria and Prince Albert spent a day in Glasgow, the first visit of a reigning monarch since the arrival of James I and VI. An enormous triumphal arch was built for the occasion at the northern end of Jamaica Bridge.

Next day, safely back in Balmoral, the Queen recorded her own impressions of that day in *Leaves from the Journal of Our Life in the Highlands*, her artless style strangely capturing her pleasure in the occasion.

Now I must describe the doings of yesterday. We embarked on board the *Fairy** at a quarter to nine o'clock, and proceeded up the Clyde in pouring rain and high wind, and it was very stormy till after we had passed Greenock. We steamed past Port Glasgow, then came Dumbarton and Erskine. The river narrows and winds extraordinarily here, and you do not see Glasgow until you are quite close upon it. As we approached, the banks were lined with people, either on estrades or on the sea-shore, and it was amusing to see all those on the shore take flight, often too late, as the water bounded up from the swell caused by the steamer.

The weather, which had been dreadful, cleared up, just as we reached Glasgow, about eleven, and continued fine for the remainder of the day. Several addresses were presented on board, first by the Lord Provost, who was knighted (Colonel Gordon's sword being

*The Royal Yacht, anchored in Rosneath Bay.

used), then one from the county, the clergy (Established Church and Free Kirk), and from the House of Commerce. We landed immediately after this, the landing-place was very handsomely decorated. We then entered our carriage, with the two eldest children, the two others following, Mr. Alison* (the celebrated historian, who is the Sheriff) rode on one side of the carriage, and General Riddell (the Commander of the Forces in Scotland) on the other. The crowds assembled were quite enormous, but excellent order was kept, and they were very enthusiastic. Mr. Alison said that there were 500,000 people out.† The town is a handsome one with fine streets built in stone, and many fine buildings and churches. We passed over a bridge commanding an extensive view down two quays, which Albert said was very like Paris. There are many large shops and warehouses, and the shipping is immense.

We went up to the old cathedral, where Principal MacFarlane,‡ a very old man, received us, and directed our attention, as we walked through the church gates, to an immensely high chimney, the highest I believe in existence, which belongs to one of the manufactories. The Cathedral is a very fine one, the choir of which is fitted up as a Presbyterian Church. We were shown the crypt and former burial-place of the bishops, which is in a very high state of preservation. It is in this crypt that the famous scene in Rob Roy is laid, where Rob Roy gives Frank Osbaldistone warning that he is in danger. There is an old monument to St. Kentigern, commonly called St. Mungo, the founder of the Cathedral.

We re-entered our carriages and went to the University, an ancient building, and which has produced many great and learned men. Here we got out and received an address. We only stopped a few minutes, and then went on again towards the Exchange, in front of which is Marochetti's equestrian statue of the Duke of Wellington, very like and beautifully executed. We got out at the railway station and started almost immediately.

From the new Queen Street station the royal couple went to Perth, where they spent the night at the George Inn, now the Royal George Hotel, and next day arrived back at Balmoral.

In 1858 Theodor Fontane, the German realist novelist, poet and drama critic (in which capacity he was one of the first to defend Ibsen), made an extensive tour of Scotland. Hutcheson, the

---

*Sir Archibald Alison (1792–1867) was the author of *A History of Europe*, which in its day was widely read.

†The Sheriff was evidently a believer in royal flattery! *The London Illustrated News* gives the figure of 40,000.

‡Duncan MacFarlane was principal of Glasgow University from 1823–58.

predecessor of David Macbrayne, had already linked the Highland lochs and islands with paddle-steamers, and Fontane's *Across the Tweed* is a delight to those who relish descriptions of early steamboat journeys. It may not prove quite such a delight to those who love Glasgow, for Fontane was one of the earliest writers to make comparisons between the cities more favourable to Edinburgh.

Disembarking from the Loch Lomond steamer at Balloch, Fontane recorded:

An hour later the express took us first to Bowling then eastwards with growing speed towards Glasgow. The sun had long set when we approached the rich capital of the Scottish west, but the dark masses of the houses were still clearly visible in the grey evening light. The question was: Should we stay or should we not? The descriptions with which a Glasgow resident, inspired by strong local patriotism, had entertained us during the journey had not failed to touch the heart and the ear of my travelling companion. For my own part I longed to return to the Canongate and to Edinburgh High Street. By way of answer, I pointed to some of the three-hundred-feet-high factory chimneys, of which a number were to be seen rising to heaven like pillars of petrified steam. The chimney is the most characteristic thing in Glasgow.

This gesture sufficed. From one side of the railway station, we hurried over to the other, where the Edinburgh train was already impatiently waiting, and was giving vent to its impatience by grumbling and hissing. Then there was a long whistle, and, passing Falkirk and its battlefields and without any kind of greeting for Linlithgow, which disappeared like a shadow picture as we passed, we were, after barely an hour's journey, describing an arc around Edinburgh's Castle rock, and could see the city's houses rising to the right and to the left of us—as always misty and fantastical.

Whilst noting that the actual journey time between Glasgow and Edinburgh seems scarcely to have improved in rather more than a century★, we Glaswegians may perhaps take some comfort from this evidence he provides of Glasgow's slipping image at the end of her Iron decades, with the reflection that, for all its romantic appeal to him, he thought Edinburgh "a city of clouds broken by flashes of light".

★Since this was written, British Rail have reduced the time to forty-three minutes.

VI

STEEL INTO SHIPS

Today, with oil and atomic energy plentifully at our disposal and the coal industry kept artificially extended partly for socio-political reasons, it is perhaps difficult for us to realize just how vital a factor coal was to everything achieved in Victorian times. "Coal," a late Victorian, Stanley Jervis, put it, "stands not beside but entirely above all other commodities. It is the material source of the energy of the country—the universal act—the factor in everything we do; without it we are thrown back into the laborious poverty of early times." It is therefore perhaps strange that in human terms the working conditions of the collier should have been the worst imaginable.

Until an Act of 1775, miners were bound for life to a particular colliery, serfs wearing a collar with their owner's name upon it, unable to get employment elsewhere and certain to be returned if they escaped. Such powers of enforced recall, which operated most strongly when there was the most widespread distress among miners, were finally removed by a further Act of 1799. When the report of the commission appointed by Lord Ashley, later Earl of Shaftesbury, came out in 1842, it was found that the most frightful conditions of employment existed in the east of Scotland, where women and very young children were still being employed to haul coal to the pithead, up to two tons a day being surfaced in this way for a daily wage of less than 2s.

While the early eighteenth-century mines in Glasgow on the banks of the Kelvin, round Jordanhill and elsewhere, merely supplied local domestic needs, the rise of the iron industry on Glasgow's doorstep greatly stepped up the demand for coal. While in the west the industry was organized, broadly speaking, on more up-to-date social lines than in the east, the construction of miners' rows—but-and-ben dwellings built as cheaply as possible and in close proximity to the pitheads—tended to make miners a race apart, and to create both human and environmental difficulties which have still not been fully overcome.

The earliest known figure for Scottish coal production was recorded for the year 1854, when just under $7\frac{1}{2}$ million tons were mined, of which about probably one-third went to the ironworks. As the iron industry declined, its share of coal consumption came down to 16 per cent by the early 1870s. By then, many of the iron masters were also coal masters, firms like William Baird and Company and Merry and Cunninghame owning substantial coal interests. After a boom in the early 1870s, particularly after production began to rise as coal was won from new pits sunk in anticipation of a continuing boom, Scottish coalmasters both in the east and the west found themselves competing against each other for export markets.* From about 1873 onwards, the industry was no longer able to rely on the ironworks as its major customer and was forced to adapt itself to the needs of foreign markets, at a time when international competition was growing and coal production in Germany was steadily increasing. That it only partially succeeded in doing so has been attributed variously to the coalmasters for failing to produce in sufficient quantity the kind of coals European customers wanted, and to the Scots miners for adjusting their output in relation to wage fluctuations, thus making it difficult for the industry to take advantage of periods of increased demand.

It was in mid-Victorian times, too, that the forerunner of the fuel which was eventually to challenge coal began to be produced. James 'Paraffin' Young, born in 1811, had learned cabinet-making in Glasgow but attended the chemistry lectures of Professor Graham at Anderson's College to such advantage that, in the easy-going academic fashion of the day, Young became assistant at University College after Graham had gone there in 1837. Later he was appointed assistant to the Professor of Chemistry at University College, London, and Chemist at Tennant's Chemical Works, Manchester. In 1848 Professor Lyon Playfair consulted Young about a petroleum spring found in a Derbyshire coal seam. Young erroneously decided that the oil was produced by the natural distillation of coal and coaly substances. In 1850, while following through his investigations at Boghead, near Bathgate, from where a sample of coal had been sent to him by the manager of Glasgow

*The Ayrshire collieries, however, kept up their traditional export trade to America, the West Indies and Ireland throughout the nineteenth century.

Gasworks, Hugh Bartholomew, Young discovered an oil shale which yielded 120 gallons of oil per ton. He therefore took out a patent for the production of oil from bituminous coal, and started distilling near Bathgate.

For a time the Scottish shale-oil industry flourished in this region mid-way between Glasgow and Edinburgh, but the winning of the shale from deep mines and the crushing and subsequent distilling made it a laborious process. The industry survived well into the twentieth century, but from 1870 onwards American competition began to tell against it, and paraffin eventually became a by-product from imported crude oil produced in the refining of petrol.

However, the development which opened up a new wave of prosperity for Glasgow depended not upon shale oil, but upon coal and iron. Malleable iron has the advantage over other forms in that it can be bent, twisted, welded or riveted. Steel was to offer malleability together with the strength of the hard but brittle cast iron.

Attempts to produce steel in Scotland began in 1857, but the unsuitability of Scottish pig-iron had defeated even Bessemer himself. Then in 1871 the Siemens-Martin acid open-hearth process—and during the 1880s, the improved Gilchrist-Thomas process, which enabled Scots pig-iron to be used with the Bessemer converter—was adopted at Hallside, Newton, this time with success, and the Steel Company of Scotland was formed. Two years later, it acquired the Blochairn Works at St. Rollox, Glasgow, a year after William Beardmore set up his works at Parkhead. Soon there were other Scottish steel producers, including David Colville and Sons at Motherwell, the Glasgow Iron and Steel Company at Wishaw, and Merry and Cunninghame at Glengarnock, where, after 1885, Bessemer steel was produced. By 1900 there were 115 open-hearth furnaces in or around Glasgow, producing just under 617,000 tons of finished steel in various forms.

From the beginning, the steel industry became closely linked with shipbuilding on the Clyde. These two industries together sustained much of Glasgow's prosperity until the First World War, while the iron industry declined in the face of the continuing importation of raw materials from the Cleveland field, and the increasing international competition facing the 'finished' product.

Because of its nearby mineral deposits and the advantages of a great waterway, Glasgow was well suited for development as a major centre of the shipbuilding and marine engineering industries. Coal, iron ore, and the technique of producing iron and steel lay to hand. At first the Clyde was not deep enough to receive imports such as copper ore from Sweden, Spain and other countries, to bring large ships up to the city or to carry the launching burdens of Clyde-built tonnage. But a series of deepening operations, beginning with the invention of piers built into the river to induce a self-scouring deepening action by the Chester Engineer John Golborne in 1768, and continuing with further deepening and widening operations in the early years of the nineteenth century, turned Glasgow into a port and changed Port Glasgow into an engineering and manufacturing town.

These were not, of course, overwhelming advantages so long as ships were constructed of wood; but Bell's *Comet*, built by John Wood of Port Glasgow and engined by David Napier, secured for the Clyde a national lead which was in due course turned to good advantage.

The early steamboats did not at first venture beyond the Clyde estuary. They then began to extend their range down the English coast, across to Ireland, and over the English Channel. The first steamship to cross the Atlantic, the *Sirius*, was built in Leith, but it was engined by Wingate and Company of Glasgow.

The Clyde came fully into its own when iron was substituted for wood in the construction of ships. The first two Clyde-built iron ships were the *Vulcan* (1818) and the *Fairy Queen* (1831), built for service on the Forth and Clyde Canal. The Clyde's first seagoing iron ships were the *Royal George* and the *Princess Royal*, both built by Tod and MacGregor for service between Glasgow and Liverpool.

In 1840 the founding of the Cunard Company, whose purpose was to maintain a regular service across the Atlantic, proved to be an enormous stimulus to Clyde shipbuilding. Early Cunard paddle-steamers like the *Britannia*, the *Caledonia* and the *Columbia* had wooden hulls. The *Great Britain*—a wreck for many decades on the Falkland Islands but recently salvaged and brought back to her native port of Bristol for conservation—was built in 1844 with a single screw instead of paddles. The advantages of screw propulsion over paddlers soon became apparent, particularly after 1830, when the Inman Line challenged the Cunard Company by putting two screw steamers on the run, the *City of Glasgow* and the *City of*

Manchester. As a result, the Cunard Company adopted the iron hull in 1855, and in 1862, went over to screw propulsion with their ship the *China.*

There was much disputation at first over the relative advantages of the two methods of propulsion but, as a contemporary writer put it: "Situated as it is at the stern of the vessel and fully immersed, the screw acts upon relatively a much larger volume of water in a given time than paddle wheels, and its efficiency is not impaired by the rolling and pitching motions of the vessel or completely nullified by variations in the ship's draught as with paddles."

Paddle steamers continued to be built for river work, or where care in manœuvring in and out of piers was essential, as in the competitive short-haul circumstances of the Clyde Estuary, where the last British sea-going paddle steamer, the second *Waverley,* was launched as recently as 1946. But in wider waters, screw propulsion quickly gained the mastery. Coasters and cargo ships continued to be built with single screws. By 1889 Clyde-built passenger ships were being equipped with twin screws.

The first steel ship was produced by Denny of Dumbarton in 1879, for the Union Steamship Company of New Zealand. The first steel Cunarder, the *Servia,* one of many of her line to win the Blue Riband, came from Clydebank in 1880.

John Elder, developing ideas derived from James Watt, invented the first compound, as opposed to single-action, engine in 1854, reducing coal consumption by from 30 to 40 per cent. Elder's invention of the surface condenser, which made unnecessary the use of sea water, damaging to boilers, followed in 1858. The perfecting of the triple expansion engine in 1886, and the quadruple in 1896, reduced coal consumption still further, and made possible the use of three or four propellers, with consequent gain in size of ship and speed.

The inability of the early steamboats to carry sufficient coal to enable them undertake long hauls resulted in the continuing construction of sailing ships, particularly for the East India and China trades with Glasgow and other parts. Alexander Stephen built the first Clyde clipper at Linthouse in 1862. Clippers were still being built on the Clyde—as many as 185 of them, between 1890 and 1894. After that year, there was a rapid falling away of their construction rate.

This was due in some measure to the invention of the turbine

9

engine by the Honourable C. A. Parsons. The *Turbinia*, the prototype of a method of propulsion described by Lord Kelvin as "the
greatest advance in steam-engine practice since the days of Watt",
was followed by the construction of two steamers for Clyde
service by Denny of Dumbarton in 1901 and 1902. In her prime
the *King Edward* reached a speed of 20½ knots and was extremely
economical in coal. She saw service on the Clyde until 1951, and
to her last sailing maintained a smoothness, an absence of vibration
few ships of her size have since equalled. Her engines are now
preserved in the Kelvingrove Art Galleries, Glasgow.

The Cunard Company thereupon adopted turbine engines for
their *Carmania* and more famous *Lusitania*, built at Clydebank in
1910 and the taker of the Blue Riband from a German rival with
an Atlantic crossing time of 4 days, 10 hours, 41 minutes, a far
cry from the eighteen days taken by the *Sirius* in 1838 from Cork
to New York. The *Lusitania*, however, was sunk by a German
torpedo during the First World War, taking with her, among
many others, the Spanish composer Granados.

Naval orders did much to help swell the total of Clyde shipbuilding in Edwardian days. By the outbreak of the 1914 war,
Clyde yards were building about half the world's tonnage, and
employing not far short of 100,000 workmen, including those
engaged in the ancillary trades.

Up to and including the development of the steam turbine,
the Clyde had consistently led the way. The distinction of building
the first oil-fired diesel ship went, not to the Clyde but to Denmark, where the *Selandia* took to the water at Copenhagen in
1912. This was, in a sense, the harbinger of bad times for Clyde
shipbuilding; but the days of decline belong to a later chapter.

Throughout the decades when steel-making and shipbuilding
were the dominant Glasgow industries, the range of manufactures and industries was constantly widening. An enthusiastic
Glaswegian of the late 1870s, declared that nothing any civilized
man could want was then not manufactured in or around the
city. This was partly because the fitting out of ships also called
for many of the products associated with domestic or hotel
use.

Opinions might differ as to the reasonable wants of a civilized
man. Certainly in 1804 Dr. John Strang, the City Chamberlain
and author of *Glasgow and Its Clubs*, was able proudly to claim
that:

Glasgow unites within itself a portion of the cotton-spinning and weaving manufactures of Manchester, the printed calicos of Lancashire, the stuffs of Norwich, the shawls and mousselines of France, the silk-throwing of Macclesfield, the flax-spinning of Ireland, the carpets of Kidderminster, the iron and engineering works of Wolverhampton and Birmingham, the pottery and glass-making of Staffordshire and Newcastle, the shipbuilding of London, the coal trade of the Tyne and Wear, and all the handicrafts connected with, or dependent on, the full development of these. Glasgow also has its distilleries, breweries, chemical works, tan-works, dye-works, bleachfields and paper manufactories, besides a vast number of staple and fancy handloom fabrics which may be strictly said to belong to that locality.

One of these 'fancy fabrics' was the Paisley shawl, woven on hand-looms and using designs of Indian origin, including the cone-like fertility symbol a cornucopia—no doubt one of the reasons why, between about 1830 and 1875, a Paisley shawl was considered an appropriate gift for a bride. Cheap printed imitations costing about a quarter of the price of the genuine article, along with changing ideas on dress, eventually destroyed the fashion for these beautiful local products.

Another form of decorative production came from the Saracen Head Foundry at Possilpark, owned by Walter McFarlane and Company, who had originally begun their operations beside the 'Saracen's Head' in the Gallowgate. Their delicately designed cast-iron ornamental railings were used by architects all over the world; but their range of products included bandstands, ornamental lamp-posts and gates, garden-seats, fountains and many other elegant objects regarded as essential outdoor 'furniture' in Victorian and Edwardian times, but despised during the neo-Georgian years and often destroyed. Today the little that survives is being reinstated for its period charm.

Carpets, mentioned by Dr. Strang, are both useful and decorative. Three Scots inventions made in the 1820s and 30s established the industry in Ayrshire, Edinburgh and Glasgow: the discovery by a Kilmarnock engineer, Thomas Morton* of a way to produce three-ply fabrics, and later the more colour-versatile two-ply, which also wear better; the discovery by Richard Whytock in Edinburgh of a new method of weaving which resulted in

---

*According to James MacKinnon in *The Social and Industrial History of Scotland* (1921), the credit should go to a Mr. Newton.

'tapestry carpets'; and the discovery by James Templeton in Glasgow of how to apply the chenille shawl principle to the making of Axminster carpets.

Templeton set up a Glasgow factory, which was burned out in 1856. After carrying on business for a time in an old mill, expansion made necessary the construction of a new factory in 1889. Because it faced Glasgow Green, the city fathers rejected several proposed designs. In exasperation, the directors of Templetons told their architect, William Leiper* (1839–1916), to copy any building which was generally accepted as a masterpiece. The result was the re-creation of something similar to the Doge's Palace of Venice, in colourful polychrome tile with stone dressing. Unfortunately, the engineer's dislike of the architect resulted in the collapse of part of the structure while it was going up, and caused the death of twenty-nine weavers who were in an adjoining shed. However, the building has outlived its unlucky beginning, and although it is not exactly one of Scotland's more native architectural treasures, at least its brilliant bizarreness has won it a place in the affections of Glaswegians.

The tradition for fine printing in the production of books founded by the Foulis brothers in the eighteenth century re-asserted itself, though adapted to suit a changed demand. Firms like William Collins, Sons and Company, Blackie and Son and Robert MacLehose and Company provided books for the general reader rather than for scholars or connoisseurs. George McCorquodale, who hailed from Argyll, set up a printing factory in Glasgow in 1854, and established a reputation for stationery, boxes and posters. Paper-making also flourished in and around Glasgow.

While soap-making seems to have been established at Greenock in 1667, and soap was one of Glasgow's staple industries by 1700, its manufacture for export was begun by Charles Tennant in 1803 at his St. Rollox Chemical works, which also specialized, as did several smaller firms, in the production of the acids and alkalis necessary to every centre of industry, and produced most cheaply locally.

---

*Best remembered for such churches as Dowanhill (1865), Belmont and Hillhead (1875), Hyndland (1886); for the Sun Life Assurance Building in West George Street (1892) and many Helensburgh villas. During the depression which followed the financial collapse of the City of Glasgow Bank, Leiper, a shy bachelor, studied painting in Paris for some years, though he later returned to Glasgow and resumed his architectural practice.

It was surely ill-luck for Glasgow that the Leblanc method of alkali production was displaced by the more efficient Solway process, which involved the action of ammonium bicarbonate solution on strong brine, and therefore made Cheshire with its salt-beds a more natural location for this method of production than Scotland. As a result of this switch of emphasis, amalgamations occurred which led to Scottish closures, the Irvine and Eglinton Chemical Companies and the St. Rollox company forming the United Alkali Company.

Other firms specialized in producing chemicals like phosphates, cyanide (used extensively in South African gold-mining) and later in the manufacture of iodine from kelp. Here, too, ill-luck befell. In the 1860s and 70s, Whiteinch Chemical Works produced virtually all the iodine for the United Kingdom. The opening up of foreign deposits of potash resulted in a decline in the value of potash salts, and the collapse of the Scots iodine industry in the ensuing competition. The company founded by Alfred Nobel in 1873 introduced the manufacture of explosives, though necessarily away from Glasgow, among the sand-dunes of Ardeer, Ayrshire, and with the opening of subsequent branch factories soon became a major employer. It is now a division of Imperial Chemicals Limited.

American industries began to arrive in the Glasgow area during the high Victorian period. Singers, the makers of sewing-machines, started their Scottish operations with a factory in Glasgow in the early 1880s and soon afterwards moved out to Clydebank. Babcock and Wilcox, the industrial 'child' of an American parent company, started their British operations at Renfrew in 1895, and in 1910 acquired premises at Dumbarton. The arrival of Swedish and American firms in the Glasgow area was hailed at the time as a Scottish triumph. No doubt it was, in the short term. These three companies are still with us. The influence of foreign-owned enterprises in the long term, however, was to prove a different proposition.

In pottery, Glasgow delft won itself a high reputation. The clay came from Devonshire, the ships that brought it returning south laden with coal. The craftsmen originally came from Holland, hence the name. Firms like the Verrefield Company, the Glasgow Pottery Company and the Britannia Pottery Company produced characteristic domestic and decorative ware, some of which, including the famous 'wally dugs' (china dogs) have now become collectors' pieces. Incidentally, in 1890 Glasgow received one of the most remarkable pieces of pottery ever devised, the Doulton Fountain symbolizing Victoria reigning over her people. It was designed by A. E. Pearce for Messrs Doulton to display at the exhibition of 1888, presented to the city and re-erected on Glasgow Green.

But for all this diversification developing alongside steel-making and shipbuilding from 1870 onwards, the accent of economic importance was upon the heavy industries. Pipes and tubes were manufactures in Glasgow in the mid-Victorian period, and A. and J. Stewart, a firm founded in the 1860s, eventually became the largest manufacturers of butt and lap-welded tubes in the United Kingdom, amalgamating with Lloyd and Lloyd of Birmingham to become Stewart and Lloyds. The production of steam locomotives, as well as the rails for them to traverse great tracts of the world upon, became another Glasgow speciality. In the early days, the manufacture of locomotives was generally combined with marine engineering, but in the 1850s the industries began to go their separate ways. A son of the inventor of the hot-blast furnace founded Neilson and Company in 1836, the first Glasgow firm to specialize in locomotive building at their Hyde Park Works, Springburn. They were one of the three firms which merged to form the North British Locomotive Company in 1903.

Throughout the final decades of Queen Victoria's reign, Glasgow concentrated successfully on its heavy engineering, but so exclusively that for the first time in its commercial and industrial history, no major new industry was coming along behind, so to say, to take over the next phase, as cotton had succeeded tobacco, iron had succeeded cotton, and steel and shipbuilding had succeeded iron.

Some light industries were introduced to Glasgow. Just before the middle of the century, Kelvin and Colville—later Kelvin, Hughes Limited—began, through its association with Lord Kelvin, the manufacture of electrical instruments, some of which were used in the laying of the first Atlantic cable. Two other indus-trially minded academics, Professors Barr and Stroud, started to produce range-finders in 1890, founding the instrument-making firm which still bears their names. Mavor and Coulson began experimenting with electrically-driven coal-cutting machinery in 1897, and eventually specialized in it. And there were others.

Unfortunately, Glasgow missed out on the two industrial

developments which were to prove most significant in the early part of the twentieth century, the motor-car and the aeroplane. Glasgow's attempts to introduce these new industries were also subjected to ill luck.

The first all-Scottish car, based on the Daimler, was produced by George Johnston, whose Mo-Car Syndicate, later the Arrol-Johnston Company, began to manufacture vehicles commercially in 1896. Fire destroyed the Glasgow foundry in 1901, but production moved first to Paisley and then to Dumfries, where it survived into the 1920s. The Beardmore company produced a car in the former Paisley works of Arrol-Johnston. The A.B.C. Company and the Bergius Company also tried their hands at car production, the latter soon abandoning the motor-car in order to develop their Kelvin engine for marine use. None of these companies survived the slump years as makers of motor-cars.

The two most successful car producers were the Albion Company, founded in Glasgow in December 1899, and the Argyll Motor Company founded in 1905. In 1912, Albion abandoned the production of cars to concentrate on making lorries, and has since become part of British Leyland, Alexander Govan's Argyll car, modelled on the French Darracq, which in turn was modelled on the Renault, was first produced at Bridgeton.

Govan realized the potential of his product, and built an imposing red-sandstone factory at Alexandria, Dunbartonshire, which opened in 1906. Unluckily, Govan died a few months later, in his fortieth year. His company struggled on, concentrating on the development of the single-sleeve valve engine, a course which led to prolonged litigation with the Daimler company who claimed infringement of patent rights, and led to the liquidation of Argyll Motors in 1914. A new company formed to continue production at Bridgeton also went into liquidation in 1920. Incidentally, the Glasgow inventor of the single-sleeve valve engine, Peter Burt, founded the firm which later became the Acme Wringer Company. They also built airships, including the R.34, the first airship to cross the Atlantic.

An unlucky death also removed the man of vision from the Scottish aeronautical scene at a crucial stage of development. Percy Pilcher, a lecturer in naval architecture at Glasgow University who achieved the first successful glider flight at Cardross in 1895, had made considerable progress in designing a powered aircraft when he was killed in a glider accident in 1899. Both the

Argyll Company and Beardmores designed aero-engines, the latter providing more engines than any other company for the Royal Flying Corps machines between 1914 and 1916. Here again, there was apparently no realization of the need for a follow-through, the market for Scotland's ships and heavy engineering products creating a false sense of prosperity given temporary buoyancy by replacement needs after the Armistice of 1918.

Men of vision had seen the dangers of concentration upon too narrow an industrial front for long enough. As early on in Glasgow's steel and shipbuilding era as 1886 Dr. John Oswald Mitchell, author of *Memoirs and Portraits* and *Old Glasgow Essays* was writing:

> Glasgow has lived through many a trying season, and probably she has still vitality to revive now. But the *felix arbor* is not sound at the roots. Chicago and Glasgow have been likened to each other, for their rapidity of Growth. But Chicago depends on wheat, which grows, and Glasgow every year more and more depends on minerals, which do not grow. Here and there grass grown blocks of slag tell where a great iron-work once blazed that has blazed its iron-stone all away; or a weather-blown heap of shale tells where the pant-engine has sent up its last batch of coal. As the exhaustion of minerals advances, our industry, and with it our commerce, must fall back, and the general suffering can only end when the population shall have shrunk in keeping with the reduced power of production.

These were to prove prophetic words; though not immediately, for job opportunities multiplied between 1878 and 1900, and the population expanded accordingly from about half to three-quarters of a million.

The city spread its acres still wider. In 1891, the independent burghs of Govanhill, Crosshill, Pollokshields East, Pollokshields, Hillhead and Maryhill, were brought within Glasgow's boundaries, along with the districts of Mount Florida, Langside, Shawlands, Kelvinside, Possilpark and Springburn. Kinning Park came in in 1905, and in 1912 the burghs of Govan, Partick and Pollokshaws, along with the district of Shettleston, Tollcross, Cathcart, Dawsholm, Temple and North Knightswood became part of the city.

So many buildings were put up between 1870 and 1900 that it is possible to mention only the most distinguished. More than 100,000 tenements went up between 1860 and the end of the century. After 1900, commercial companies lost interest in building homes for letting, there being more profitable ways of investing money.

Whatever may have been its good intentions, the Rent Restrictions Act of 1915 turned out to be a death warrant for much of Glasgow's stock of tenements. Landlords who had no way of shielding themselves against rises in the cost of repairs brought about by inflation (which, after several decades of more or less stable prices, gathered momentum during World War I) eventually had no money at all to spend on routine maintenance, and the builders' equivalents of moth and rust were left to do their corrupting will.

But these days of decline were still far off when Glasgow's buildings were striving to beat the housing shortage by covering acre after acre with tall grey or golden ashlar tenements, using stone from local quarries until it began to run out during the early 1890s, and then turning to the red sandstone quarries of Arran and Dumfriesshire to provide material for their late-Victorian and Edwardian successors.

The fact that these builders simply could not keep pace with the housing needs of Glasgow during its flowering Victorian years—for such, indeed, they were, the industrial canker which had already fastened upon the vital stem of her major industries producing few apparent blemishes on the bloom of the city's prosperity before 1900—meant that more and more people took to letting rooms, and the old early-nineteenth-century problem of overcrowding began to repeat itself in the rebuilt heart of the city, and in the older areas of the cotton era New Town and in its suburban extensions.

The bloom of prosperity also resulted in the construction of so rich a profusion of public and commercial buildings that Glasgow became, and to some extent still is, not only the repository of a major part of the United Kingdom's Victorian stone-and-mortar heritage, but as J. M. Reid put it, "*the* Victorian city."

The most exciting contribution to Glasgow's built environment in the 1860s and 70s undoubtedly came from Alexander Thomson (1817–75), dubbed 'Greek' because of his fondness for classical detail. The most obvious feature of Victorian architecture is that it evolved no real style of its own, the 'battle of the styles' being really an argument as to whether this or that ancient manner, Greek or Gothic, was the more appropriate to copy for an age whose upper and middle classes enjoyed a degree of affluence never before experienced, but which nevertheless felt sufficiently insecure to believe that the physical reflection of that affluence should be based upon the greatness of past ages.

Thomson was born at Kippen, Stirlingshire, the seventeenth child of John Thomson, an upholder of the United Presbyterian Kirk who came of Covenanting stock. Alexander Thomson came to Glasgow with his brothers and sisters after their father's death in 1824. He was employed as a clerk in a lawyer's office, where he attracted the attention first of Robert Foote, then of John Baird, whose chief draughtsman he became. Thomson married a daughter of Peter Nicholson, the designer of Carlton Terrace. With another John Baird, no relation to Thomson's former boss, he set up in architectural practice, later to be joined by brother George, who was not himself an architect. Thomson rarely went to London, preferred Arran to anywhere else for his holidays, and so far as is known never left the shores of the United Kingdom.

He was highly regarded even in his own day, becoming President of the Glasgow Institute of Architects in 1871. His presidential address included consideration of the question: "How is it that there is no modern style in architecture?" He was enormously prolific, and at his death sufficiently wealthy for his wife to be able to endow a travelling scholarship for young architects, one of the recipients of which was to be a young man called C. R. Mackintosh.

Thomson gave a series of lectures in the Glasgow School of Art in 1874. In one of these lectures he declared the fundamental qualities of Greek architecture to be "Beauty and symmetry of form, and harmony of relative perspective . . . the only style of architecture which harmonizes with the higher class of sculpture and painting". In another lecture given the same year he declared his antipathy to Gothic: "Every part of a Gothic building looks as if it was trying to stand on end. . . . Gothic does not express greatness; it is only great where it is actually of large dimensions." To him, it suggested the Dark Ages. He rightly observed that it was no more native to Scotland than Greek or Renaissance, and in his view, to call it a 'Christian' style was an impudent assertion, since the early Christian buildings were Greco-Roman.

Such were the beliefs which earned Thomson his sobriquet. J. M. Reid, however, perceptively suggests that "memories of the Old Testament surely coloured his mind and work", pointing out that he would borrow "as readily from ancient Egyptian models as from Greek ones—Egyptian columns, pylon-like openings, lotus forms and even Greco-Egyptian chimney-pots". Though he was no more the innovator of a true Victorian style than any other nineteenth-century architect, his 'borrowings' were so thoroughly assimilated and his rich invention so consistent and contained that he at least achieved an immediately recognizable personal idiom in his best work, whether churches that were temples, spacious villas, large-scale terraces, commercial buildings or tenements.

Thomson is best known today for his churches and his terraces. Caledonian Road Church, his first, went up in 1856, and, as has already been remarked, its beautiful shell stands as a motorway monument to twentieth-century mindless vandalism. His St. Vincent Street Church, built in 1859 for the United Presbyterians and presently occupied by Spiritualists, occupies a dramatic hillside site, rendered somewhat less so by Heron House, which dominates and partly obscures the church from certain angles. A plinth contains basements and the ground floor of the church carries the temple, columned at its ends with square columns down either side between the aisles. One of Thomson's most remarkable steeples, suggesting Indian rather than Greek inspiration, crowns this noble building. Its interior has a deep pillar-supported gallery, banked as in a theatre. "One can almost see the blind Samson laying his hands on one of those climbing pillars," wrote J. M. Reid, "cast iron beneath the paint though these are, to bring down the Philistines about his head;" a pleasant fancy, for no Samson has yet been found who might undertake what would be in Glasgow so encompassing a task.

Thomson's third major church, built at Queens Park and also for the United Presbyterians, with "its sloping Phœnician doorways, its Greek ornament, its dwarf Egyptian columns and its Assyrian-looking high door", to quote William Power, must in some ways have been the most exciting of all his churches, Indian and Egyptian inspiration predominating over Greek. It was struck by German bombs in 1942 and totally destroyed, one of the most serious of British architectual losses sustained in the Second World War.

Thomson, great creative artist that he was, no more repeated himself in his churches than in his terraces. Walmer Crescent, begun in 1857, is scarcely classical at all. As David Walker and Andor Gomme remark, "the tremendous and nearly unbroken sequence of large square mullions on the top storey" form a kind of "residual colonnade". There are twice as many 'columns' on the top floor, an effect Thomson developed in Moray Place, built in 1859, which, with its imposing end pavilions, inspired Professor Hitchcock to dub it "the first of all Greek Terraces". If one ignores the non-Greek detail, and apprehends the Greekness rather than subjects it to technical analysis, one sees what he means.

The most famous of Thomson's terraces is undoubtedly the serenely imposing Great Western Terrace, begun in 1869, in one of the houses of which this book is being written. A two-storeyed terrace on a raised mound set back from Great Western Road, its basements concealed by ornamental railings, it achieves a balanced dignity. This is no doubt due in part to the fact that its two pavilions are placed not at the ends of the terraces, but six bays in from each end, and have each an extra storey.

Thomson's last terrace,* Westbourne (1871), now numbering 21 to 39 Hyndland Road, has a highly characteristic ground floor, but the inclusion of auriols or bays, apparently forced upon Thomson by the taste of his clients, introduces a discordant feature which detracts from the overall balance.

Thomson's personal accent can be read even in his tenements. The finest of these blocks is Queens Park Terrace, Eglinton Street, the ground floor of which carries a row of shops. The decorated pediments on the first and second floors, the little columns between the top-floor windows, and the arrangement of the chimney heads are highly characteristic.

Thomson built houses and villas throughout most of his career, not all of them yet documented. He was influenced to some extent by the German architect Karl Friedrich von Schinkel, both in his linked bands of windows, and in the so-called 'round-arch' style, the latter manifesting itself in some of his houses in the vicinity of Kilcreggan, on the Clyde Coast, and in Pollokshields. 'The Knowe', 301 Albert Drive, is certainly his, dating from 1853, as is 200 Nithsdale Road, Pollokshields. The most complex of Thomson's houses is probably Holmwood, Netherlee Road, Cathcart, now a convent, which also has an exceptionally fine interior.

*There is no direct evidence to show that Northpark Terrace, Hamilton Drive (1860) is Thomson's, though confident stylistic evidence suggests the strong probability that it is.

Of Thomson's public buildings, the most frequently looked at, but the least seen, is the Grosvenor Building opposite Central Station, which went up in 1860. It was owned and let by Thomson and his brother, but a continual worry to them. In 1907 J. H. Craigie, an architect of distinguished tastelessness, added an over-powering additional storey in Renaissance style. As the Grosvenor Restaurant, the grotesque Edwardian Assembly Hall, its roof supported by muscular men and generously-breasted maidens stripped to the waist, the whole slaistered in gilt, was the scene of innumerable Glasgow dinners and wedding receptions before it was badly damaged by fire in 1969.

The Buck's Head replacement building, which went up in 1863, is an iron-frame structure of considerable interest, though suffering from the fact that the two sides are of different lengths (not, of course, Thomson's fault), and that the attics seem fussy. It is much less successful then the first and finest iron-frame building to be put up in Glasgow, Gardner's Warehouse in Jamaica Street, the work of John Baird I, finished in 1856.

Of the remainder of Thomson's surviving public buildings, the most fantastic is the Egyptian Halls in Union Street (1873) with its powerful cornice, its increasing number of windows on each ascending storey, and its vigorous decorative details. More delicate are the Grecian Buildings in Sauchiehall Street (1865), wretchedly painted over. Presumably one has to accept that in modern times when ever-increasing consumption is regarded as an end in itself, shop-fronts are likely to go on being shoutingly tasteless, paying scant regard to the nature of the buildings they disfigure. Developers should be severely discouraged from laying hands on either of these fine buildings in order to replace them with prefabricated arrangements of undistinguished clichés varied by 'faceless' towers, producing higher plot ratios and richer rateable returns.

By the nature of their work, architects are, or should be, part artist, part technician. It is easy to condemn them for giving in to a client's insistence, though the technician persona in some cases seems to have put up singularly little resistance to assaults against the conscience of the artist. It is interesting to note that with Thomson in mind, his contemporary and fellow architect Campbell Douglas—builder in 1878 if what is now the Citizens' Theatre, Gorbals (but whose columns came from Hamilton's Union Bank in Ingram Street)—should say: "In my experience I

have only known one man who confined himself to one style, and
if his proposed employers insisted on building in a different style,
why, then, he let them go elsewhere. That architect was a great
man, who probably made less money than some others did, but
he left behind him monuments more worthy of his genius."

Thomson prepared a plan for the university on Gilmorehill.
The first disaster of the Senate's decision to abandon their
medieval university was succeeded by a second disaster—
their failure to choose what must surely have been the most distinguished entry submitted to them for the design of the new
buildings. Alas! They preferred the farrago of imitation Gothic by
Sir George Gilbert Scott (1810–78), who, in 1870, four years later,
built the much more chaste and restrained St. Mary's Cathedral.
His son, John Oldrid Scott (1841–1913), added spires to both
buildings in 1887 and 1893 respectively, the fretwork nature of
the university spire being the result of Lord Kelvin's calculation
that the weight of a solid spire could not be borne by the central
tower.

Of Thomson's successors, the most obvious classicist was James
Sellars (1843–88). His St. Andrew's Halls, in Berkeley Street
(1873), with its magnificent pillared west front, had a splendidly
panelled interior, resulting in it being, according to the B.B.C.,
acoustically the finest hall in Britain. It was destroyed by fire in
1963. When the decision to incorporate the shell of it in an extension to W. B. Whittie's rather heavier Renaissance-style copper-
domed Mitchell Library (1911) was taken, it was decided to
conserve the Granville Street ornamental elevation, but only three
of the bays on the returns, a sad error of taste on someone's part.*

Sellars was also responsible for Kelvinside Academy (1877),
which is reminiscent both of Thomson's work and of Hamilton's
much more sympathetic Edinburgh Royal High School. Perhaps
Sellars' finest work was his City of Glasgow Bank (1878), a
Renaissance delight though never given its intended top storey,
which, sad to say, was demolished in 1959. Some of his other good
things, like the Queen Insurance Building (1879) in St. George's
Place, have also gone. His churches rarely represent him at his best.

John Honeyman (1831–1914), on the other hand, has three of
Glasgow's finest churches to his credit: Barony North Church
(1878), in Cathedral Square, richly inventive with a suggestion
of the eighteenth century; Lansdowne (1862), a delicate exercise

---

*The author's gentle charity precludes the naming of names.

in Gothic Revival with a slender spire of breathtaking poise; and the beautiful classical Westbourne Church (1880). Comparing the three, it becomes obvious that Honeyman was the gifted Victorian imitator *par excellence*, with, unlike Thomson, no identifiable 'voice' in stone of his own, yet able to create masterly buildings in whatever manner he turned his hand to. The gay, Italianate Ca d'Oro (1872) in Gordon Street, once a furniture warehouse and now a restaurant (though with a hideous slamming-down mansard attic added in Edwardian days by J. G. Gillespie), provides yet further evidence of his stylistic versatility.

One or two other Glasgow classicists ought to be mentioned. Thomas Lennox Watson (1850–1920) showed his disapproval of Gothicism-run-riot by building the Roman temple with its massive Corinthian portico that is Wellington Church (1883) on the north side of University Avenue. St. Georges-in-the-Fields (1886), by Hugh and David Barclay, is Ionic, more obviously Thomsonian, but with rich figure sculpture by Birnie Rhind. The Barclays were also the builders of Glasgow Academy (1873), Kelvinbridge, though the addition of large attic windows has distorted its proportions. Elgin Place Congregational Church (1834), an earlier example by John Burnet senior, brings us to the work of a father and son who together gave Glasgow many of its most spectacular later Victorian, Edwardian and even neo-Georgian buildings.

John Burnet (1814–1901), born in Kirk o'Shotts, began life as a carpenter, but rose to be President of the Glasgow Institute of Architects for two years from 1876. Fitzroy Place, Sauchiehall Street, an early work dating from 1847, was his contribution to what is now the Park Conservation Area. The Merchants' House in George Square is also his, being fitted in to the Italianate pattern already begun by Rochead with his Bank of Scotland building in 1869, further added to in 1874 by Sellars who provided a matching central building. Burnet's tower, however, somewhat disturbs the balance of the range as a whole, the additional two storeys added later by his son completing the 'ogee' appearance, rising up by steps from the St. Vincent Street end to the tower on the Queen Street–George Street corner of George Square.

The elder Burnet's three main public achievements stand within a few yards of each other. The head office of the Clydesdale Bank (1870) provides a fine red sandstone Italian-influence Baroque flourish, even although the east range was never finished, the

Evening Citizen securing the site for their building. Lanarkshire House (1876) in Ingram Street, now the Sheriff Court, is a Venetian palazzo originally built as a house, made into a bank by Hamilton, and given its present façade by Burnet. Splendid sculptured figures by John Mossman fill the niches between the columns on the top floor. It reflects little credit on the then Ministry of Works that some of the friezes which surround the building were removed during a botched-up restoration of the 1960s. Officialdom and the Law between them ought to set a better example. Finally, there is the Stock Exchange Building (1875) in Buchanan Street, Italian Gothic of high inventive originality, which now wears a totally new structure within its shell.

Burnet's contribution to the Great Western terraces was Cleveden Crescent, Kelvinside (1876), a simple and dignified series of houses stepping down a gentle slope.

His son, Sir John James Burnet (1859–1938), was born in Glasgow, and, after an extensive education and apprenticeship that included three years in France and both Continental and American travel, joined his father's firm in 1878.

His first notable work was the classical Fine Art Institute in Sauchiehall Street, which became part of Pettigrew and Stephens, but regrettably was destroyed by fire in 1964 and subsequently demolished. The fantastic, Frenchified Charing Cross Mansions (1891–7) with chateau-like roof detail, sweeps round what used to be Charing Cross but now dominates the eastern cliff of the inner ring motorway. When the reconstruction of this area is complete, the owners and occupiers of Charing Cross Mansions should club together to reinstate the huge clock, which was clearly intended to be the central focal-point of the elevation.

The Athenaeum (1886), now part of the Royal Scottish Academy of Music and Drama, and the related Athenaeum Theatre (1891) in Buchanan Street are the younger Burnet's, as is Waterloo Chambers (1899) in Waterloo Street; similar to, though less assured than, his Atlantic Chambers in Hope Street, dating from the same year. Both these buildings rise up from narrow Georgian frontages, and cope admirably with the problems set by this ground restriction.

American influence, particularly that of Louis Sullivan, was reflected in the construction methods employed by Burnet in his Alhambra Theatre (1910)—now alas! a victim of changing

Central Station and the signal box

fashions in entertainment—and in the magnificent balance of McGeoch's Warehouse (1905) in West Campbell Street—now, alas, a victim of Glasgow Corporation's failure to produce overall practical plans for the conservation of its finest central area buildings, and government tardiness in backing its admirable Civic Amenities Act of 1967 with hard cash!

Burnet's lesser buildings are too numerous to detail here, although one must note that they include the Cenotaph in George Square, Glasgow (1922), the ornamental Forsyth's buildings in Princes Street, Edinburgh (1907), and Kodak House, Kingsway, London (1911).

Working at the same time as Burnet was J. A. Campbell (1859–1909), who joined forces with Burnet in producing the Athenaeum Theatre. Campbell's masterpiece is the Northern Insurance Building (1908) in St. Vincent Street, with its soaring lines of windows and its functional but impressive steel-frame fenestration at the rear elevation.

Another contemporary was Sir Robert Rowand Anderson (1834–1921). In Govan Old Parish Church (1884) and the Pearce Institute (1903) he provided Govan with two of the very few public buildings of quality likely to survive the comprehensive redevelopment of the area. Pollokshaws Burgh Hall (1897) is a delightful reinterpretation of Scottish Baroque. Anderson's main Glasgow achievement is the Central Hotel (1884), curiously Scots in feeling yet, as many people have remarked, bringing successfully together a Swedish tower, Amsterdam gables and both Florentine Renaissance and English Jacobean windows. In a sense it is the most spectacular embodiment in Glasgow of that assimilation of, and variation upon, foreign styles which was the deliberate achievement of Victorian architecture.

The most obvious visual sign of the confidence which Glasgow felt in itself as it sailed upon its high tide of Victorianism was the new City Chambers, built upon the site of Alexander of Ballochmyle's* town house and opened in 1888 by the Queen herself. A London Scot, William Young (1843–1900), won the competition to build it. It, too, is an astonishing amalgam of styles, capped by a great tower abounding in Renaissance detail. The noble central staircase, its ceiling and the interior decoration and furnishings of the public rooms put one in mind of a Renaissance nobleman's palace. As a boy I used to laugh at it; but I had not then lived

*The descendants of Burns's supercilious "Bonnie Lass o' Ballochmyle".
10

The Broomielaw: circa 1800; and circa 1900

long enough to experience our age of prefabricated design, staining concrete and shoddy finish. There is never likely to be another palace like the sumptuous City Chambers built again in Glasgow. For its sheer magnificence of craftsmanship alone it should be highly valued. The arches which link the additions at the rear of the building are by Watson, Salmond and Gray, and date from 1923.

A word should perhaps be said here about Glasgow's statues, particularly those in George Square. A favourite quiz test on Glasgow invites the contestant to name them. Few can, which is hardly surprising in an age out of sympathy with the Victorian belief in permanence and the consequent fondness for bronze Valhallas. The taste for such things had passed even by Edwardian times, for Neil Munro makes "Erchie", his "Droll Freen", report King Edward VII to have said, on first arriving at Queen Street Station from Edinburgh: "Whit 'na graveyaird's this?"

The dominating statue of Scott (1838) is by A. Handyside Ritchie, to a design by John Greenshields, a self-taught Lesmahagow man. Sir Walter Scott visited him in his cottage by the Clyde, the last visit taking place a year before Scott died. Greenshields was on his own deathbed when he learned that his statue had been accepted to stand on top of David Rhind's tall fluted doric column on a plinth at the centre of George Square. By then the statue of Sir John Moore of Corunna by John Flaxman was already a familiar landmark, having been erected in 1819, and reputedly made from smelted-down cannon. Once surrounded by railings, as were all the statues, it was the object of an attempt by Glasgow hooligans to destroy it, according to a drawing published in *The Northern Looking Glass* in 1825. Colin MacIver, who took his uncle's name of Campbell and served under Moore, became first Sir Colin Campbell and then Lord Clyde, for services during the India Mutiny. His statue, the work of J. H. Foley, joined the George Square bronze set in 1867.

James Watt's statue by Sir Francis Chantrey went up in 1832. Three former rectors of Glasgow University are represented. The statue of Sir Robert Peel (1859) is also by Mossman. Peel, whose repeal of the Corn Laws won him wide popularity in Glasgow, had a banquet given in his honour in a marquee erected in a Buchanan Street garden when he was elected Lord Rector in 1837. Another politician, William Ewart Gladstone, whose statue is by Hamo Thornycroft and went up in 1904, was a speaker at that dinner. Gladstone delivered his rectorial address in the Kibble Palace, a fascinating structure originally erected by the engineer John Kibble at his Clyde Coast home in Coulport about 1860, but gifted to Glasgow and re-erected in the Botanic Gardens in 1873. It contains tropical vegetation interspersed with romantic white-marble statues by Hamo Thornycroft, Goscombe John and others. The Botanic Gardens, originally opened only to private sub-scribers, were taken over by the Corporation in 1887 and opened to the public in 1891. The gardens were bought at a cost of £59,531.

The statue of the third rector, the poet, Thomas Campbell, another of Mossman's contributions to George Square, went up in 1877. It was he who, in *The Pleasures of Hope*, pointed out to us that:

> 'Tis distance lends enchantment to the view,
> And robes the mountain in its azure hue

and is said to have coined a phrase popular with authors:

> Now Barabbas was a publisher.

Thomas Graham (1805–69), a friend of David Livingstone, was lecturer in chemistry in the Mechanics' Institute, and successively Professor of Chemistry at Anderson's College at University College, London. In 1855 he became Master of the Mint in London. His representation joined the George Square Valhalla in 1872 and was the work of William Brodie. Marochetti was responsible in 1855 for the likeness of James Oswald, his hat in hand an ageless temptation to small boys to lob things into it. Oswald was a Reform Bill supporter and a Glasgow Member of Parliament twice—from 1832 to 1837 and from 1839 to 1847. He is said to have been in his day "one of the most influential Scottish members in the House of Commons". That the mere suggestion of erecting a statue to any Glasgow member of the House of Commons in our own day provokes instant risibility may not wholly be due to the twentieth century's lack of enthusiasm for statuary.

Robert Burns arrived in 1876, the year before his fellow poet, Campbell. His statue, by C. E. Ewing, was paid for by more than 40,000 shilling subscriptions, and unveiled before a crowd of 30,000.

Finally, there are the equestrian statues of the Prince Consort and the Queen herself, both by Baron Marochetti, of Turin and Vaux. They arrived together in 1864, the Queen's statue having come from Charing Cross, where she had been since 1849.

Other notable examples include Mossman's representations of David Livingstone, the explorer,* and the Reverend Dr. Norman Macleod, an eloquent minister of the Barony Church, which went up in Cathedral Square in 1877. Alexander Skirving's monument to the Battle of Langside was erected at Battlefield in 1887. Lord Kelvin, pensive, went up in Kelvingrove in 1813, the work of Macfarlane Shannon, three years after Paul Montford's figures on Kelvingrove Bridge. Ernest Gillick was responsible for the lions that flank Burnet's Cenotaph of 1922.

To complete our survey of the fabric of late Victorian and Edwardian Glasgow, several rather more minor figures who provided an exciting flourish or two should be mentioned. James Salmon senior (1805–88) built the first Langside College (1870), originally a Deaf and Dumb Institute, but superseded by Boissevain's and Osmond's new college in 1965. Salmon's famous grandson, also James Salmon (1874–1924), built 'The Hatrack', 142 St. Vincent Street (1899), an exuberantly-detailed realization of another narrow Georgian frontage drawing inspiration in many respects from Art Nouveau. It contrasts with his more severe Lion Chambers (1906), 170–72 Hope Street, the first building in Glasgow to have a reinforced-concrete frame. His University Gardens (1900), in which J. G. Gillespie may have had a hand, has been restored amongst the complex of new university buildings of which it now forms a part.

Because the former Liberal Club (1909) has been incorporated with the Royal Scottish Academy of Music and Drama in one of Glasgow's most architecturally exciting precincts, its builder, Alexander Nisbet Paterson (1862–1947), who worked with the firm of Burnet Son and Campbell, deserves mention.

There remains John Keppie (1863–1945), whose main claim to our interest here is that Charles Rennie Mackintosh (1868–1928) joined the firm of Keppie and Henderson as a draughtsman, and Keppie had the young Mackintosh working in association with him in *The Glasgow Herald* Building (1893) in Mitchell Street, the annexe to Northpark House (1893), now Broadcasting House, Queen Margaret Drive, and, in the same year, Martyrs Public School at Townhead.

*Removed from George Square to make way for an Information Kiosk.

Mackintosh is generally hailed as the founder of twentieth-century design. Although his father was a Police Superintendent of Highland extraction, Glasgow provided the environment of Mackintosh's formative years. After five years of apprenticeship to a Glasgow architect, John Hutchinson, during which period he studied at the Glasgow School of Art, Mackintosh joined the firm of Honeyman and Keppie. In 1890 he won the 'Greek' Thomson scholarship, which took him to France and Italy. During the 90s, he became associated with Herbert McNair and the sisters Frances and Margaret Macdonald—Margaret later became his wife—who, as 'The Four', exhibited graphic and craft work in the then novel Art Nouveau manner. At the age of 28, perhaps as a result of some influence upon the governors by its director, Fra Newberry, Mackintosh won the limited competition for the Glasgow School of Art.

This building, his masterpiece, went up in two sections, the eastern in 1897, the western in 1907. Between these years, Mackintosh built two inventive houses, both with his belief in total design carried through to include the furniture: Windyhill, Kilmacolm, Renfrewshire in 1901, which has had its interior altered and is no longer equipped with all its original furniture; and the still intact Hill House, Helensburgh, Dunbartonshire, the following year. Queen's Cross Church went up in 1897, its interior a minor instance of Mackintosh's remarkable skill in manipulating spatial relationships in the way that a composer must. It has a Gothic-influenced exterior. Nevertheless, the fact that it has been scissored by motorways and roads, depriving it of its church hall, puts some urgency upon the need for its eventual removal and rebuilding in an area where there is felt to be a need for a new church.

Scotland Street School, built in 1904, though half-obscured by a post-Second World War factory and restricted in its internal arrangements by the regulation requirements of the day, is, with its two Gropius-like glass-fronted towers, also so original a building as to make its conservation essential, possibly on a rebuilt site and adapted internally for a different use.

But the School of Art seems safe. The range and quality of the invention, even today let alone in 1896, is truly astonishing. Thomas Howarth, Mackintosh's most considerable biographer, speaks of its "synthesis of traditional craftsmanship and twentieth-century engineering", and rightly calls it "the first important architectural monument to the new movement in Europe".

Whereas all Mackintosh's Victorian predecessors had synthesized combinations of the five basic architectural styles, achieving excellences that, with the exception of Thomson's work, had no continuing personal 'thumbprints'. Mackintosh synthesized feelings and achieved a new and instantly recognizable individuality. Even the greatest of artists show their influences from time to time, since art, like life, is a continuing process, and—contrary to the ill-considered dogma circulated by our late-twentieth-century drop-outs—we cannot disown our ancestry. The tower of *The Glasgow Herald* Building may indeed, as Gomme and Walker suggest, have been inspired by J. M. MacLaren, who built a farmhouse and the hotel at Fortingall, Perthshire, at the turn of the previous decade. Certainly, the names of Boysey and Halsey Ricardo have been commonly mentioned as other possible influences. Yet what ultimately matters in art is not which influences show but what asserts its own life. A Scottish cliff-cum-castle feeling shows itself in the eastern and southern façades of the art school, while possibly the northern façade, as J. M. Reid puts it, catches "a faint reminiscence of the old University building, transformed in a mind that was re-thinking everything for itself". The detail, including the "iron gates that hint at portcullises", adds satisfaction to the whole conception, inside and out, in a curiously integral way. The finest interior is undoubtedly that of the library. Here, the spatial relationships that were Mackintosh's speciality, the strength of creative power yet of containment, call to my mind Beethoven's late String Quartet, opus 132, where there is displayed the same absolute mastery of a great mind operating economically and effortlessly at full stretch, for its own satisfaction.

Mackintosh left Glasgow when he was 48, and, with the exception of the house he built for Basset Lowke at Northampton, his creative days were virtually over. A difficult temperament not helped by too great a reliance on drink may have hampered the getting of further major commissions; or he may, as some suggest, though with no evidence to support them, simply have been played out, the French and other water-colours of his last years providing a kind of therapy against decline.

I have devoted considerable space to the buildings which went up in the steel and shipbuilding era of Glasgow and the men who created them, because, in spite of depredations already made upon our stock of them, they form a major part of the United Kingdom's stone-and-mortar heritage. The inevitable limbo into which newly-dead artists and just-passed eras are necessarily plunged as their successors strive after original variations on the basic themes of life has now released the Victorians and their achievements from the darkness of its contempt, and a fresh realization of the measure of these achievements has developed.

One aspect of Mackintosh's work which unfortunately has not re-emerged from the decades of neglectful limbo, being by its very nature fashionably ephemeral, had considerable social significance. This was his association with Miss Kate Cranston, to all intent and purpose the inventor of the Glasgow tea-room.

Stuart and Kate Cranston, members of the family who owned the Crow Hotel in George Square, where the Merchants' House now stands, were responsible for this innovation, Stuart Cranston opened his tea-room in Argyle Street, while Kate had her first tea-room in Ingram Street. Mackintosh began designing for her in 1896, along with his wife Margaret Macdonald: furniture—his chairs offered greater visual than physical satisfaction, but perhaps the intention was to discourage patrons from staying too long!—interior decor, cutlery, and, in the case of 'The Willows' (inspired by Sauchiehaugh, 'the willow meadow', on which Sauchiehall Street was built), the whole tea-room. Its façade above ground-floor level may be seen incorporated in Daly's. The Ingram Street tea-rooms, with their Oak and Chinese rooms, were in the possession of Glasgow Corporation for almost a quarter of a century. For a time they did duty as a warehouse store. Mackintosh's interiors have now been stripped for assembly elsewhere, and the building itself demolished.

That composite writer James Hamilton Muir* claimed a major reason for the success of the tea-rooms to be the fact that women, who were not then popular in Glasgow pubs, were able to go to a Cranston's tea-room on their own. Wrote Muir: "It is believed (and averred) that in no other town can you see in a place of refreshment such ingenious and beautiful decorations in the style of new art as in Miss Cranston's shop in Buchanan Street."

A Glasgow man's overheard commentary on an uncompleted building is quoted: "It is so kind o' artistic, ye know, wi' a' that sort o' light paint. Oh, it'll do! It's quite Kate Cranston-ish."

The design sense of successive generations of Glaswegians was widened by a series of exhibitions which flowered out of the

*Pseudonym for James Bone, Archibald Hamilton Charteris, Muirhead Bone.

city's sense of prosperity, and its belief that at last it had something to show off to the world.

The first of Glasgow's International Exhibitions was held in Kelvingrove Park during the summer of 1888. The theme of the exhibition was oriental, and white stone palaces with domes and minarets went up to house the various objects on show. A replica of the Bishop's Palace was built on the Gilmorehill slopes, and extra bridges were thrown across the Kelvin on whose waters gondolas glided up and down.

J. J. Bell, whose autobiography *I Remember* provides a vivid account of the day-to-day lives of what he calls "Little Victorians", remembered a festive glimpse of Victoria herself.

Bank Street led to the University and it was therefore a thoroughfare of some little importance, but in August 1888 it attained, for a few minutes, honour and glory, by the progress of Her Majesty passing through it to Kelvingrove Park, there to visit Glasgow's first International Exhibition;* a little elderly lady in a bonnet, sitting erect in a big landau, giving every now and then a nod—so she passed by, looking severe and not bored. A year ago, the land had acclaimed her Jubilee—fifty years on the throne yet with, as reigns go, many years to come. The Exhibition had been opened in May by the Prince and Princess of Wales, her Royal Highness wearing a tight-fitting costume with a very decided 'bustle', a floral bonnet, with a veil to the tip of her nose, and carrying a prim little muff.

Not long after Queen Victoria and her retinue had passed, and the pavements and windows had become vacant, an aged Italian with barrel-organ and monkey appeared. Possibly he knew nothing of the importance of the hour of Glasgow's first International Exhibition, of the august Personage who had so lately preceded him. It was his day for Bank Street, and calmly he began to grind the 'Carnival of Venice', lifting peering rheumy eyes to the windows.

There was, indeed, a cosmopolitan feeling in the air, a feeling even more apparent when the exhibition of 1901 opened on the same site. The profits of the previous exhibition had been used to

---

*The date of this official visit was 22nd June. She later paid a private visit, as did her son, the Duke of Cambridge, and, amongst other royal personages the King of the Belgians, to say nothing of nearly 6 million non-royal personages.

help provide a red sandstone wedding-cake of an art gallery,*
built by Sir J. W. Simpson and Milner Allen on the apparent
assumption that the more variegated the detail the greater the
effect of sumptuousness. It is said that Simpson wanted his gallery
built the other way round, and that because he did not get his
own way, he committed suicide. Simpson, however, lived to a
ripe old age, and the myth probably arose because of the early
death of Allen. In any case the gallery put on a notable opening
show of painting.

The 1901 exhibition, known as 'The Groveries', was both more
extensive and more ambitious than its predecessor. Its architect,
James Miller—who built the Royal Infirmary which replaced the
Adam Infirmary—laid it out over 73 acres, intending it to wear
a Spanish air. Its purpose was to demonstrate the development of
art, industry and science during the century that had just ended,
particularly during the reign of Queen Victoria, who died while
it was in progress. There were numerous innovations; an industrial
hall with a dome crowned by a Statue of Light balanced on one
toe, several Russian pavilions and a display of motor-cars. The
railway companies, who in 1888 had cut an hour off their
journeys from London, this time enticed the southern British to
the exhibition with tempting excursion fares. The occasion was
marked locally by the introduction of electric tram services,†
powered by the new generating station at Pinkston. This innovation harmonized with other electrical manifestations at 'The
Groveries'. Electricity apart, the weather was magnificent,
and a new generation of Glaswegians relaxed and enjoyed
themselves.

The 1911 exhibition had the purpose of raising money to found
and endow a Chair of Scottish History and Literature at Glasgow
University. It was smaller in scale, if more ingenious in the range
of its delights, which included a Highland village, a 'Scottish
Toonie', a West African village, a Palace of History that housed
the most comprehensive collection of bits and pieces out of
Scottish history hithertofore brought together, an aerial railway,
a mountain slide, and motor boats instead of gondolas on the yet
unfouled Kelvin, where a flotilla of model ships also floated.

*Alfred Waterhouse, the competition assessor, turned down much finer
designs by Honeyman and by Keppie and Mackintosh, for which no seeing
Glaswegian will lightly forgive him!

†Electricity had been introduced to Glasgow for domestic use in 1893.

German and Hungarian bands in immaculate uniforms flapped the tunes of the day against the summer air, and there were sessions of massed hymn-singing, to placate the god of prosperity. A great storm blew up on the final day of this last Glasgow exhibition before the First World War, carrying the roof of the Aviation Pavilion up to Park Terrace and severely damaging many of the others.

Exhibitions apart, regular opportunities for Glaswegians to enjoy themselves had both improved in quality and multiplied in quantity between 1870 and 1914.

For one thing, the theatre-going habit had spread. Glasgow acquired further scarcely less inflammable theatres, to say nothing of music-halls, a zoo and a skating palace, which stood on the site of what became the first building to show films commercially in Glasgow, later the Regal Cinema in Sauchiehall Street and now the A.B.C.1.

For those whose tastes did not reach the higher flights of dramatic fancy, there was the Scotia Music Hall, which later became the 'Metropole', a house of barn-storming melodramas like *Maria Martin* and *The Face at the Window*. Its burnt-out façade still faces the Goosedubs, allegedly so-called after a goose-keeping bailie who had a house in Stockwell Street with a garden stretching to the Briggait, the goose-puddles providing the name for the lane that later connected these two streets. Among the many famous artists who appeared at the 'Scotia' was the young Harry Lauder, facing his first audience as a professional entertainer.

The Britannia Music Hall, newer than the 'Scotia' and located in the Trongate, near Glasgow Cross, was another popular haunt of our ancestors, though by Edwardian days it was reputed to have become a known rough house, where bad fruit and rotten eggs were sold outside, so that patrons could arm themselves before entering in case a performer turned out not to be to their taste. 'The Britannia' and its neighbour, MacLeod's Waxworks, both came into the hands of an eccentric Yorkshireman, A. E. Pickard, who turned the 'Britannia' into the 'Panopticon', which then alternated films with variety acts, and MacLeod's into Pickard's Waxworks, beneath which he ran a zoo of sorts. Neither of these establishments managed to survive the slump between the wars.

The Theatre Royal had been rebuilt in Cowcaddens after the

Dunlop Street Theatre Royal went up in flames in 1869, after a performance of the pantomime *Bluebeard*. Fire removed this theatre in 1879, and badly damaged its successor in 1895. However, the third rebuilding carried the 'Royal' over two wars and into the television era, when it became the studios of Scottish Television Limited.

The Royal Princess's (now the Citizens') Theatre in the Gorbals, and the 'Grand' in Cowcaddens (burned down in 1917), specialized in melodrama and pantomine. Indeed, the very essence of Glasgow pantomine lived on into the 'Citizens'' occupancy through pantomine with such traditional thirteen-letter titles as *Gaggiegalorum* and *Bletherskeite*.

For East End folk, the Queen's Theatre at Watson Street, which had begun life as the 'People's Palace', provided good strong music-hall fare. 'The Gaiety', later rebuilt as the 'Empire', provided music-hall fare for posher customers. It was mostly a mixture of Scots comics like Neil Kenyon and such popular artists from England as Nellie Wallace and Bill Bennett, who filled these halls, as well as the smaller 'provincial' theatres, which, by the 90s, had sprung up in Partick, Anderston and Govan.

Music-hall artists also appeared at both the City Hall and St. Andrew's Halls. Charles Coburn was a popular favourite with Glasgow audiences, singing such hits as 'Two Lovely Black Eyes', 'If you want to know the time, ask a P'liceman' and 'The Man who Broke the Bank at Monte Carlo'. Albert Chevalier was amongst those who came to St. Andrew's Halls about 1890, delighting audiences with 'Mrs. 'enry 'awkins', 'The Nipper's Lullaby', and 'My Old Dutch'.

Scots comics such as J. C. Macdonald and W. F. Frame, did not emerge into popularity until the late 80s. The line of Scots comics that burgeoned from them included Will Fyffe (who, like Lauder, came from the east coast, in spite of his famous song 'I belong to Glasgow'), Tommy Lorne, George West, Tommy Morgan and in our own day, Duncan Macrae, Jimmy Logan and Stanley Baxter, Macrae and Baxter versatile actors as well as comedians. Sir Harry Lauder openly acknowledged Macdonald's influence on his own later successful career.

Many of the early Scots comedians relied heavily on songs and jokes about drink. J. J. Bell quotes a typical example of early Scotch comic lyricism, obviously dating from the end of the beginning of the new century:

Oh, my, I'm thenkfu that it's by—
That dreidfu Exhibeetion, ma temper it did try,
For every time oor Jock gaed there
He cam' hame roarin' fu,
And he always blamed it on the tea
He got at the Bungaloo.

I remember an uncle of mine quoting the verse of a song by Frame which ran:

The River Clyde is verra wide
Especially whaur it's narra.
There's mony a chiel stauns at the bar
That couldnae wheel a barra.

though whether this inability was due to drink or sheer absence of skill I was never really sure.

Even Lauder on occasion, used drunkenness as a theme for his melodious humour.

Edwardian Glasgow, fonder even than the 90s of foot-tapping tunes, had more theatres and a wider range of 'shows' to choose from. 'The Alhambra' ran variety, the 'Royalty' (later the 'Lyric'), 'rep'. 'The Pavilion', the 'Savoy' and the 'Coliseum' also catered mainly for the music hall public. The new King's Theatre, opened in 1904, vied with the 'Royal' in offering plays and opera. To most people, Lehar's operetta *The Merry Widow*, with its languorous waltzes and its saucy gaity, symbolizes the leisured side of Edwardian life. The *Widow* made her first Glasgow curtsey in the King's Theatre on Christmas Eve 1907. By then internationally famous, she had a tremendous reception. Robert Turnbull, the music critic of *The Glasgow Herald*, deplored the liberties taken with the music in the interest of laugh-raising by George Edwards and his cast, but was otherwise full of praise for the performance. "Last night the piece, presented by an entirely capable company, never flagged for a moment. The singing, both solo and concerted, was always good; there was plenty of verve in the dancing; and in matters of setting, dresses etc., 'The Merry Widow' left no room for criticism."

The famous waltz in the second act had to be repeated three times. While Glasgow's middle and upper classes were not nearly as sophisticated as London society—it is doubtful if many copies of that clandestine publication *The Pearl*, from which respectable Victorian gentlemen were able to draw pornographic sustenance between the rigours of appearing to be upright pillars of society and generous dispensers of charity, sold in Glasgow*—the "Golden Age with the gilt off", as J. B. Priestley calls Edwardian England, would have sufficiently affected Scotland for that King's Theatre audience of bosomy women and moustachioed men to experience something of the cosmopolitan sensuousness of Lehar's measures, before driving back to their West End houses, still well staffed with servants to stoke up their coal fires.

Incidentally, the prices of the seats for that performance on Christmas Eve 1907 were: orchestral stalls, 5s.; dress circle, 4s.; upper circles, 2s.; pit, a shilling; and gallery, 6d.

In the 1880s, orchestral concerts moved from the City Hall to St. Andrew's Halls, and chamber concerts were held in the Queen's Rooms. Glasgow had a second Festival of Music in the City Hall in 1873. It lasted five days, during which the celebrities included the singers Tietjens and Santley and the conductor Sir Michael da Costa. The choral works on this occasion included Mendelssohn's *Elijah*, at which the audience was requested not to applaud for religious reasons, and Costa's own oratorio *Eli*. Beethoven's *Pastoral* and Schumann's *Spring* symphonies were the main orchestral items.

This festival seems to have given the necessary encouragement for the creation of a new and 'permanent' orchestra, proposals for which had been mooted nine years before. From 1874 to 1891, the Glasgow Choral Union's orchestra gave concerts all over Central Scotland under such conductors as Sir Arthur Sullivan, Hans von Bulow, and Augustus Mann. A group of music-lovers then engineered a break-away. While the Choral Union continued to give their concerts, the Scottish Orchestra Company Limited ran a rival series. By 1894 the two bodies had merged to become the Choral and Orchestral Union. A long series of foreign conductors and foreign leaders then dominated the musical scene, Glaswegians believing, in common with most British audiences, that a musician who was not a Herr, a Monsieur or a Signor could not possibly be any good, although informed British opinion thought otherwise. As long ago as 1914, the *Musical Times* greeted the appointment of Wilhelm Bruch to the conductorship of the orchestra with a brave nationalistic protest: "What becomes

---

*I am not suggesting that pornography is a measure of sophistication; rather indicating the continuing restraints kept upon taste by Scottish Calvinism when such restraints no longer prevailed throughout London society.

our boasted progress in music if important appointments . . . are not to be filled by native musicians? Cannot we raise the article on our own soil? Are we always to import it? Would such a stigma be tolerated in any other European country?"

The answer, of course, was 'no': but tolerated it was in Glasgow. Even the providers of light music for balls and dinners had to have names like Monsieur Claude Jaquinot and Herr Wilhelm Iff. Until the appointment of Alexander Gibson as musical director of the Scottish National Orchestra—the permanent successor from 1950 to the peculiarly impermanent old Scottish Orchestra, whose season at most never stretched to more than six months of the year and for much of its existence lasted for only three—this dreadful unmusical snobbery resulted in preference being given to a third-rate mittel-European rather than to even a first-rate English conductor.

The taste for painting greatly increased during the 70s, the leaders of city life having homes with plenty of wall space and money to spend on pictures they liked. The work of the Barbizan group and their Dutch followers was much sought after in the 70s and 80s, imported to Glasgow by the art dealers John Forbes White and Alexander Reid. The *plein-air* method of painting—setting the easel in front of the subject and painting direct from nature—had brought home to Glaswegians the excitement of light. The influence of Whistler on young painters was also considerable. Revolt was in the international air.

The Glasgow Group of painters came together about 1880. The 'father' of the movement was W. Y. Macgregor (1855–1923), a powerful painter "glorying in the quality of the medium for its own sake", to quote Ian Finlay: "deriving inspiration from it, in stark contrast to the infilling of colour upon careful drawings which had become the established tradition in the academies".

Not all 'The Boys' who gathered in Macgregor's studio were Scots. Joseph Crawhall (1861–1913) was a Northumbrian hunting man, the delicacy of whose birds and beasts still seems remarkable. Sir James Guthrie (1859–1930), who caught fleeting moments at tennis parties or on the golf course, and whose early portraits abound in character, came from Belfast. E. A. Hornel (1864–1933) was influenced by the decorative qualities of Japanese painting, and created his rosy-cheeked children in laid-on daubs of sheer colour. George Hendry (1858–1943) also visited Japan, and produced what has come to be regarded as the key-picture of the

movement with his *Galloway Landscape*. The others included
E. A. Walton, Stuart Park, Alexander Melville and, a younger
recruit, D. Y. Cameron.

A show at the Grosvenor Gallery in London, where they were
welcomed by the followers of England's rebels against the
academies, the New Art Club, brought the Glasgow Group its
first major success. Other successes followed in Munich, Dresden
and Vienna, where the German Secessionists welcomed them.

They were never really a 'school' in any unified sense, and the
nearest they came to having a manifesto was the short-lived
Scottish Art Review, which included as fellow contributors characters as diverse as James Matthew Barrie, then still full of unful-
filled Kirriemuir ambition; that inverted Calvinist rebel-poet from
Greenock, John Davidson, whose later plays hammered home
with Knoxian obstinacy his belief that God was dead; and the
Russian revolutionary writer Kropotkin.

All that 'The Boys' had in common was a freshness of approach,
a certain emphasis on colour,* and chance that brought them
enthusiastically together at a moment when the rich Philistines
were ready to buy. By the turn of the century, they were going their own diverse ways, Hornel to Kirkcudbright to repeat
his coy little girl-pictures so endlessly as almost to suggest a
psychological obsession, and Guthrie to become the fashionable
President of the Royal Academy. But for about twenty years
they produced a remarkable range of impressive pictures, as an
exhibition of the work of the movement mounted by the Scottish
Arts Council in the Kelvingrove Gallery in 1968 clearly demonstrated.

Interest in Art Nouveau perhaps helped to make the movement
seem old fashioned by Edwardian times. Of the Scottish Colour-
ists who succeed them, Peploe and Cadell had no real Glasgow
links, only the lyrical Leslie Hunter (1879–1936) belonging to and
drawing inspiration from Glasgow and the West, whose citizens
on the whole neglected him.

In literature, the latter part of the Victorian era in Scotland
was dominated by Robert Louis Stevenson (1850–94) and James
Matthew Barrie (1860–1937), the novelist who, so to say, preceded
the playwright with such things as *Auld Licht Idylls* (1888) and
The Little Minister (1891), part of which is set in Glasgow. Neither

*A characteristic of later Scottish painting, and of nearly all Scottish poetry,
as if in defiance of our predominantly grey skies.

of these men had Glasgow connections, any more than had the
Kailyaird, or back-green cabbage-patch school of Gallovidian
S. R. Crockett (1860–1914) and the Reverend John Watson,
'Ian MacLaren' (1850–1907), whose novels *The Lilac Sunbonnet*
(1894) and *Beside the Bonnie Briar Bush* (1895) showed a coy
archness of sugar-sweet sentimentality never before achieved,
though doubtless devoured avidly by many Glasgow readers, to
whom the novel that jerked the fashionable validity out of such
saccharine literary pietism, Ayrshire-born George Douglas
Brown's (1869–1902) *The House with the Green Shutters*, must
have come as a disagreeable shock.

But the darling of the circulating libraries in the 70s and 80s
was undoubtedly Trongate-born William Black (1841–98), who
took the journalist's road to London. After two false starts he
produced *The Daughter of Heth* (1871), a love story painting contrasts of manners and conventions through the arrival of a French
girl at a country manse in the West.

Into almost all his novels, Black contrived to introduce his
native city. Thus in *The Daughter of Heth*, Coquette, the French
heroine of the book who captures the fancy of the minister of
Airlie's eldest son (known by his nickname, the 'Whaup'), comes
up from Ayrshire by train to see him, chaperoned by Lady Drum,
one of the minister's aristocratic parishioners.

As Coquette and Lady Drum drew near to Glasgow, the impatience of the girl increased. Her thoughts flew on more swiftly
than the train; and they were all directed towards the Whaup
whom she was now about to see.

"Will he be at the station? Does he know we are coming? Or shall
we see him as we go along the streets?" she asked. "Dear me," said
Lady Drum, "Ye seem to think that Glasgow is no bigger than
Saltcoats. Meet him in the streets? We should scarce see him in the
streets if he were dressed in scaurlet."

It was growing towards dusk when the two ladies arrived. Lady
Drum's carriage was waiting at the station; and presently Coquette
found herself in the midst of the roar and turmoil of the great city.
The lamps on the bridges were burning yellow in the grey coldness
of the twilight; and she got a glimpse of the masses of shipping
down the dusky bed of the river. Then up through the busy streets—
where the windows were growing bright with gas, and dense
crowds of people were hurrying to and fro', and the carts, and
waggons, and carriages were raising a din that was strange to ears
grown accustomed to the stillness of Airlie.

Bridges over the Clyde
Cityscape

"Alas!" said Coquette, "I cannot see him in this crowd. It is impossible." Lady Drum laughed and said nothing.

And so they drove on—the high, old-fashioned chariot which ought to have been kept for state purposes down at Castle Cawmill,* swinging gently on its big springs,—up to the north-western districts of the city.

For those who really cannot bear not to know what happened, Coquette never married the 'Whaup', for she fell in love with a dashing earl who perished when his yacht *Caroline* was run down by a steamer bound for Ireland. Coquette, after visiting the spot where his body had been washed ashore, fell ill with one of these fatal 'fevers' which Victorian doctors could not accurately diagnose, and for which they knew no cure.

Black's other successes included *The Strange Adventures of a Phaeton* (1872) and *MacLeod of Dare* (1878), after which, as J. H. Millar put it, he merely repeated his stock effects, "impulsive tomboys, Highland seas, polychromic sunsets." There is perhaps an air of contrivance about all the tales which has no doubt militated against their survival. Nevertheless, *The Daughter of Heth* could well bear reprinting as a period piece.

Nor was the output of the verse department in Glasgow much more distinguished. Throughout the 70s and 80s, Robert Buchanan (1841–1901), Staffordshire born but brought up and educated in Glasgow, was thought by some to be the equal of Browning; but the rhetoric of such pieces as "Judas Iscariot" has worn decidedly thin, and he is really better remembered now for his onslaught on Rossetti and his friends of the so-called 'Fleshly School of Poetry', and for thus providing W. S. Gilbert with the theme for the Gilbert and Sullivan opera *Patience*, than anything he achieved during his London career as a somewhat pugnacious Man of Letters.

Glasgow-born Sir James George Frazer (1854–1941) produced between 1890 and 1914 his enormous Spencerian attempt to unify life through the interpretation of myth and legend. It aroused considerable interest, and was still spoken of in tones of hushed awe by *savants* when I was a boy, though more recent scientific inquiry has discredited some of its conclusions.

Bret Harte, the American writer, was American consul in Glasgow for four years from 1880, during which time he lived

---

*Seamills, as Airlie represents Fairlie.

11

Buchanan Street: looking south; looking north

at 113 West Regent Street, where he wrote his Glasgow tale *Young Robin Gray*.

Edwardian prose-writing was dominated by the remarkable popularity of *Wee MacGregor* (1902) and *Wee MacGregor Again* (1904) by James Joy Bell (1871–1934) which began to appear in the *Evening Times* in 1912. Its humorous portrayal of Glasgow working-class life won it a popularity which even spread to America. The novelist who best captured the atmosphere of Edwardian Glasgow was Frederick Niven (1878–1944) with *The Staff at Simsons*, though there is also real merit in *The Setons* by Anna Buchan (1877–1948). Neil Munro (1864–1930) succeeded to the Stevenson tradition with romantic historical novels like *John Splendid* (1898), *Doom Castle* (1901), and many others still popular. He became editor of Glasgow's *Evening News*, lived latterly in a house next the building that had once been Henry Bell's hotel in Helensburgh, and endeared himself to Glaswegians and many others, with his *Para Handy* tales of the West Highland skipper of a Clyde 'puffer' or coal-boat, and his pawky crew; tales that have achieved a wider popularity through television, but which have been over-extended and temporarily devalued in the process. Munro's autobiographical reminiscences *The Brave Days* do for middle-class Edwardian Glasgow life what Bell's *I Remember* did for the late Victorian city.

The *fin de siécle* 90s and most of the Edwardian decade had John Davidson (1857–1909), the Barrhead-born Greenock-bred writer, as Glasgow's nearest *Yellow Book* literary representative. He taught in various schools, including Kelvinside Academy, before going south, where he battled with the usual odds against making a living as a poet and essayist, odds stacked high by depressions stemming from the strain of insanity in his family.

While his best poem "Thirty Bob a Week", which powerfully influenced both T. S. Eliot and 'Hugh MacDiarmid', is couched in Cockney terms, the hopeless position of the struggling London clerk he depicts was probably little different from that of his Glasgow counterpart.

> And its often very cold and very wet,
>   And my missis stitches towels for a hunks;
> And the Pillar'd Halls is half of it to let—
>   Three rooms about the size of travelling trunks.
> And we cough, my wife and I, to dislocate a sigh,
>   When the noisy little kids are in their bunks.

But you never hear her do a growl or whine,
  For she's made of flint and roses, very odd,
And I've got to cut my meaning rather fine,
  Or I'd blubber, for I'm made of greens and sod:
So p'r'aps we are in Hell for all that I can tell,
  And lost and damn'd and served up hot to God.

Being lost and damned brings us to that section of Victorian society who might reasonably have supposed they were: the poor. By a 1579 Act of the Scottish Parliament, magistrates in burghs and justices of the peace in rural parishes had had conferred on them the right of assessment for poor relief, a right later transferred to heritors and kirk sessions. Very few parishes made use of these powers of compulsory assessment by the beginning of the nineteenth century, the Scots preferring to give relief through voluntary church contributions. Begging, by and large, was regarded as a suitable means of augmenting this tardy charity.

After twenty years' opposition to the corporation's proposal that it should municipalize the city's water supplies, Glasgow Corporation Water Works Act finally got through Parliament in 1855, enabling the corporation at a cost of a million pounds, to harness Loch Katrine and bring the water by pipeline to Milngavie reservoir, a supply later augmented by feed-ins from several other nearby mountainy lochs, notably Lochs Vennacher and Drunkie.

Thirty-four miles of tunnelling were completed, and a reservoir built at Mugdock all for £70,000. A million and a half pounds had been spent before the final link-up was complete, and the city was receiving 50 million gallons a day.

On 15th October 1859 the Queen and Prince Albert went by rail to Callander and then by coach to Loch Katrine. Although the day was wet and blowy, a large crowd turned out, making use of the cheap railway excursion fare offered. The guard of honour included detachments of the 42nd and 59th Highlanders. Lord Provost Stewart met the Queen, and aboard the *Rob Roy* they sailed to the mouth of the tunnel. "Such a work is worthy of the enterprise of Glasgow," said Her Majesty, turning the handle which caused the water to flow, "and I trust it will be blessed with complete success."

It was, and is: various extensions have kept Glasgow thoroughly on top of its water problem.

Various other Acts were passed in the 60s relating to nuisances, sanitary reform and the better organization of the police.

Most important of all, however, was the appointment of Glasgow's first Medical Officer of Health, Dr. W. T. Gairdner, in 1862. The vital importance of hygiene and of preventative medicine finally began to be recognized during the 70s, though not until the Medical Officer of Health in the 80s, Dr. J. B. Russell, revealed in frequent speeches that 25 per cent of Glasgow's families were living in single-roomed houses and more than half of these were also taking in lodgers, did the extent and degree of the squalor and human degradation prevalent in the city begin to be generally realized. Even then, some wealthy Glaswegians were none too keen to provide finance for the speeding-up of improved conditions.

The Glasgow Improvement Act of 1866 resulted in the setting up of the Glasgow Improvement Trust, which, though empowered to levy a rate of 6d. in the pound, was inadequately financed. It cleared over 15,000 houses from the old heart of the city, aided also by the demolition work of the railway companies as they swathed their way through slum areas. It is not to underestimate the social urgency of the problem the Trust had to face to say that the pressure put upon them by the railway company to abandon the old university, and their failure to provide new houses for those who were displaced by their demolitions, were both to prove disastrous. Had the university stayed where it was, additional buildings would inevitably have been added to the old, and the creation of a new future central problem area would thus have been avoided. Without new houses in which the displaced slum-dwellers could be accommodated, they simply flooded into areas like the Gorbals and Cowcaddens, which then in turn entered upon their decades of overcrowded decline.

Under a later Act a further six central acres were cleared. While tenements were now provided for the poor, the mixed land-uses of the rebuilt areas set in being other problems for the passing years to hatch.

The continuing failure of any authority adequately to provide for those thrown out of work and hard put to it to avoid destitution, bred in Glaswegians a dislike of rent originally based on sheer inability to pay. This dislike of rent has had some curious consequences. Just before the First World War, for instance, when overcrowding was still widespread, one house in ten was actually standing empty, lodgings being cheaper than a place of one's own. Out of this situation has arisen the belief that, regardless of the income of the tenant, housing should be a 'social service', a manifestly absurd proposition in our affluent society.

By 1909, the corporation had built more than 2,000 houses, just over a quarter of which were for poorer tenants. In his budget that year, Lloyd George introduced a 20 per cent tax on the increment value of all heritable property. This, on top of the unfavourable Scots rating system, put an end almost immediately to private enterprise building for the working class, or, indeed, any other class.

Along with the rest of Scotland, Glasgow was affected by the Scottish Education Act of 1872, which set up the school board system in which was vested control of parish and burgh schools, the Scotch Education Department (as it was at first called) becoming the central authority responsible for the qualification of teachers, the approving of grants and the election of the members of the school boards.

Glasgow's first school board of fifteen members was voted into office the following year. It later became the practice in Glasgow for three members to be nominated each by the Church of Scotland, the Free Church and the Roman Catholic Church, three by Labour organizations while three members remained independent. That first school board decided that thirty new schools with accommodation for 22,000 pupils were needed immediately; so, borrowing over £1¼ million, it set in hand a modest building programme. Compulsory attendance was at last introduced for children between the ages of 5 and 13, the leaving age being raised to 14 in 1902. By 1892, education up to leaving age was, in general, free. It is interesting to note that it took England until 1899 to provide an equivalent to the Scotch Education Department, when the English Board of Education was formed. Scotland's continuing lead in Victorian times gave substance to the belief that her education was ahead of England's, a belief from which the substance has long since evaporated although the myth lives on.

In 1888, Glasgow children first presented themselves for the examinations of the Scottish Leaving Certificate. The department's inspectorate soon had under state control a more or less uniform curriculum, varied only by a few independent schools outside their authority. The most famous of these schools in the city were the Glasgow Academy, founded in 1846 and first located in Elmbank Street, vacating its original building in favour of the High School for Boys (as the old grammar school, formerly in Rottenrow, George Street and after 1835, John Street, was now called) in 1878, when the academy moved to Kelvinbridge; Allan Glen's (1853), and Kelvinside Academy (1878).

The Co-operative and Trade Union movements also grew during these years. Both organizations could possibly be described as encouraging a process of self-education. There had been stirrings of early co-operatives among the Fenwick weavers in 1769, and at Govan, Tradeston, Lennoxtown and Kilmarnock around 1800. When Robert Owen returned from America, he threw much of his energy into trying to further acceptance of the idea of the Co-operative Movement. He met with many setbacks, and in the end much of the credit for persistently carrying on in spite of initial discouragement went to his disciple, Alexander Campbell, a Glaswegian. The movement received parliamentary sanction in 1852, through the Industrial and Provident Societies Act, although the right of co-operatives to exemption from income tax, provided goods were sold only to members, came only with an amending Act of 1893. But the Glasgow Co-operative Society collapsed in 1864 as a result of overextending its branches, and it was not until 1871 that the Kinning Park and St. George's Societies reasserted Glasgow's stake in the enterprise. In the meantime, the Scottish Co-operative Wholesale Society was formed in 1868, beginning business in Madeira Street. It then employed six people, had capital of £1,795 and had sales of just under £10,000 in its first year. In 1897 it was to build itself the imposing palace which had won second place in the City Chambers competition, designed by the firm of Bruce and Hay, on the south side of the river, as if to assert with a grandiose flourish its own success—a success reflected in its capital of more than £2½ million, its sales of over £4½ million and its staff of almost 4,800.

The smaller grocer always resented the advantages thus given to the Co-operative Movement, and middle-class housewives often refused to support it. To shop at 'the Co-op', was regarded as some kind of unthinkable betrayal by my own relatives when I was a child. But its social value has been immense, only now perhaps becoming less useful in an affluent society and against fierce competition from supermarkets some of which are owned by international operatives with enormously greater resources behind them.

It had been the enterprise of the weavers which had provided the impetus behind the first moves towards establishing the co-operatives. It was the miners who were principally behind the first practical steps towards the formation of Trade Unions. Since the trial and deportation of the Edinburgh advocate Thomas Muir and other Friends of the People in the 1790s, there had been substantial opposition to any kind of unions, opposition strengthened by the Combination Acts of 1799 and 1800. Alexander Campbell became one of the leaders in the formation of Trades Councils, which began to be set up in industrial centres after 1858. Campbell's friend Alexander MacDonald, a Lanarkshire miner who qualified at Glasgow university by working at his studies in the winter and going down the pits in the summer, and who had then become a teacher, co-operated in helping to have carried through the Reform Act of 1867 which gave working men in towns the vote, and an Act of 1871 which gave trade unions greater financial security. Macdonald, having unsuccessfully contested the Kilmarnock Burghs seat in 1868, entered Parliament in 1874 as the member for North Stafford—one of the first two Labour members ever elected—and was instrumental in having the Master and Servant Act, which discriminated against the servant, superseded by the Employers and Workmen Act, which put both on an equal footing and recognized the right of collective bargaining. The Act restricting strike action was also repealed.

In the late 80s, Keir Hardie (1856–1915) was associated with John Burns and Tom Mann in a movement which looked forward to the overthrow of the capitalist system by 1889, the anniversary of the French Revolution. Hardie, a Glaswegian, was responsible for the formation of the Scottish Miners' Federation before he stood unsuccessfully as Labour candidate in a Lanarkshire by-election, having been refused the Liberal nomination because some Liberal supporters would not vote for a working man.

Because of Roman Catholic antipathy, and a tendency to engage in internecine war, the pre-First World War Labour Party never really got anywhere until 1909, by which time the British Labour Party had tempted all the contending Scottish Labourites into its centralized political fold. It is interesting to note that Scottish Labour at first took over several of the causes upheld by the Scottish Liberals, including temperance, Home Rule, and shorter working hours; and perhaps a sad reflection on the Scottish variety of human fallibility that temperance was eventually abandoned, because it was simply impossible to sustain, and that Home Rule for Scotland was ditched because by 1945 it had become inconvenient to Big Brother in England.

In 1914 three out of Scotland's forty M.P.s were Labour, Keir Hardie having been elected to an English seat in 1892.

That temperance cause which the Labourites espoused had its origins in a Maryhill movement of 1829, out of which grew the Glasgow and West of Scotland Temperance Society. Various bodies followed, notably the Scottish Temperance League in 1844, the Scottish Lodge of the Independent Order of Good Templars in 1869, and the Band of Hope Union the following year.

There was a real problem to fight, because drink shops were both the poor man's only apparent refuge from misery, and the certain means of increasing his destitution. Unfortunately, many of the earliest opponents of the misuse of drink nullified their efforts by failing to tackle the social miseries which drove the victims to the gin parlours. Nor was it helpful to make the drinking shops as uncomfortable as possible, since sordid surroundings merely encouraged increasing squalor.

Although a mild attempt at controlling drinking had been made with the Home-Drummond Act of 1828, the first effective control measure was the Forbes-Mackenzie Act of 1854, named after its sponsor, the Member for Peeblesshire, which set down the hours between which drink could be sold—from 8 a.m. to 11 p.m.—abolished the Sunday sale of drink and prohibited the sale of liquor within 6 miles of a tollhouse, the first blow to be struck against 'one for the road'. Later legislation followed, relating to such matters as the granting of licences by magistrates, the sale of drink to children under 14, the discretion of magistrates to order ten o'clock closing, and giving the police increased powers of supervision. Following a Royal Commission's report in 1899, an Act of 1903 set up licensing courts in burghs of 4,000 and over and in counties. It also increased the penalties for drunkenness. The Scottish Temperance Act of 1913 set up a system whereby the electors could vote for no change, no licence or the limitation of licences. While the majority has always voted for no change, the option system has led to the possibility of small intemperately temperate pressure-groups forcing the withdrawal of established licences through a well-organized campaign. This merely pushes the problem into someone else's bailiewick.

In the case of the once dry burgh of Kirkintilloch, the local police had regularly to deal with home-coming drunks from neighbouring parishes.

Many of the old restrictions designed to curb nineteenth-century working-class drunkenness have been carried over into the twentieth century and are quite out of line with the rest of Europe. Consequently, they adversely affect the tourist industry. It is sad to reflect that the churches oppose drink law reform as they have opposed many recent laws designed humanely to ease the position of such social unfortunates as homosexuals or the unhappily married. Truly, Calvin and Knox have much for which to answer!

The rate of alcoholism remains high in Glasgow, partly due to the Scots custom of absorbing 'pint and chaser'—in English parlance, sending a whisky down the gullet along with a pint of beer —but the despair of poverty need no longer be a cause of drunkenness. Other means and different agents to combat the contemporary misuse of alcohol must be found, since those well-meaning bodies which sought to grapple with the Victorian manifestations of the problem have either gone out of existence, or, as a result of their own extreme lack of tolerance, fallen into disrepute.

Public occasions, sad and gay, meant a good deal to the inhabitants of late Victorian and Edwardian Glasgow.

Not all of them were pleasant.

There were river tragedies, due to the overcrowding of the ferries crossing the Clyde. On 6th April 1861 the paddle-steamer *Lochgoil*, returning from Lochgoilhead with a full cargo of intoxicated Saturday excursionists, hove-to off Govan to allow some passengers to disembark on the Govan ferry, which came alongside. The drunken excursionists tumbled into the little ferry boat in such numbers that she was swamped. Half a dozen passengers were drowned.

Worst still was the sinking of the overcrowded ferry boat at the foot of Clyde Street at the end of November 1864, when the boat left the ferry-steps just as the *Inveraray Castle* was passing. The steamer's paddles were of the old-fashioned non-feathering type, which set up so considerable a wash that the ferry-boat capsized and some nineteen lives were lost (for some reason the exact number was never established). This accident led to restrictions on the number of passengers which these old row-boat ferries were allowed to carry, and to the placing of an order for the first steam ferry-boat with Hedderwick of Govan.

Then there was the murder of Jessie Macpherson, a servant to the Flemings in Sandyford Place, in July 1862. She had been visited by her friend Jessie McLaughlan on Saturday 4th July, and two days later was found dead in her bed by young Fleming, in the Fleming home. McLaughlan tried to maintain that she, Jessie Macpherson and old Fleming had been drinking together on the Saturday night, and that old Fleming committed the murder in a drunken passion. But the jury decided otherwise. Found guilty, McLaughlan was sentenced to be hanged, but reprieved.

The third Scottish banking disaster, the City of Glasgow failure, took place in 1878. In this case not only had the directors made unsound advances of millions of pounds, but they had manipulated their books to conceal the true facts from the shareholders. The final deficit was over £5 million. As the bank was unlimited, most of the directors were ruined. Several were tried and imprisoned, but the effect on individuals who had lodged most of their savings with the bank, and on the business world generally—firm after firm failed for many weeks—was no less disastrous. Sellars' splendid new building, into which they had moved only the previous year and which was never completed, became a warehouse and survived until 1959. As a result of the financial crash, the Scottish banks had to register under an Act of 1879 as limited liability companies, but further to help restore public confidence they commenced the practice of having their books audited by independent accountants.

The last public hanging in Glasgow, that of Dr. Edward William Pritchard, took place in 1865. He was a fashionable, dapper Sauchiehall Street medico whom some thought little more than an elegant quack. He murdered his wife and his mother-in-law, the latter quickly because she had become suspicious about the lengthy illness of her daughter, who was in fact being given regular doses of antimony, a poison used in preserving bodies. The good doctor, prominent public lecturer and Freemason, was meanwhile having an affair with their Highland maidservant. He was wearing a new pair of patent leather boots when he took his enforced departure from this life between the pillars of the old South Jail, facing David Hamilton's Nelson's Monument, on Glasgow Green. A huge crowd turned out to watch. Sermons were preached while pockets were picked. The doctor, whose career was to provide 'James Bridie' with the theme for his play *Doctor Angelus*, seems to have regarded these sordid proceedings with dignified contempt, and made a good end.

Glasgow readers must have been as shocked as those in the rest of Scotland when they learned about the Tay Bridge disaster. The bridge gave way while a train was crossing it during a stormy evening late in December 1880, its passengers being thrown into the waters below. Of more direct concern was the capsizing of the steamer *Daphne* while she was being launched from a Linthouse yard on 3rd July 1883; the 124 workers aboard her were drowned.

The following year a false fire alarm in the Star Music Hall, Partick, resulted in a stampede that killed fourteen people and injured twenty-four.

Queen Victoria's Jubilee provided the public with a happier interest, when, on 16th June 1887, in a city gaily decorated for the occasion, 1,000 poor people were entertained to dinner by the corporation, after a cathedral service; a Grand Review of regulars and volunteers was held on Glasgow Green, when the weather was fortunately kinder than it had been on the occasion of the famous 'Wet Review'; there was music in Kelvingrove, the Queen's and Alexandra Parks, a corporation banquet at night and great ball in St. Andrew's Halls. Her Majesty requested that a replica of the statue of Prince Albert which stood in George Square should be erected in Windsor Great Park.

Similar celebrations were held to celebrate the sixtieth year of her reign in 1897, and in addition there was "a display of pyrotechnics" in the evening.

Edwardian Glasgow's most talked-of murder was that of an old lady, Miss Gilchrist, who lived with her maid in West Princes Street. On 21st December 1908 her downstairs neighbour became suspicious that all was not well, and, on going to investigate, met the maid, Lambie, who had been out buying a paper. As she opened the door a man came out, greeted them and disappeared. Inside was the body of Miss Gilchrist, who had been murdered with considerable brutality. Papers were scattered about the floor, but her jewels were untouched, except possibly for a crescent brooch: 'possibly', because the testimony was Lambie's.

Because a dishonest character called Oscar Slater had been trying to sell a diamond ring pawn ticket, and had gone off to America on the *Lusitania*, the police formed the suspicion that he must have some connection with the crime. On very dubious identification by a passing message girl, one or two passers-by in the street and Lambie herself, Slater was tried, convicted and sentenced to death.

The sentence was changed by the Secretary of State to one of life imprisonment. Conan Doyle, the creator of Sherlock Holmes, pressed for a new trial. Edgar Wallace, the author of a stream of enormously popular detective novels, wrung from Lambie, by then married and in America, the admission that she might have mentioned the wrong name to the police, though she insisted that Slater had previously visited Miss Gilchrist's house.

Although Lambie refused to give further evidence when a new trial was eventually ordered, Slater got off on the technicality that the judge at the original trial had misdirected the jury by allowing the prosecution to blacken Slater's moral character. Slater, a far from attractive man, got less compensation than was his due; Conan Doyle felt that because of the work he had done he should share in Slater's £6,000; and no one in Glasgow believes that the mystery of Miss Gilchrist's death has yet been, or ever will be, solved.

The available opportunities for indulging private pleasures widened considerably.

By the 80s, most factory workers had Saturday afternoons free, although those who served in shops had to be behind their counters until ten o'clock at night on what consequently became the busiest shopping day of the week. Generally, leisure time increased.

Cricket had been played on Glasgow Green since the end of the eighteenth century, but although it has a surprisingly large following—as the B.B.C. in Scotland discovered some years ago when they decided to devote less time to cricket results—it is not a game which flourishes naturally in a rainy climate.

Football is by far the most fundamental Glasgow game. Its three famous teams were all founded within a few years of each other: Queen's Park in 1867, Rangers in 1872, and Celtic in 1874. Queen's Park today are not professionals as are the other two, but in 1867 they brought Association Football to Scotland and helped to formulate modern playing conditions out of what had previously been little better than a rough and tumble scramble. Celtic (1874) and Rangers (1872) have had competing religious overtones since their foundation, with results frequently neither good for the reputation of football nor for Scotland. The Scottish

Football Association was founded in 1873, and, through its Scottish Challenge Cup, helped the spread of the game.

Enormous crowds still turn up for Rangers-Celtic matches at Ibrox Stadium or Parkhead, or for the biennial international match with England. At one such international at Ibrox in 1902, the wooden platform collapsed killing twenty-three spectators and injuring more than 500. This disaster was exceeded by the even worse disaster of 2nd January 1971, when someone fell as the crowd was streaming down the steep steps of the eastern exit from Ibrox. In the resulting catastrophic human pile-up, sixty-six people died and more than 100 were injured.

Football has been the Glasgow man's absorbing passion now for nearly a century. Headlines which, were they not printed on the pink or green paper of the sports editions of the *Evening Times* or *Citizen*, would seem to portend international doom, stand above stories as eagerly read by those who have attended a match as by those unable to be present.

Interest in football seems to exist at different imaginative levels. To some, the game is a counterpoint of rhythmic motions, a kind of rudimentary ballet. To others its value is the usually harmless sublimatory release of tensions it provides through emotional identification with the 'hero' figure. Most fans probably just think it good fun, a game they like to watch and which can nearly always triumph over the Glasgow climate.

Rugby is played mostly by the pupils of Glasgow's fee-paying schools. Although it has a large following in the Borders, in Glasgow "the general public takes comparatively little interest in it, and the support accorded it comes pretty much from the better class school element".*

Golf has continued to be a Scottish preoccupation since it was introduced from Holland in the fifteenth century, though it tends to be the recreation of the professional or business man rather than the artisan. Bowls, an even more ancient game, has always had a strong Glasgow following among all social classes. Rowing and quoiting became popular in later Victorian times, as did cycling, after the development of Dumfriesshire-born Kirkpatrick Macmillan's invention of 1838†, and, in winter, curling.

*John K. McDowall, *The People's History of Glasgow* (1899).
†But the Chevalier de Sivrae got in first with his wheeled 'hobby horse' of 1790, and Baron Karl Drais von Sauerbronn in 1810, with his 'Draisene'. Neither of them developed their invention commercially.

Yacht-racing is now a popular pastime. In Victorian days it was the pastime of the rich. The annual Clyde Regatta was then the occasion for the big yachts to spread huge sails and race the various vintages of *Shamrock* built by Sir Thomas Lipton (1850–1931)—who made his money from a chain of stores that cut out middlemen, brought produce direct from the 'Green Isle', and blended tea to suit the differing textures of water in the towns where his chain had branches—but who never realized his ambition to win back for Britain the Americas Cup.

Between 1884 and 1903 Glasgow used water-buses on the Clyde, the Cluthas, eventually twelve in number and covering the 3 miles between Victoria Bridge and Whiteinch Ferry. For most Glaswegians, the Clyde was still the pleasure-ground for the annual holiday. Clyde steamers grew more and more luxurious and even the competition of the railway companies for a time did not take the edge off the operating profitability of the surviving private owners. The most famous of the Clyde steamers, Mac-Brayne's *Columba*, built by J. and J. Thomson, made her first appearance on the river in 1878, and sailed every summer until 1936, most of her life paddling up and down the 'Royal Route' from the Broomielaw to Ardrishaig and back. Her sister ship the *Iona*, built in 1864, though less luxurious, achieved even greater longevity, surviving in service to the record age of 72. Laurence Lockhart, a nephew of John Gibson Lockhart, described the scenic and the cosmopolitan delights of a sail on the *Iona* from the Clyde to Oban in his novel *Fair to See* (1891):

What is there to do? What is there not to do? And see? First, if you have ever so little of an artist's eye or an artist's soul—that is to say, if you love nature at all—very surely you will find that love stirred and quickened within you all the live-long day—if you will only keep your eyes open—while threading with the *Iona* the wondrous labyrinth of her beautiful course. The mountain panorama which greets you as you start, noble though it may be, is but the noble promise of still better things. . . .

The steamer is a varying stage, on which you can see going on, side by side, no end of little dramas; and as for the dramatis personae, who are they? or rather, who are they not? Honeymooning couples huddled together under umbrellas to screen them from the sun, and from the world's garish eye: inevitable reading parties from Oxford and Cambridge: indigestive blue-stockings, 'inverted' philosophers, saucey persons and leathery-looking lawyers; sportsmen *en route* for their shootings, yachting men for their yachts, gamekeepers, ghillies and figure footmen; bleary Germans and dyspeptic yankees calculating the exact number of cocked hats into which the Mississippi knocks the Clyde; jocund schoolboys, bread-and-butter misses, 'cock-lairds' and Cockneys; Highlanders and Mile-Enders; ladies and gentlemen—all sorts and conditions of men, natural and artificial, shamming and detective, bragging and counter-bragging, appreciative and depreciative, a *farrango*, a *pot-pourri*, *Olla Podrida*, a dainty dish to set before Democritus.

Other famous pre-war ships, which doubtless carried a similarly varied human cargo, and whose names were once summer music to Glaswegians' ears, included the Buchanan Steamers Limited's *Isle of Arran* (1892); the Caledonian Steam Packet Company Limited's *Duchess of Rothesay* (1895) and *Duchess of Fife* (1963); the Glasgow and South Western Railway's *Juno* (1898), *Jupiter* (1896) and *Waverley* (1899); Captain Williamson's *Benmore* (1876) and *Kylemore* (1897); the 'dry' paddler *Ivanhoe* (1880) and the *Lord of the Isles* (1891), as well as the turbine steamers *King Edward* (1901) and *Queen Alexandra* (1912).

When the First World War broke out in 1914, forty steamers were plying between Glasgow, Gourock or Greenock and the Clyde Estuary, calling at piers or meeting ferries at eighty-five places. Alan J. S. Paterson has chronicled the late Victorian and Edwardian Clyde fleet in a book which he calls *The Golden Years of the Clyde Steamers (1896–1914)*. Myself, I am no more a believer in years of gold or lead than in acts of black or white. But if one accepts such oversimplified conceits, then in a sense the late Victorian and Edwardian periods were also the Golden Years of Glasgow. It is doubtful if, in those summery August days of 1914, when an unheard-of European nobleman was murdered in Sarajevo, many Glaswegians bothered much about the news when it first reached them. Yet the outcome of that far-away murder ended the 200-year-long era of Glasgow's success story. Nothing would ever be the same again.

VII

THE FIRST WORLD WAR AND AFTER

By the time war came in 1914 there was already a long tradition of voluntary military service in Glasgow. When the threat of Napoleon's invasion had seemed a reality, nine regiments of Glasgow volunteers were formed, including the Glasgow Light Horse (1796) and the Glasgow Volunteers (1803). Although they never had to fire a shot in anger, they were called out more than once upon rumours and alarms, and until Napoleon was finally defeated, slept with their muskets and their uniforms to hand.

During 1849, Europe's year of revolution, a volunteer cavalry force was formed. This became the Queen's Own Royal Glasgow Yeomanry.

After the Crimean War, menacing noises from the Paris of the Third French Empire resulted in renewed efforts being made to revive the volunteers, and in 1859, the Old Guard of Glasgow became the forerunners of the 1st, 2nd and 3rd Lanark Volunteers, the 1st recruiting from the West End, the 3rd from the South Side. The twenty-first birthday of the Volunteers was the occasion of Queen Victoria's 'Wet Review' on Glasgow Green, held in 1881 during torrential rain, which subsequently resulted in the deaths of some of the less robust of the 40,000 officers and men who had been on parade. This was also the year in which the voluntary forces were first grouped under territorial regimental designations, the 1st, 2nd, 3rd, 4th and 7th Lanarkshire Volunteers becoming the Cameronians (Scottish Rifles) and the 5th, 6th, 8th, 9th, and 10th forming the Highland Light Infantry. It was a Lieutenant W. A. Smith of the First Lanark Rifles, a volunteer later to become Sir William Smith, who in 1883 founded the Boys' Brigade. The B.B., whose members still wear their dark-blue pill-box hats wrapped with a band of white, was organized on military lines and run in conjunction with a Sunday school, but was aimed at inculcating military-style discipline into working-class lads.

The Boer War produced eleven serving companies from Scotland. Many Glaswegians enrolled as regulars. In 1908, those who had volunteered became the core of the new Territorial Army. At the same time the Officers' Training Corps scheme, which was designed to produce what used to be called 'officer material' began to operate in public schools.*

Field Marshal Earl Roberts, whose equestrian statue still looks exultingly across Kelvingrove Park towards the university, addressed the students and others in May 1913, warning them of the need for a citizen army capable of engaging with the Germans at short notice should war come as a result of the German Kaiser's scarcely-concealed belligerence. But it was not easy for Lord Roberts to make his message carry conviction, because earlier in the year, Lloyd George had been thundering away about the folly of expenditure on armaments. While an audience in St. Andrew's Halls attending the last of Lord Roberts' series of meetings passed a resolution which, had it been implemented, would have amounted to compulsory service in the Territorial Army, the war when it did come nevertheless took the British by surprise.

On the British side, there was a belief that Germany could not stand up for long against the combined forces of Britain, France and Russia. War, if it should come, would be a short-lived affair, over by Christmas, a belief it seems, also held by the Germans, though they, of course, envisaged winning it. Glasgow, like the rest of the United Kingdom, was quite unprepared for the long years of struggle and of fearful slaughter which were unleashed by the declaration of war on Germany by Britain, her Dominions and Empire, on 4th August 1914.

The exalted idealistic mood of the sensitive young men who went eagerly into the fight is enshrined in Rupert Brooke's well-known sonnet "Now God be thanked who has matched us with this hour", and in less familiar lines by Lawrence Binyon, from his poem, "The Fourth of August":

> Now in thy splendour go before us,
> Spirit of England, ardent-eyed,
> Enkindle this dear earth that bore us,
> In the hour of peril purified.

*In Scotland, public schools are, in fact, private schools!

> The cares we hugged drop out of vision,
> Our hearts with deeper thoughts dilate.
> We step from days of sour division
> Into the grandeur of our fate.

The British Expeditionary Force of the regular army at first consisted of one cavalry division and four infantry divisions, later supplemented by a further two. Known as the Contemptible Little Army, it not only turned the first thrust of the German horde but secured the Channel ports, giving Britain time to arm.

Because the country was thought not to be ready to accept conscription, the first appeals were for volunteers to fill additional Territorial battalions. The Secretary of State for War, Lord Kitchener, appealed for 200,000 volunteers, using the famous finger-pointing poster. By 1915, Glasgow had contributed substantially more than its quota. The regiment most closely associated with the city was the Highland Light Infantry. Members of professions and trades formed their own fighting groups. Thus the 17th Battalion was largely recruited by the Chamber of Commerce and the 15th by the Corporation Tramway Department, spurred on by its manager James Dalrymple, who used illuminated tramcars, banner posters round the Transport Department's offices in Bath Street and other startling publicity methods as part of a highly persuasive advertising campaign.

All in all, the H.L.I. had twenty-six battalions in action during the First World War. The Cameronians (Scottish Rifles), naturally also attracted Glaswegians. So, rather surprisingly, did the Cameron Highlanders, many Glasgow men responding to an appeal in *The Glasgow Herald* by the clan chief, Cameron of Lochiel, which had really been aimed at the men of the north-west.

The war had immediate effects on the wives and children of the private soldiers who responded to the call. The inadequate state of the national welfare arrangements resulted in numerous cases of hardship and privation, epitomized by a newspaper headline drawing attention to the plight of *The 12/6d. Woman*. The Prince of Wales immediately organized a National Relief Fund, to which Glasgow alone had subscribed nearly £240,000 within six months. It was the first of several such charities, a later one having the catch-phrase title of 'Jock's Box'. The extent of the need for such arrangements was made plain by Lord Provost Dunlop, who, in September 1915, announced that 100,000 women and children had already "received relief".

Amongst those who stayed at home, there was at first an attempt to carry on 'business as usual'. But the war's grip soon tightened. The German U-boat blockade began in February 1915, conscription was introduced in January 1916, and by early 1917 compulsory food rationing had replaced voluntary meatless days.

By 1916, the men who fought in the trenches knew the full horror of twentieth-century warfare. The bloodiest engagement was the Battle of the Somme, really a series of battles, fought between July 1916 and the end of the year. Huge hordes of men flung themselves against the entrenched positions of armed masses.

The histories of most of the battalions which fought in what used to be known as the Great War have been written up. The description which L. B. Oatts gives in his book *The Highland Light Infantry*, of what happened to some of the Glasgow men was more or less the common experience of all British regiments in France at that time.

The Glasgow Highlanders lost four hundred and twenty one all ranks at High Wood, but fought on until within six weeks their casualties had mounted to thirty-three officers and seven hundred and fifty men, which was just about all they had. They were reinforced by three hundred and fifty-five men drawn from other Scottish regiments, of whom some were young, some rather old, and some were just out of hospital. But they went on fighting, day after day, week after week, in conditions which the devil himself could scarcely improve in hell. . . . By the autumn, the battlefield had become such a sea of mud that men and animals were sometimes swallowed up in it; but there was still no let-up, although when the Battle of the Ancre had commenced in November, it had begun to snow.

Struggling through snow and sleet, the 16th and 17th H.L.I. advanced together against the Redan Ridge at dawn—November eighteenth. The whole of the 17th and the right company of the 16th were decimated by machine guns and rifle-fire. But the survivors pressed on into the German Munich and Frankfurt trenches, overcame all resistance with the bayonet, and sent back fifty prisoners. Attacks on either side having failed, the remnants of the 16th H.L.I., about one hundred men under a sergeant major, then became isolated in the Frankfurt trench, which they held for eight days. At the end of it there were only fifteen left, who were then taken prisoner because they had become so weak from lack of food that they could no longer stand up.

After that, there were still two years of bloody battles to be footslogged through, the 15th and 16th H.L.I. being amongst those who faced up to Ludendorff's last desperate assault, which began on 21st March 1918.

Glasgow contributed to the other fighting services as well as to the army, although until comparatively recently the navy has remained very much an English service. More than thirty Clyde yards and engineering works turned out ships, many of which fell victim to German U-boat attacks and had to be replaced. A large repair programme was also carried through. The Mercantile Marine, who manned the Clyde-built ships, played the decisive part in defeating the German intention of cutting Britain off from the rest of the world.

Munitions in huge quantity, aeroplanes and uniforms were among the other requirements of a nation at war in the making of which Glasgow specialized.

There were, of course, sour overtones to be heard now and again. Some women who, for one reason or another, could not work, told vicious stories about the alleged excesses and extravagances of their earning sisters. Some of those at the front accused those at home of profiteering. A Glasgow academical, D. S. MacCall, neatly capped a speech by the Minister of Munitions in 1915, who, referring to the strategy at the western fronts, had declared: "We must keep on striking, striking, striking . . .", with four topical lines titled "The Miners' Response".

> We do: the present desperate stage
> Of fighting brings us luck;
> And in the higher war we wage
> (For higher wage) *We struck.*

Women came into the factories, and in long tartan skirts took over from the men as conductresses on the trams, making Glasgow the first city to employ women in this role. The war, indeed, hastened the emancipation of women, the vote being given to them in February 1919.

In September 1918, more than four Christmases after the war had started, Bulgaria asked for a truce. Although there was general realization that an armistice was probably in the offing, the suddenness with which it came surprised many people.

On the morning of 11th November a poster appeared in *The Glasgow Herald* office window emblazoned with a Union Jack and carrying one word—VICTORY!

A special edition of the paper was soon on sale in the streets. The chimes of the university gave the news to the West End. Classes ceased immediately. Hooters sounded in factories, sirens on ships. Flags and tricolours miraculously appeared from drawers and cupboards. Factory workers laid down their tools. A great crowd gathered in the streets, and the Lord Provost pronounced the civic joy from the back of a lorry in George Square.

"The greatest day of rejoicing Glasgow has ever known," was how *The Glasgow Herald* summed it all up, telling us that: "In the absence of military bands, a huge effort was made to import a melodic note to the jubilations by solo cornet and melodeon players and by solitary pipers. Now and again an unexpected bugle note was added, and the happy discord was increased by the clanging of the impatient warning bell of the tramway cars as they made their way through the surging crowd."

That day there was a victory flight over the city, and in the evening the students organized a torchlight procession.

Banquets and celebrations were held during the weeks that followed. Field Marshal Sir Douglas Haig, as he then was, received the Freedom of the City in May 1919, and the Prince of Wales was given the same honour in March 1921 when he declared: "Glasgow's achievements in the war stir one indeed."

Glasgow had high hopes that its pre-war prosperity would continue through the days of peace. But by nightfall on 12th November the city was shrouded in a cold yellow fog, which was to prove symbolic of what was to come.

The end of the war had certainly taught the fighting men the meaning of disillusion. What had there been of 'grandeur' about the fate met by nearly three and a half million of Britain's young men on foreign fields? The mightiest human struggle the world had ever seen may have begun in a mood matched by Brooke's poetic heroics. It certainly ended with the realistic bitterness of Siegfried Sassoon's attacks on incompetent leadership, and the bitter pity of Wilfred Owen's poem "Futility":

> Are limbs so dear achieved,
> Full-nerved—still warm—too hard to stir?
> Was it for this the clay grew tall?

Even that imperialist's darling Rudyard Kipling celebrated the finish of "the war to end wars" with an aphorism, "Common Form":

> If any question why we died,
> Tell them because our fathers lied.

With the return home of the ex-servicemen, it was not to be long before "sour division" opened up again.

Early in the nineteenth century, Glasgow had gained a reputation for political militancy, mainly because of its Chartist riots. This reputation was further increased as a result of wartime labour troubles, chiefly in the munitions industry where the necessary dilution of skilled workers with unskilled labour caused resentment. This was not helped by the inevitable deterioration in housing conditions, bad enough in 1914 but worse after four years during which no resources could be spared to build new homes.

Even during the war, in 1915, strikes and violence, stimulated by the Clyde Workers' Committee, had resulted in a visit to Glasgow by the Prime Minister, Lloyd George. However, the Welshman's verbal wizardry failed to work its accustomed magic upon the Clydesiders, and there was nothing left for the Government but to resort to strong-arm tactics. The militants were imprisoned in Edinburgh, among them the communist schoolteacher John MacLean (who has surely inspired more good poets to produce bad verse than any other Scot!).

There was an ugly scene in George Square on the last day of January, 1919, when a crowd of strikers gathered outside the City Chambers to be told by the Lord Provost that two Glasgow men in high office, the Prime Minister, Bonar Law, and the Minister of Labour, Sir Robert Horne, had refused to intervene. A clash with the police ensued, and among those arrested was Emmanuel Shinwell. The day was dubbed by the press 'Black Friday'.

Three years later, Glasgow attracted more permanent political attention when a group of Independent Labour Party men known as The Clydesiders got themselves elected to Parliament. In 1914, Glasgow had only one Labour M.P. in the House of Commons. By 1922, after the apparent settling of the Irish question had freed Catholic voters from the need to support the Liberal Irish Home-rulers, ten out of the fifteen Glasgow seats were captured by I.L.P. members, along with a further five elsewhere in Scotland. Nine seats went to trade-union-nominated Labour M.P.s.

Long-haired 'Jimmy' Maxton, belligerent 'Manny' Shinwell and Thomas Johnstone, literary hater of *Our Noble Families*, amongst others, made the Clydeside presence audible in the House, sometimes beyond the breaking point of its traditional tolerance. One I.L.P. man, John Wheatley, reached the Cabinet as Minister of Health in 1924. Though they were at war with conventional Labour M.P.s like Ramsay Macdonald, most of them eventually outgrew their extreme Marxist convictions. Johnstone became an outstandingly able and patriotic Secretary of State for Scotland under Churchill, and later the leader of many Scottish enterprises, including the North of Scotland Hydro-Electric Board. Lord Shinwell, as he now is, became a Minister in Attlee's post-Second World War Government. David Kirkwood eventually accepted a peerage. Not all the others managed to preserve, as did James Maxton, a personal charm which mellowed with the years to make him one of the best-loved members in the House.

Post-war Glasgow's dissatisfaction with men and affairs also played a part in the founding of the Scottish National Party. The position of Secretary for Scotland was abolished after 1745, Scottish matters were then dealt with by a series of 'managers' who controlled Scottish patronage, the most famous of them being Henry Dundas, Viscount Melville, "the uncrowned ruler of Scotland" as Lord Cockburn called him. Early in the 1880s nationalist feeling pressed Gladstone and the Government towards the eventual reinstatement of a Scottish administrative head, resulting in the creation of the Scottish Office in 1885. A Scottish Home Rule group was set up in 1886, and within a decade there was strong Liberal support at Westminster for a Scottish Parliament; support in fact which culminated in 1913 in the passage through the House with a majority of 145, of the second reading of a Home Rule Bill, which might have brought practical results but for the outbreak of the war with its overriding supra-national concerns. By 1923 the Liberal Party had been fragmented, the Scots backing the emergent Labour Party. A Glasgow Labour M.P., George Buchanan, put forward a Home Rule Bill in 1926, which failed, as did the 1928 bill of the Reverend James Barr. In 1928 the Scottish National Party was launched with the support of Robert Bontine Cunninghame Graham, the writer and traveller who had a home on the north bank of the Clyde; R. G. Muirhead, whose family tanning business was at Bridge of Weir, in Renfrewshire; the Duke of Montrose, whose seat of Buchanan Castle (now a ruin) at Drymen, was less than 20 miles from Glasgow; novelist Compton Mackenzie and poet C. M. Grieve ('Hugh MacDiarmid'). Though the Scottish National

Party scored no political successes in the between-the-war years, indirectly they helped to stimulate a fairly widespread revival of Scottish consciousness, to say nothing of that literary revival dubbed somewhat grandiosely by the Frenchman, Professor Denis Saurat, "The Scottish Renaissance".

These were real grounds for the dissatisfaction of which the temporary success of the Independent Labour Party and the arrival on the scene of the Scottish National Party were political reflections. After a vigorous short-lived spurt, all the traditional Scottish industries based in and around Glasgow went into decline.

The textile industry, with the exception of carpet-making, was so squeezed by both Lancashire and foreign competition that it virtually went out of existence within a decade, taking with it the last of the 'job' weavers who worked to special order in the East End of Glasgow.

The coal industry, faced again with the pre-war lessening of demand from the iron industry, continued to decline and had little success in meeting competition in foreign markets during the 20s. It was, indeed, the coal-owners belief that reduced wages could alone remedy a situation producing huge losses that spearheaded the General Strike of 1926.

The proposal upon which the miners and the employers failed to reach agreement was that there should be either a reduction in miners' wages or an increase in their working time in an effort to achieve profitability. For example, a hewer's wages were to come down from £3 18s. per week to £2 5s. 10d., or his hours to go up from seven to eight a day. On 1st May 1926 *The Glasgow Herald* commented grimly on the news of the breakdown of negotiations, declaring: "The country now finds itself plunged into an industrial struggle the end of which it is exceedingly difficult to tell." The Trades Union Congress called for a sympathetic strike. The Government asked King George V to declare a national emergency. Unwisely, the Trades Union Congress responded by declaring general strike action from midnight on 3rd May, and thus found itself in a direct constitutional clash with the Government.

In the hours between, the politicians were busy with their speeches. Lloyd George said: "There is one thing I dislike about the situation more than anything. There is a great similarity in it as to the methods that led to the great war—desultory and dilatory diplomatic exchanges, leisurely negotiations, never touching the

Playgrounds old and new style
(overleaf) *The changing face of Glasgow*

real issues, and then the parties hurling ultimatums at each other." George Lansbury thought it unfair that the miners should be asked to take less money or work an hour a day longer prior to discussions on the reorganization of their industry. J. H. Thomas, with remarkable originality of phrase, declared: "The outlook is indeed black." And Emmanuel Shinwell seemed to hint at the remoter realms of metaphysics and theology by reminding his hearers that the miners were standing out for a weekly wage of 50s., and asking: "Can a man be a Christian on such a wage? He might think he was, but it was very difficult."

For the first time, though possibly not for the last, the Trade Union Movement overestimated its strength and underestimated the point at which the wider public will not put up with arrogant, bullying, sectional interests. The National Citizens' Union appealed for patriots to help man essential public services. The Roll of Voluntary Workers asked people to sign on at St. Andrew's Halls. Sign on they did, and, for the six days the general strike lasted, they drove tramcars, moved supplies and kept life going. *The Glasgow Herald*, *The Bulletin*, the *Daily Record*, the *Glasgow Evening News*, the *Evening Times* and the *Citizen* all combined to produce a slim sheet called *Emergency News*.

The T.U.C. soon realized that it had made a bad miscalculation and could not possibly win the struggle, although the return to work was gradual, and long delayed in the case of the miners.

"A victory for common sense," said Stanley Baldwin. "It had been once more demonstrated," said *The Glasgow Herald*, itself now resolved to employ only non-union labour, "that the people of Britain will not accept the dictation of any section, and that the community has within itself resources, vitality and adaptability equal to the overcoming of any emergency." The unions' "big battalions", it added, were "neither so reliable nor so important a section of the community as they had imagined." The following year the Government passed the Trades Disputes Act, prohibiting sympathetic strikes, an Act which, had it not been repealed by the Labour government of 1945, might have allowed the United Kingdom to compete against other trading nations after the Second World War with less 'wild-cat' disruption and loss of production arising out of industrial disputation than has, in fact, been possible.

The day after the return to peaceful normality, Messrs Paisley's advertised on the front page of the *Herald*, "summer living suits

Studies in Victorian detail

for chauffeurs in blue, brown, claret, green or grey" for £7, with a matching cap at 12s. 6d. A Rolls-Royce to go with the suit and cap could be had for a little over £1,900 pounds, while a humbler car you could drive yourself could be yours for a little over £200 —a Bean, perhaps, or a more dashing Voisin. A packet of ten Players cigarettes to smoke while you drove, or were driven, to the Palais de Danse—of which there were nearly fifty in the city during the 20s, all offering new dances like the Charleston, the Foxtrot and the Black Bottom—cost 6d.

Something of the violence which bad social conditions and outworn religious rivalries engender was reflected in the gang warfare which troubled Glasgow's conscience through much of the 20s. It had reached a climax when Percy Sillitoe, later knighted, came from Sheffield as Chief Constable and proceeded to break up those bands of hatchet-wielding, bicycle-chain-slashing thugs. There was also an alarming number of prosecutions among the city magistrates for fraud, five in all being sent to prison—giving rise to a music-hall joke about a wee man who arrived with his horse outside a pub and asked a pompous passer-by to 'mind' it for him." "My man, d'ye no ken who I am?" the pompous one asked—"No, sir."—"I'm a Glasgow magistrate"— Pause while the wee fellow digested the information, and thought for a moment. "Och it's aa' richt. I'm only gaen in for a quick yin, an' ye'll no get faur wi' the beast in that time."

During the 30s, some increased home demand for coal and export agreements concluded with the Scandinavian countries, Canada and Ireland helped to absorb production for a few years. But confidence in the coal industry was gone, and in the Lanarkshire coalfields alone the labour force fell by 50 per cent between 1914 and 1932.

The iron industry was also in trouble. There was a drastic decline in the production of Scottish pig iron while the decline of locally produced ore and the closure of Glengarnock works in 1926—the only works in Scotland producing the kind of basic Bessemer they required—induced Stewart and Lloyds to move to Corby in order to be nearer their English source of supply. There then followed amalgamations among the steel makers, until by 1936 the Steel Company of Scotland and the Lanarkshire Steel Company were both under the control of Colvilles. Thereafter, Colvilles went in for improvements and for modernization. Although these changes had not resulted in Scotland possessing a fully-integrated steel works by 1939, at least they prepared the way for such a step in post-Second World War years.

Shipbuilding in some respects fared worst of all. After a brief post-war boom caused by the need to replace war-lost tonnage, and a further brief boom caused by the hold-up of orders due to the General Strike, the Depression set in. The rusty hull of John Brown and Company's order 'Number 534', later to become the Cunard liner *Queen Mary*, towered in its uncompleted state above Clydebank, a symbol of the stagnation which had overcome not only the industry but the whole of the business world. Government help towards finishing '534' in 1933 made John Brown's yard a busy place until the launch the following year; but not even a 'scrap-and-build' recommendation from the Government did much to help the Upper Clyde yards.

There were a number of reasons for the severe decline in shipbuilding orders. Foreign buyers were no longer ordering from the Clyde, many countries which were formerly customers having established shipbuilding industries of their own. Even British shipowners were finding it cheaper to build in foreign yards. Indeed, but for increased naval construction as the 30s wore on and the building of the *Queen Elizabeth*, launched in 1938, the social disaster which occurred would have been even worse than it was.

The fact is that the Slump of the early 30s was virtually worldwide. Tramp steamers for which there were no cargoes lay idle and rusting at anchor in the Gareloch and the Holy Loch. Unemployment in the United Kingdom was nearly 3 million by the end of 1931, and by the following year approximately 30 per cent of the working population of Scotland, most of them in or around Glasgow, were unemployed. Dole queues and straggling processions of hunger marchers became familiar sights, and posed in my young mind, as I set out in my parents' car on a weekend afternoon drive to the country, the problem of the haves and the have-nots, an antithesis which social measures have very considerably ameliorated throughout the United Kingdom, but to which there is fundamentally no ultimate solution under any known system of Government, since no amount of egalitarian adjustment can counter the handiwork of non-egalitarian Nature.

But the 20s and 30s in Glasgow were by no means all gloom. The British Broadcasting Corporation set up its first studios at 141 Bath Street in 1922, moving the following year to 202 Bath

Street. After a brief period when its headquarters were at 5 Queen Street, Edinburgh, it returned to Broadcasting House, Glasgow, developing around the former Queen Margaret College.

In the days when the programme came out of Bath Street, there was for me the memorable experience of listening in the parlour of our Ashton Terrace home to the 'aunts' and 'uncles' of "Children's Hour", pricking the crystal with the cat's whisker to get a clearer sound through the headphones. I made my own first appearance before the microphone as a broadcaster singing "Linden Lea" in my piping, unbroken treble voice. Later, there was the extraordinary fascination of Christmas Eve 1929, when my father brought home a 'wireless' which gave forth its own sound—Christmas carols, comedians, a Mozart symphony and of course the well-loved 'aunts' and 'uncles' in a new round aural dimension. Not even the introduction of television, for all its greater cleverness, ever managed to reproduce for me such a glimpse of boundlessly enriching possibilities as did the first sounds out of that self-amplifying radio set.

In these early days, and for several decades thereafter, the B.B.C. accepted the duty, incorporated by implication in its charter, of fostering the Scottish languages and the nation's culture. But in spite of that remarkable series of broadcasts the *Foundations of Scottish Music*—the voluminous research material for which was accidentally turned over to the paper-salvagers by an over-zealous clerkess during the Second World War—the Scots plays and the dialect verse-readings, the smoothing out of our native Scots sound from our ears and our tongues was inevitably accelerated by the mere invention of broadcasting. The process was further hastened through the cinemas when 'the talkies' reached Glasgow in 1929.

The first cinema to install the new invention was the 'Coliseum' on 7th January showing *The Singing Fool*. Even in the days of the silent films, when the plushier cinemas had instrumental groups, while the cheaper ones made do with vamping pianists, 'the filums' became the Glasgow rage, and new stucco film-palaces went up in every suburb, and multiplied in the centre of the town. One of them, Green's Playhouse, was, until the removal of a gallery in the 60s deprived it of that distinction, the largest cinema in Europe.

Theatres did well too. The 'Alhambra' alternated variety with drama, as did the 'Kings'. Opera companies went to the 'Royal', where the lushest pantomimes in town were to be seen. There was an enormous vogue for 'light' plays, purveyed throughout well-attended 'seasons' for many years by the Brandon Thomas Players and later by the Wilson Barrett Company.

The Scottish National Players, a company of talented amateurs seeking to encourage native drama, drew into their circle the playwright Dr. Osborne Mavor, first in the guise of 'Mary Henderson' then later as 'James Bridie'. They usually played in the 'Royalty', later the Lyric Theatre. It became the custom in our family to go to a 'musical' on Hogmanay, and while I must admit that I found those long ago performances of 'musical comedies' like *No, No, Nanette*, *The Desert Song* and *The New Moon* neither very musical nor particularly comic, the sense of red-plush occasion was certainly something to savour.

Variety was so popular between the wars that it sustained the 'Pavilion' and a new enlarged Empire Theatre built on Sauchiehall Street opposite the 'Lyric', the one now replaced by shops and offices, the other by an Electricity Board's headquarters.

Some old favourites among Glasgow's periodicals disappeared in the 20s. The *Scots Pictorial* merged with *The Bulletin*, and the *Bailie*, which had long delighted Glaswegians with its pithy comment and pungent cartoons, ceased publication. The *Scottish Daily Express* joined the dailies, and the *Scottish Field* became a national monthly, much read in Glasgow though produced in Perth.

Between the wars the physical scene underwent major changes. In 1918, a Royal Commission on Housing was set up. It found that more than 45 per cent of the people of Scotland were living in overcrowded conditions, by which was meant more than two people to a room. The majority of the members of the commission came down heavily against the private builder, declaring that "most of the troubles which we have been investigating are due to the failure of private enterprise to provide the necessary houses sufficient in quantity and quality".

This was not wholly a fair judgement. Not only were Glaswegians reluctant to pay as much in rent for a house as their English counterparts, making it very difficult for a private builder to operate at the profit level without which he could not for long have remained in business, but the Rent Restrictions Act effectively discouraged builders from putting up houses for renting. On top of all this, there was the peculiar Scottish rating system, whereby part of the rates were at that time paid by the owners, who, prior to 1914, had been able to recover rate increases from their occupiers in the form of increased rents. As a result of all this, tenements which, had they been properly maintained, might have had a long lease of useful life, fell into disrepair, a process of decline accelerated by renewed overcrowding brought about by the bad times of the 20s and 30s. Some older 'spec' tenements, of course, had, so to say, been equipped with built-in obsolescence, and were thus unacceptable in terms of human dignity even when they were new.

A controversial pamphlet *Cancer of Empire*, reporting upon Glasgow's housing conditions, was published in 1924. Its author, William Bolitho, described his visit to a tenement 'backland' single-end, or one-room home.

On each landing opens the water-closet, which the municipality installed thirty years ago. This is clean—the municipal inspectors are vigilant; but on an average twenty-five persons share its use. In some houses this number is nearer fifty. On the other side of the tiny landing opens a long, impenetrably black gulf; the central corridor of five homes. We feel our way, knock at a door and enter, calling out "Sanitary". A small room, one side of which is taken up by the Scots fireplace, like an enclosed iron altar, with two hobs on which the teapot is kept everlastingly on the boil. The floor is worn wood, there are irregular square inches of frayed oilcloth. An enormous drabbled woman, who is dressed in the same dish clothes which do not show the dirt so plainly, however, as her face, explains the arrangements. . . .
She has five children. . . . There is the bed, set into a niche, deep, evil-smelling, strewed with heaps of the same material as her dress. . . . Bed, hearth and chair: humanity's minimum. . . . Under the window is the 'jaw-box', the boarded greasy sink, with polished brass syphon tap. . . . On the mantel-piece are two china dogs . . .

The conclusion reached by the majority of the Royal Commission was that responsibility for rehousing such unfortunate families as these should rest with the local authority. So Glasgow Corporation began to build houses for letting—'council houses', as they were called—for the most part semi-detached cottage-type dwellings each with its own garden. All round Glasgow 'estates' of these grey-harled brick houses sprang up. The rents were low, the subsidies being found, in effect, by the property-owning rate-payers and by the tax-payer at large. Although there was, and is, a huge waiting-list for a council house in Glasgow, a millionaire is as eligible a tenant as a motor-mechanic. Scots folk have always objected to means tests, the method of income assessment employed to calculate entitlement to the dole during the Slump. By 1939 about 20 per cent of Glasgow's population was living in subsidized council houses, regardless of family income and therefore of the genuine social need for subsidy. By 1939 Glasgow had extended its boundaries to take in such districts as Knightswood and Cardonald.

All these new areas were designed to relieve pressure on the overcrowded slum area of a city which by then had the highest population density-rate in Europe.

Public buildings went up too, but in nothing like the rich profusion of the high Victorian period. The Glasgow head office of the Bank of Scotland, 110–12 St. Vincent Street, originally the head office of the Union Bank, was the work of James Miller in 1927. In spite of its simpler Greek detail, it is very much the kind of imposing large-scale building which Victorian and Edwardian architects had been putting up for banks all over Britain— "temples of Mammon", some humbug or other called them. Much more original, though naturally still reflecting the idiom of a previous age, is 200 St. Vincent Street, Sir John Burnet's last design, built in 1929.

Churches of the inter-war period usually also held fast to elements of traditionalism, whether as is shown by the severely modified Gothicism of James Taylor Thomson's St. John's Renfield Church, Beaconsfield Road, built in 1931, or in Sir Robert Lorimer's St. Margaret's Church, Knightswood, with its Baltic-looking saddleback tower.

But there were signs that the uneasy architectural compromising of the 30s would soon give place to something new.

The Cosmo Cinema, which opened in 1939 to specialize in showing Continental films, is a dignified brick building with some glazed ceramic 'faience' showing Scandinavian influence. T. Harred Hughes's and D. S. K. Waugh's reading room for Glasgow University, dating from the same year, and circular in design, excited much comment when it first went up and still manages to maintain its distinctive dignity in the company of massive post-1939 war structures.

An apt flamboyance rather than dignity is the keynote of the most ambitious and forward-looking addition to the Glasgow scene during the between-the-war years, Sir E. Owen William's Scottish Daily Express and Evening Citizen building, its black glass facings and long lines of windows looming effectively against its western neighbour, St. David's 'Ramshorn' Kirk.

In a way, perhaps the most exciting buildings that Glasgow had the chance of experiencing between the wars were the best of what went up in Bellahouston Park for the Empire Exhibition (Scotland) 1938, the last of the city's great spectaculars. The scene was dominated by Thomas S. Tait's 300-feet-high tower, rising up from a hill in the centre of the park. The two Scottish Pavilions and the acoustically splendid concert hall raised visions of an exciting environmental future which the Second World War dampered in more senses than one; for Tait's Tower, intended to be a permanent memorial to the exhibition, had to be hurriedly dismantled when it was realized that it was giving navigational assistance to German airmen.

My own memories of the 1938 exhibition are of the exceptionally wet and windy weather (which, although it forced a claim on the guarantors, did not prevent the turnstiles clicking up a total of 13½ million visitors); of the appearance of Queen Mary, powdery and frail-looking as an Oscar Wilde heroine, driving through cheering crowds whose acclaim she acknowledged with a small wave of the hand and an ever so slight inclination of the head; and the shimmering cascades of floodlit water which flowed down the central liquid 'staircase'.

There were other vigorous manifestations of contemporary trends in the Glasgow of the 30s. Erik Chisholm (1904–65) in 1930 founded his Active Society, and through it and the concerts which succeeded it between 1930 and 1937 brought to Glasgow some of the then leading *avant garde* composers including Bartok, Casella and Hindemith, as well as the romantic Medtner and the native Francis George Scott.

They usually performed in the Berkeley Hall, mostly to tiny audiences. Chisholm was more successful in attracting wider support for his pioneering productions mounted by the Glasgow Grand Opera Society. With this entirely amateur body, Chisholm managed to stage the first performance in English of Mozart's *Idomeneo*, Berlioz's *The Trojans* (with Guy MacCrone, author of *Wax Fruit*, in the role of Aeneas in 1935) and a Scottish opera by W. B. Moonie, *The Weird of Colbar*. It was not as successful as its predecessor, *Jeanie Deans*, by Greenock-born Hamish MacCunn

(1868–1916), which has several times been revived. MacCunn's freshly youthful overture *Land of the Mountain and the Flood* firmly held its place in the repertoire of the Scottish Orchestra's Saturday evening concerts, and recently featured in a long-playing recording by the Scottish National Orchestra. The Tuesday concerts, where one's presence in evening dress was expected at least in the more expensive seats, were deliberately 'highbrow'. Looking back now on the supposed 'difficulties' of Bartok, Sibelius and the others who featured on these programmes,* it seems strange that their music should have come to seem almost a refuge of familiarity from the serial and electronic probings of so much of the 'difficult' music by the younger composers today. Many of them seem to have achieved successfully a kind of non-masterpiece neo-eighteenth-century cosmopolitanism which makes the export or import of their product pointless, more or less the same being available from native pens in every European country.

Scotland has never produced a great composer, but it can claim one outstanding composer of songs. 'Hugh MacDiarmid's' English teacher at Langholm, Francis George Scott (1880–1958), having graduated as Bachelor of Music at Durham University, spent the last twenty-five years of his working life as lecturer in music at Jordanhill Training College for Teachers. He wrote many of his finest settings of the poems of Burns, MacDiarmid and others at his Glasgow home, 44 Munro Road. Scott had no Scottish art-song tradition to build upon, so he set about creating his own. Under such unsettling circumstances he was tempted into occasional harmonic and figurative errors of judgement; but these cannot obscure his many characteristic successes. Although his music, full of national flavour, has for the moment fallen somewhat out of favour, it is impossible to believe that songs like "Milkwort and Bog-cotton", "The Old Fisherman", "The Tryst" and many others are not surely made of the stuff of survival. Certainly I have always considered Francis George Scott a great song-writer of the second order, evoking deeper responses than Warlock or Quilter or Gurney.

William Montgomerie, an east-coast man, has a little poem of the 30s, "Glasgow Street", which goes:

*I retain a precise visual image of Hindemith, a stockily bespectacled profile playing his own viola concerto, *Der Schwanendreher*, with stolid Germanic efficacy, before a St. Andrew's Halls Tuesday audience.

> Out of this ugliness may come,
> Some day, so beautiful a flower,
>   That men will wonder at that hour,
>   Remembering smoke and flowerless slums,
> And ask—glimpsing the agony
> Of the slaves who wrestle to be free—
> "But why were all the poets dumb?"

The question is rhetorical, but nevertheless there was a practical answer. Glasgow did not have very many poets during the 20s and 30s. Indeed, apart from William Jeffrey, who wrote his cool classical verses between daily bouts of journalizing, there were none of any consequence. But 'Hugh MacDiarmid', though a Borderer, knew enough about Glasgow to be anything but dumb.

> The houses are Glasgow not the people—these
> Are simply the food the houses live and grow on
> Endlessly, drawing from their vulgarity
> And pettiness and darkness of spirit
> —Gorgonising the mindless generations,
> Turning them all into filthy property
> Apt as the Karaunas by diabolic arts
> To produce darkness and obscure the light of day.
> To see or hear a clock in Glasgow's horrible,
> Like seeing a dead man's watch, still going though he's dead.
> Everything is dead except stupidity here.

Like most of MacDiarmid's polemic, while containing a basis of truth the detail was inaccurate and unfair. Joe Corrie (born 1894), a miner-turned-playwright, whose one-acters were for long the staple diet of amateur drama companies in Scotland was neither 'dead' nor stupid when he wrote *A' Jock Tamson's Bairns* and *The Auld Blue Cup*. Nor, in still lighter vein, was W. D. Cocker whose "The Deluge" reflected a faint glimpse of that ironic blend of the serious and the absurd frequently reflected in MacDiarmid's own early poems in Scots.

The most frequently read novel about Glasgow between the wars was *The Shipbuilders* by George Blake (1894–1961) which, like James Barke's *Major Operation* published in 1936, the year after Blake's book appeared, deals with the devastating effect on middle-class husbands of the breakdown of their marriages. Read in their day, too, were Dot Allan's *Hunger March* and *Charity Begins at Home*, both set in Glasgow.

John Buchan, the first Baron Tweedsmuir, could hardly be

claimed as a Glasgow novelist, although he arrived in Glasgow as a boy, lived in the villa suburb of Pollokshields, and was educated at Hutcheson's Grammar School and Glasgow University. At Oxford he formed those connections which were later to help him combine the roles of man-of-letters and political figure, leading him eventually to the Governor Generalship of Canada, in which country he died in 1940. The references to Glasgow in his autobiography *Memory Hold the Door* are nowhere nearly as sympathetic as the uses made of the city's background in the novels of Anna Buchan, his sister, who wrote under the pseudonym 'O. Douglas'.

The Glasgow novelist who had the widest reputation in the 30s was Dr. A. J. Cronin. His *Hatters Castle* deals with the Turkey-red dyeing industry established in the Vale of Leven by the Stirling family. *The Green Years* has also a Clydeside setting. The mythical Dr. Finlay of television case-book fame was originally Cronin's creation, though Cronin cannot be held responsible for the melodramatic puerilities on which this over-prolonged return to the Tannochbrae of the 20s expired after a run of nearly a decade.

Just as J. J. Bell's *I Remember* recorded recollections of late Victorian middle-class life in Glasgow, so Neil Munro's *The Brave Days* (1931) similarly recorded a slightly later period, his remembrances, written in retirement, carrying across the First World War.

Of the same generation as Cronin was Dr. Osborne Mavor, who, as 'James Bridie', produced a series of divertingly discursive plays which pleased both London and Scotland, and have held their place in the repertoire: *A Sleeping Clergyman*, *Tobias and the Angel*, *Mr. Bolfry*, *The Anatomist*, *Daphne Laureola* and many others. His own autobiography, *One Way of Living* (1939), gives a racy account of a Glasgow-based life in the 20s and 30s.

Edinburgh rather than Glasgow has provided the background to most of our more distinguished twentieth-century painters; but J. D. Fergusson (1874–1961) whose best work was done in early life abroad and whose associations were with the French post-Impressionists, lived the latter part of his life in Glasgow. A fine collection of his work has been presented to the University of Stirling.

By far the most varied and generous single gift of works of art came to Glasgow through the munificence of Sir William Burrell, a Glasgow shipowner who left a collection worth, by the standards of 1970, somewhere in the region of £4 million, along with a sum of money to build a gallery in which to house it. Unfortunately, there has been a delay of more than a quarter of a century in beginning work on the gallery, partly because the money was never adequate for the purpose for which it was intended, and partly because Sir William, making his will in the days before internal atmosphere-control was as sophisticated as it is now, originally insisted that his art treasures should be housed more than 17 miles beyond the centre of the city. However, the generous gift of Pollok House and its spacious grounds by Mrs. Maxwell Macdonald to the National Trust for Scotland and Glasgow Corporation, has enabled a site to be chosen in the park of Pollok. An architectural competition limited to United Kingdom architects has been organized, and more than 400 architects have shown interest. The gallery which will house the Burrell collection towards the end of the 70s is certainly likely to be one of the outstanding buildings of the last quarter of Glasgow's twentieth century.

While the business use of the motor-car developed between the wars, pleasure motoring increased in popularity, though not yet to the detriment of the traditional Glasgow pleasure, 'doon the watter' sailing. In the 1939 summer season there were still twenty-seven steamers in the Clyde fleet, although the last of the independents, the Williamson-Buchanan Line, had sold out to the London Midland and Scottish Railway's subsidiary, the Caledonian Steam Packet Company in 1935. Their turbine steamers *King Edward* and *Queen Mary II*—the numeral a courtesy gesture towards the younger but larger Cunarder of the same royal name —appearing thereafter in the yellow-and-black topped funnel of the L.M.S., while the *Queen Alexandra*, with a third funnel added, and re-named the *Saint Columba*, wore the red-and-black colours of MacBrayne and took over from the veteran *Columba*. The *King George V* also went to MacBrayne to undertake the Staffa and Iona summer sail from Oban, a trip she is still making.

The departure of the *Columba* was the beginning of the end of the great days of Clyde pleasure cruising. Some years later a senior MacBrayne executive who happened to be sitting next to me at a dinner, told me that during her last few seasons, the frailties of age lay so heavily upon the old ship that whenever he and his colleagues thought about her they felt slightly apprehensive.

During these last few seasons she was the ship which carried me

off every summer to our holiday home at Innellan, on the Cowal
Coast. In a book of mine, *The Lowlands of Scotland: Glasgow and
the North*, published in 1953 and now, like so many of the County
Series of which it formed a part, out of print, I set down my
recollections of one of these 'doon the watter' trips which have
now ceased to be a possibility after an unbroken run of more than
150 years. Since this is avowedly a personal portrait of my native
city, and the traditional sail 'doon the watter' was for me a
keenly anticipated annual pleasure, it seems appropriate to quote
it here.

We were to set out, I think, on the first day of July; mother
and father, nurse, four children, dog, cat and goldfish. Although
we could depend on being able to purchase rather more than
could the Reids, nevertheless, a great deal of luggage had to be
taken. The packing was done systematically during the last days
of June. I do not think I slept much on the night before the day of
our departure.

It began early. We got up at five in the morning, and had
breakfast half an hour later. For some reason, that breakfast had a
special quality of its own. Its ingredients were those of many
another breakfast eaten since—porridge, bread and butter, and a
boiled egg—but I can still remember the extra flavour those
comestibles seemed to acquire that morning. (No doubt it was in
a similar mood of anticipation that the poet Southey generously
praised the excellence of Scottish breakfasts while staying at
Old Meldrum.)

After breakfast, we children were expected to keep out of the
way of our elders, for a horse-drawn lorry arrived outside the
house at six o'clock to cart the luggage down to the quay. I was
given the job of guarding the cat while the luggage was being
grunted and manœuvred round the bends of the staircase. The
cat, a venerable beast who lived to be 18 and would then be
about 12, had the idea that if he managed to escape while the front
door stood open to let the carters move freely in and out, he
would not have to undergo his annual holiday ordeal of transportation by basket; hence the need for one of the family to stand
guard.

At last the luggage had rumbled away, the cat had been safely
basketed, and it was time to prepare ourselves for the arrival of the
taxi. That taxi-drive itself was something of a novelty. Usually, I

went to children's parties in a cab: a musty affair, upholstered in faded green, and driven by a red-nosed mufflered coachman, whose characteristic smell was almost as strong as that of the horse that pulled the contraption.

Ordinary mortals who go about their affairs during the hours of daylight would do well to take an occasional ride through an industrial city at half past six in the morning, if only to remind themselves how large a section of the community has to do "day labour, light denied" in order to keep essential public services running. The new sun shone out from a clean sky this July morning, glistening the roof-tops of the tenements, and lighting up even the drabbest side-streets with the promise of a fair day.

The *Columba* lay on the south side of the river, her two red-and-black funnels setting off nobly her huge, gilded paddle-boxes. The moment you climbed up her gangway, your nostrils were assailed by a peculiar aroma that was all her own. After some years, I discovered that it was a mixture of heated engine oil, good galley cooking and well-scrubbed cleanliness, to which, down the river, the scudding tang of salty spray was added. But at that time, analysis did not matter. The smell was wholly entrancing.

We were to establish ourselves in the cabin, or the 'saloon' as it was more grandly called. The 'saloon' consisted of a number of seated bays lined with dark-red velvet plush, and richly draped with similar hangings. It gave an impression of well-established opulence and time-saturated sea-going. All went well at first. I carried the cat's basket down the companionway, and the cat remained obligingly silent. But at the entrance to the 'saloon', a liveried steward looked at me and my burden with an unmistakable air of hostility.

"What's in that basket?" he demanded.

"Provisions," I answered, with a happier promptitude than I have displayed on many a more important occasion since. He grunted and let us past. We chose an empty bay, and comfortably dispersed our bits and pieces.

Those final moments of waiting seemed the most interminable of all. Above our heads, busy feet tapped out their walking patterns on the deck. In the orange glow of the engine-room, the great gleaming monsters hissed and sizzled quietly to themselves, as if anticipating the moment when the flicker of a dial and the loosening of a lever would send them plunging backward and forward in all their pride of power.

Seven o'clock! Five minutes past! And then the mishanter occurred. A long, thin stream of clear liquid suddenly raced down the floor. Its place of origin was unmistakably the basket at my feet.

In a moment the steward was at my side.

"Your provisions seem to be leaking, sir," he observed acidly. (That "sir", to one of my tender years, seemed an additional humiliation.) "You'd better take them on deck."

I was delighted. I certainly had no desire to spend my first voyage in the feminine confines of the cabin. Now, someone would *have* to stay on deck to see that the cat was not shipped prematurely ashore.

Up there, things were happening. The captain, an impressive and recognizably Highland figure even beneath the disguising weight of his gold braid, was pacing his bridge, which straddled the ship from one paddle-box to the other between the two funnels. (It has always seemed strange to me that, until about 1920, it apparently never occurred to the designers of paddle-steamers that the funnel was a fairly major obstacle in the way of the helmsman's vision.) The captain took one final look at his watch; then he pulled the clanging brass levers at his side. The paddles began to thresh the water, nosing the ship's bow out towards the centre of the river; with a couple of dirty splashes, the ropes were tossed into the water, to be retrieved fussily by puffing steam capstans at bow and stern; and then the long, lean hull, shuddering a little at first, began to slide slowly forward.

Past close miles of shipyards, resounding with the racket of the riveters welding together the rusty hulks of the ships that would sail tomorrow's seas; past docks, full of towering ocean-going liners, and queer-looking tramp ships with foreign characters scrawled across their sterns; past grumphed-up, dirty old dredgers, squatting in the middle of the river, digging away the mud that forever strives to slip back into its ancient bed; past low-built hoppers carrying the mud far down the Firth to be dumped in the deeps around Ailsa Craig; past the chain-drawn car ferries of Renfrew and Erskine; past Bowling, with its stone-pencil monument to Henry Bell, and its huge oil port and depot cut back into the hills; past Greenock and Gourock, and over the broad Firth to Dunoon and Innellan.

My generation grew up under the certainty of a developing war threat that neither my immersion in literature nor my determination to become a violinist could shut out from my awareness for long. After the Munich affair of 1938 I joined a searchlight battery of the Territorial Army in order to put in the necessary service to enable me apply for a commission in my father's old regiment, The Cameronians (Scottish Rifles).

Glasgow's Territorial Battalions began to double themselves between Munich and the invasion of Poland. I went to my first camp in the early summer of 1939 with the 7th Cameronians at Dunfermline. Summoned by telephone from a summer lawn, I crossed the Clyde in a motor-boat from Innellan to Gourock to join the 9th Cameronians on 2nd September, our headquarters down a lane opposite Langside Public Hall. Although we spent the morning on which the Second World War was declared piling sandbags against the battalion office's windows, Glasgow heard its first air-raid warning—a false alarm as things turned out. At sea it was a Glasgow ship, the Anchor-Donaldson liner *Athenia*, newly out of the Clyde on her way to Canada with evacuees, that was to be the first British casualty of the war at sea. Thus in a sense, the war which one hoped by some miracle might yet not happen but knew in one's heart could not be avoided, struck one of its first blows at Glasgow children.

VIII

WAR AND PEACE

There was considerable bitterness among Clydeside industrialists just before and during the early months of the Second World War because of a belief that an unfair proportion of government contracts since Chamberlain plucked the sting out of the Munich nettle had gone to the South. C. A. Oakley who, during the war, was to become Scottish Controller of the Ministry of Aircraft Production and later Scottish Controller of the Board of Trade, and therefore has authority behind his opinions, has gone on record as saying: "An impression does remain that the English firms who doubled or trebled their capacity in the 1938–40 period —taking their opportunity of doing so at the taxpayers' expense— were willing to put their younger executives in charge of their new plant, and that the West of Scotland firms, who would not make any major extensions to their factories, or open new ones, denied to their youngest executives comparable chances".

Unlike its predecessor 'the war to end wars', the war of 1939, so long expected, affected everyone from the start. This time there were no public heroics. The mood was one of sober resignation mingled with a curious amalgam of disgust, guilt and, inevitably, a fear of the unknown perhaps best caught by the self-exiled W. H. Auden:

> I sit in one of the dives
> On Fifty-Second Street.
> Uncertain and afraid
> As clever hopes expire
> Of a low dishonest decade. . . .

The decade was low and dishonest because most of us chose to shut our minds to the terrible things which were happening to the Jews in Germany and to the Ethiopians in Africa; dishonest, because most of us kidded ourselves into believing that without commitment on our part, something would somehow happen which would let us off the hook, the bad turn suddenly good and our islanded lives be no longer threatened or disturbed.

Long before it could be the time for voyaging back, when "the lost traveller, with sun bleached hair/Dazed on the gangway" could "come home again"* from distant battlefields, six long years were to be lived through. This time at least, no one thought it would "all be over by Christmas", in spite of stories about friends holidaying in Germany in 1938 whose 'Baby Austins' had fashionable collisions with German tanks, which turned out to be made of papier mâché.

Gas masks were a universal issue, and were supposed to be carried everywhere. Dave Willis, then one of the most popular of the long line of 'Scottish Coamics', delighted Glasgow audiences with a song that went:

> In my wee gas mask
> I'm working out a plan,
> 'Though all the kids imagine
> That I'm just a bogey man.
> The girls all smile
> And bring their friends to see
> The nicest-looking warden
> In the A. R. P.
>
> Whenever there's a raid on,
> Listen for my cry
> An aeroplane, an aeroplane
> Away up a-ky
> Then I'll run helter-skelter
> But don't run after me
> You'll no get in my shelter
> 'Cause it's far too wee.

Children and old people were tearfully evacuated from Glasgow and Edinburgh to safer country places. Many of them drifted back again after about six months, when it began to look as if the urban dangers might not be as serious as had been supposed.

Other townies remained 'exiles' in the country almost for the duration. The novelist Robin Jenkins has dealt amusingly yet profoundly with the difficulties which the introduction of city

---

*"The Armistice" by John Lehmann.

children and their often difficult parents into rural families sometimes produce in *Guests of War* (1956).

Air-raid shelters were built, those at the bottom of our gardens being dubbed Anderson shelters, named after Sir John Anderson, the Home Secretary in 1938. The entrances to tenement closes were faced with baffle-walls. Barrage balloons floated above the city.

Clothes rationing froze fashions. A scheme for food rationing had been prepared well in advance, but although delicacies, especially fruit, were often in limited supply, there was always plenty to eat. Restaurants were limited to a maximum charge of 5s. per head, and it was astonishing how much continued to be offered for that sum throughout the war. Some food myths were created, like the supposed efficacy of carrots for increasing sharpness of vision at night in the severely blacked-out streets. (By a curious coincidence, Woolton Pie, another war-time speciality also commended by the Minister of Food, Lord Woolton, contained carrots as a major ingredient.) Glasgow swallowed the carrot-myth along with the lave [the rest.]

There were shortages from time to time particularly during the middle years of the war. Cigarettes were difficult to come by, and so was paper. The paper shortage sometimes made it difficult to meet the full demand for them. It also forced some limitation on the number of books which could be published. Many of those that appeared used a poor-quality paper which was often a dirty grey when new and speedily yellowed in the post-war years. Books, though produced under licence number, were nevertheless in steady demand, as was entertainment of all sorts.

Driving at night, with masked headlights showing only little rectangles of light, was an unpleasant experience. Petrol was only available for essential purposes, though it was surprising how apparently unessential some essential purposes managed to seem. Even among the services in training, restrictions on transport were severe.

Public transport presented problems too. Glasgow's tramway service operated at a reduced level. Long-distance travellers found themselves faced with conscience-troubling posters asking: "Is Your Journey Really Necessary?" To most people the need to struggle for a place in an overcrowded train only arose once a year at holiday time. Thousands of Glasgow men and women in the Forces no doubt still have memories of long journeys to and from points of leave overcrowded in compartments or crushed in corridors.

Many of the Clyde steamers sailed out beyond the arms of the Firth to become mine-sweepers. An anti-submarine steel-net boom which stretched across the Clyde from the Cloch to Dunoon divided the estuary in two, Dunoon and the Holy Loch being served from Gourock, Rothesay and the Kyles of Bute piers from Wemyss Bay.

It is right and fitting to begin any survey of Glasgow's 1939 war with the civilian population, since this was the first war affecting the United Kingdom in which those out of uniform were liable to be as dangerously involved as the soldiers at the front—a good prospect for the future of peace, I remember reflecting when air-raids started to take their toll of civilians on both sides. Scotland had to bear only a small share of the brunt of the air war launched against these islands by the Germans. Most of that share, however, was directed against Glasgow and the Clyde.

There was a minor daylight raid on 19th July 1940. The first night raid came on 18th September, when bombs dropped on George Square but missed the major buildings, Queen Street Station and the tunnel which leads into it. It did, however, remove the building at the east end of Royal Exchange Square, the site on which Glasgow Corporation Planning Department was later erected in an early post-war undistinguished style. Another bomb set fire to the cruiser *Sussex* at Yorkshill, causing the evacuation of the nearby Royal Hospital for Sick Children because of a danger that her magazine might blow up.

The most serious attacks on Clydeside were made in 1941, when Clydebank and Greenock took the full weight. In the three days, or rather nights, between 13th and 15th March, 1,083 people were killed and over 1,600 injured, mostly in Clydebank, where only seven houses remained entirely undamaged. As a result, this town with a population of 55,000 had to evacuate its fifty thousand or so survivors. Many of these folk were involved in vital production work, and their spirit in quickly overcoming the need to travel substantial distances to and from work was wholly admirable.

Between 5th and 6th May the raids against Greenock killed 341 people and injured 312. Whisky stores and sugar refineries were a major hazard in the fires which broke out. Worse still could have been the dangers which would have followed if the Admiralty oil storage tanks at Bowling, containing more than 12 million gallons, had been hit by any of the hundred or so bombs which the Germans tried to land on the site. 'Greek' Thomson's splendid Queen's Park St. George's Church was unfortunately totally destroyed by fire in the last raid on Glasgow, on the night of 23rd March 1943.

Glasgow had thirteen raids in all, and had dropped on it 183 high explosive bombs, 37 parachute mines, 3 oil bombs and thousands of incendiaries. By comparison with that which Bristol or Coventry endured, this was slight punishment. But the Secretary of State for Scotland was later to describe the Clydeside raids as being "as severe as any other areas of Britain".

Towards the end of 1943, the main tide of the war turned. Because of this, and because German technology was consequently prevented from improving the range of its V–1 'flying bombs' and its V–2 rockets, Glasgow was spared the renewed ordeal which London and other English cities and towns had to face from rocketry long after the offensive power of the Luftwaffe against the civilian population had been broken by 'the Few' in the Battle of Britain. Amongst the Spitfires which swept the Germans out of the skies was the City of Glasgow Fighter Squadron (602). Many other Glasgow men served in the air force, either in the Glasgow squadrons formed subsequently, or as individuals on Atlantic duties, protective and offensive, in the Far East and above Normandy beaches in the summer of retribution, 1944.

The loss of life among service personnel in the Second World War was mercifully much less severe than in its predecessor, there being less actual fighting. As the added names on war memorials show, only about a third of the total of those killed between 1914 and 1918 fell between 1939 and 1946.

Conscription was introduced from the start of the 1939 war, and once again the Territorial battalions of both the Highland Light Infantry and the Cameronians (Scottish Rifles) included many Glasgow men, enrolled or conscripted. It is probable that about 150,000 Glaswegians in all served in the armed forces. To many of these men and women, the war took them for the first time away from their native place. While travelling under wartime conditions must certainly have broadened their minds it sometimes also induced understandable nostalgia, distance lending a focusing enchantment to the remembered view, an experience I reflected in a poem now included in *The Oxford Book of Scottish Verse*, "The Exiled Heart."

Two purple pigeons circle a London square
as darkness blurs and smudges the shadowless light
of a winter evening. I pause on the pavement and stare
at the restless flutter of wings as they gather flight
like rustling silk, and move out to meet the night.

And my restless thoughts migrate to a Northern city—
fat pigeons stalking the dirty, cobbled quays,
where a sluggish river carries the cold self-pity
of those for whom life has never flowed with ease,
from a granite bridge to the grey Atlantic seas:

the bristling, rough-haired texture of Scottish manners;
the jostled clatter of airless shopping streets
where lumbering tramcars squeal as they turn sharp corners;
the boosy smell from lounging pubs that cheats
the penniless drunkard's thirst with its stale deceits:

where my heart first jigged to the harsh and steady sorrow
of those for whom mostly the world is seldom glad;
who are dogged by the flat-heeled, footpad steps of to-morrow;
for whom hope is a dangerous drug, an expensive fad
of the cushioned rich, or the young and lovesick mad:

where chattering women in tea-rooms, swaddled with furs,
pass knife-edged gossip like cakes, and another's skirt
is unstitched with sharp words, and delicate, ladylike slurs
are slashed on the not-quite-nice or the over-smart,
till their cigarette smoke is a lazy, prickled hurt.

I remember Glasgow, where sordid and trivial breed
from the same indifferent father; his children side
with the mother whose sour breasts taught them first to feed
on her hot, caressing hates that sear and divide,
or swell the itched, distorting bladder of pride.

Yet my casual smile is the tossed-down beggar's penny
the goaded heart throws out in vain to procure
the comfortable forgetfulness of the many
who lie in content's soft arms, and are safe and sure
in the fabled Grecian wanderers' lotus-lure:

who forget the sullen glare of the wet, grey skies,
and the lashing Northern wind that flicks the skin
where hum-drum poverty's dull and listless eyes
are pressed to the window, hearing the friendly din
of the party, watching the lights and the laughter within.

But oh! I cannot forget! So I wait, and wonder:
how long will the thinly-dividing window hold?
How long will the dancing drown the terrible anger
of those, the unwanted, who peddle their grief in the cold,
wrapped in their own despair's thick and unkindly fold?

Yet evil is no pattern of places
varied, like terraces from town to town.
A city's charms and individual graces
are but the sculptor's bleak and basic stone,
the photographic face without a frown.

The wound is in this bewildered generation,
unfriended, lost within the Freudian wood,
its compass-point no longer veneration
of that lost God who rewarded the simple and good,
vivid and real, now, only in childhood.

For we, the children of this uncertain age,
breathing its huge disasters and sad airs,
have seen that our warm, humanitarian rage
is impotent to soothe war's animal fears,
and cannot quell the lonely exile's tears.

So the heart, like a wounded seabird, hungers home
to muffled memories on fainter-beating wings
which once soared over history's clouded foam;
to that first shore where each new hero flings
his careful stone that fades in slow, concentric rings.

One other more prosaic confession of nostalgia I must record.
On a Sunday afternoon in 1942, walking in Lowestoft, I suddenly
recognized the unmistakable lines of the Clyde steamer *Duchess of
Rothesay*. There she was, lying in the harbour camouflaged in the
grey paint of a minesweeper. I felt as if I had suddenly come
unexpectedly upon an old familiar friend with whom I had shared
happier days!

Glasgow's most important functions between 1939 and 1946,
were probably as a sheltered port and as 'the arsenal of the

Empire'. During the war years more than 300 merchant ships were built in Clyde yards. The total tonnage of 1,634,216 included H.M.S. *Howe*, the aircraft carriers *Indefatigable* and *Implacable*, the battleship *Vanguard* and a huge quantity of smaller ships, including submarines, corvettes, escort vessels and landing craft. More than 25,000 repair jobs were also rushed through, some of them major undertakings, like the putting together of a ship blown into two sections by a mine.

The Clyde also became the chief port in the United Kingdom, handling about 80 per cent of our incoming merchant shipping. Some of the ships that arrived berthed at a new specially built port in the Gareloch; others were unloaded at anchor in the lochs of the Clyde, a fleet of little ships and barges ferrying their cargoes to the nearest railhead. Fleets of fighting ships, British, Canadian and American, assembled in the Clyde. So did the Norway convoy of May 1940 and others, including convoys to Malta and to North Africa. Many of the D-day landing rehearsals were carried out on the Clyde, and the famous Mulberry Harbours, without which the Normandy landing could not have been sustained, were organized in the Gareloch. More than a hundred Scottish firms were involved in making piers and other parts of this remarkable enterprise, all within a fixed delivery schedule.

The Clyde's great liners *Queen Mary* and *Queen Elizabeth* steamed 950,000 miles between them, carrying $1\frac{1}{4}$ million soldiers, the speed of their camouflaged hulls fortunately making them a difficult target for German U-boats.

Enormous quantities of ammunition and equipment were manufactured in and around Glasgow. Even the Kelvin Hall was turned into a factory where barrage balloons and inflatable rubber dinghies were produced.

Womenfolk spent their energies generously in running service canteens for visiting soldiers, sailors and airmen. It is said that about 90 per cent of American troops spending leave in the United Kingdom came to Glasgow. A tile showing a Free Dutch Army soldier, and presented to Glasgow women who had organized wartime club facilities, stood by a fireplace in my parents' home long after a generation had grown up to whom the war was merely part of history.

There were local excitements ranging from the surprising arrival of Hitler's deputy Rudolf Hess, who baled out of an M.E.110 over Eaglesham on the night of 10th May 1941, to the dreadful explosion of a French destroyer, the *Maille Breze* at Greenock on 30th April 1940, killing most of her crew and causing severe damage to the town.

Although an end to the war had so often seemed so impossibly far away during these long six years, when it came at last, on 9th May 1945, Glasgow celebrated V.E. (Victory in Europe) Day with energetic gaiety. According to *The Glasgow Herald* report:

> People of all ages, conditions and sizes who had been thronging the city streets as if waiting for nightfall made George Square their resort when night settled down.
>
> Long before the lights had sprung up to shed beauty and carnival gaiety upon the Square, over which towered the mass of the Municipal buildings, the junketing had begun. Dancing had gone on intermittently among the young, the leadership of which seemed to fall upon high-spirited liberty men from the Navy.
>
> They danced jigs and eightsomes in front of the City Chambers, performed sweeping wonders with the palais glide, and wound in long serpentine columns, singing and laughing in happy eddies, round the staider islands of civilian sightseers.

The 1945 election returned a Labour government with a majority of 200, a result which to our European Allies seemed to smack of ingratitude to Churchill, the man whose determination had at one stage seemed almost all that stood between Hitler and the achievement of his territorial ambitions for the Third Reich. Just as the mood of realistic determination in which the 1939 war had begun differed from the feeling of exalted crusade which accompanied the outbreak of the 1914 war, so the mood of 1945 differed from that of 1918. With fighting less continuous and the expectation of survival among members of the armed forces much greater than the life-expectancy of a week which faced the average second lieutenant on his way to the trenches in 1916, there was more time for thinking. Soldiers given compulsory instruction in current affairs were actively encouraged to plan the brave new world which every generation feels so certain it can build out of the failures of the past.

Yet Glasgow played virtually no part in the political shift that brought the Attlee Government into power, only one seat—Kelvingrove, which Walter Elliot lost by a small majority to the Labour candidate J. L. Williams—changing party allegiance. Glasgow was represented in the 1945 House of Commons by five Conservatives, seven Labourites and two I.L.P. members.

One result of the introduction of the newly-created Welfare State was that progress towards improvements in the social services were plain for all to see. Perhaps because of this, in the immediate post-war years, strikes were few and comparatively small. It was not, of course, V.E. Day that finally marked the end of the conflict, but V.J. Day, 15th August 1945, when Japan capitulated after the dropping of two atomic bombs, which undoubtedly saved the lives of thousands of Allied soldiers, sailors and airmen. The severe cost to the civilian population of the nation which elected to enter the war with the aggression of Pearl Harbour has always seemed to me to have been entirely justified in the balance.

The events which for some time thereafter dominated the thoughts of Glaswegians were mostly international: the Berlin blockade, the political fermentation of the Middle East, the Russian achievement of the atomic bomb, the war in Korea.

Inevitably, these years were not easy at home. Food rationing dragged on until 3rd July 1954 and in 1947 there was a power shortage aggravated by one of the severest winters of the twentieth century.

The worst problem which Glasgow had to face was housing. 'Pre-fabs', quickly erected little bungalows originally intended to last for ten years, went up on vacant sites all over the city. By the end of 1970 78 temporary pre-fabs were still occupied in Glasgow.

Mandatory planning came into force for the first time with the Planning Act of 1947. A survey of Glasgow's permanent housing stock was then carried out. Over 100,000 dwellings, or nearly one-third of all the houses in the city, were found to be at, or beyond, the end of their structural lives. In human terms this meant that 100,000 families were living in houses where the fabric was damp or crumbling, and where there was neither hot water of any kind nor internal sanitation. This, too, in spite of the fact that between 1919 and 1939 the corporation had built more than 50,000 council houses for letting.

Between the wars the concept of the 'garden suburb' caught the imagination of people. Most of the houses which went up in suburbs like Knightswood, Mosspark and Carntyne were of this type, having their own front and back doors leading into their own gardens.

After the war suburban building was begun again with commendable energy, covering to the east and north-east districts,

Ruchazie, Garthamlock, Barlanark and Easterhouse; to the north-west, Blairdardie and Drumchapel; and to the south and south-west, Pollok, Householdlwood and Castlemilk. Some of these houses were variations of the traditional tenement theme, reduced in scale. Unfortunately, serious mistakes were made. In some cases, the wholesale transfer of the inhabitants of an old slum area into a new estate simply prepared the way for the re-emergence of social problems which, in theory, new and better housing standards were supposed to eradicate. Drumchapel, a new housing suburb with a population the size of Perth, was built without any shopping or social amenities, the shortage of accommodation persuading the politicians that extra houses were a more justifiable use of material and labour resources than shops, cinemas, picture-houses, pubs and clubs. A good deal of local unrest developed before resources were eventually diverted to put right this omission.

One of the problems created by the pre-1939-war garden suburb development, was that a lot of land was needed to house people. The density in some of the tenemented parts of the city is about 400 people in roughly 115 dwellings per acre. In the garden suburbs, the comparable density was approximately 50 people in 14 dwellings to each acre. Even the modern tenement-style block resorted to in the 50s only raised the density to about 100 people in 29 dwellings to the acre. Although this doubled the density of pre-war housing schemes, it was only a quarter of the density encountered in the worst tenemented areas in the older districts of Glasgow.

Having ringed the pre-1939-war city with new housing, by 1960 Glasgow had no more land left upon which to build. For topographical reasons it could not extend its boundaries. Yet despite the massive building programme of the previous forty years—a programme which included the clearing of slum areas like the notorious Gorbals—Glagsow still suffered from over-crowding.

The only solution available was for the older parts of the city to be rebuilt. Twenty-nine zones in Glasgow were therefore designated Comprehensive Development Areas, among them Gorbals,* Anderston, Townhead, Bridgeton and Gallowgate;

*Made notorious by MacArthur's novel *No Mean City* (1935) and by Sir Arthur Bliss's ballet *Miracle in the Gorbals* and Robert MacLeish's play *The Gorbals Story* (both 1946).

areas lying round the centre of the city, and with tenements about 120 years old; areas, too, in which mixed uses had developed in the nineteenth century, partly because of the need for workers to be within walking distance of factories, partly because of haphazard chance.

Comprehensive redevelopment still allows for mixed land usage in certain circumstances, but in a planned manner. Thus at Anderston, a centre has been built which makes provision for shops, offices, the parking of cars, and for small firms which had perhaps previously functioned in ramshackle buildings wedged into backlands among rows of slumland tenements. Allowance has also to be made for the inescapable fact that so great was the density in these run-down old areas that when redevelopment does take place, only 40 per cent of the people thus displaced can go back into the new buildings. As a result Glasgow, for a century and a half the 'second city', its populations having exceeded the million mark by 1913 has begun to shed some of its numbers with a consequent decline in its rateable return; and this at a time when the work of renewal demands more money than has ever been needed before.

Obviously, the displaced 60 per cent must be accommodated somewhere. Two solutions have been tried. In 1957, Glasgow began to enter into overspill agreements with other towns. The idea was to settle displaced Glaswegians in expanded older towns like Haddington and Grangemouth. But the overspill plan, though successful on a small scale, could not possibly provide a full solution to the problem. For one thing, some of the towns willing in theory to accept Glaswegians were situated at so great a distance from the Scottish megalopolis that there could be little hope of attracting the necessary industries to provide work for the newcomers.

The major solution to Glasgow's problem therefore lay in the creation of new towns far enough beyond the green belt around the city to prevent an eventual join-up, yet near enough to enable industrialists to make use of Glasgow's communications system and other facilities.

East Kilbride, the first of these new towns, is a pleasantly hilly green-spaced garden town which has been remarkably successful in attracting industry. It now has a population target of 100,000. Glenrothes, in Fife, begun in 1948, is made up of 'neighbourhood units'. It was originally intended to serve the East Fife mining area when the potential of the Fife coal fields and the post-war demand for coal were both thought likely to be greater than they have in fact turned out to be. Glenrothes has become a centre of the electronics industries. Many of its inhabitants came from Glasgow.

Cumbernauld, built in 1956 around a windy spine of land between Glasgow and Stirling, has been designed to take a much larger proportion of Glasgow's overspill population than the others. More compact than its predecessors, its designers have successfully resolved the dangerous conflict between vehicles and pedestrians which complicates urban life in older towns and cities originally built to cope only with horse-drawn traffic. Both East Kilbride and Cumbernauld have developed their own identities, resulting in the evolution of a vigorous range of community activities. It is perhaps not without interest that at the time of writing, the elected councils of both these new towns are led by Scottish National Party provosts.

Other new towns designed to help Glasgow with its overspill problem are Livingstone in West Lothian, begun in 1962; Irvine in Ayrshire, begun in 1966; and Erskine in Renfrewshire, begun in 1970.

Within the city itself, the environmental quality of those Comprehensive Development Areas on which work has already begun varies. The Gorbals has Sir Basil Spence's 'hanging garden' flats, and a less exotic block by Sir Robert Matthew. It also has a variety of pre-fabricated types of housing block ranging from the harmlessly faceless to the hopelessly tasteless, though all of them are being laid out spaciously and suitably landscaped.

Finance naturally influences decisions as to what kind of housing is to replace the bull-dozed tenements in a particular area. Scots unwillingness to pay for environment and the obvious limitations on the total amount that a traditional low-rent policy can be allowed to impose upon the generality of ratepayers are also factors which have to be given consideration.

The development of high-rise housing has altered drastically the Glasgow skyscape during the 60s: white or grey towers like piled-up children's bricks; or oblong blocks, like upended gargantuan cigarette packets. Multi-storey tower dwellings were originally conceived as a useful method of stacking-up on small land-areas families without children of school age. Their designers intended them to be merely one method of housing for use in redeveloped areas which would also include terraces or maisonettes near the ground to accommodate families with children under 15.

Glasgow's land shortage is so acute, however, that high-rise towers have been built in isolation where small parcels of waste-land were available. Some are tenanted by families with young children. In such cases there is evidence to suggest that this high-rise living, though matched to modern standards of comfort and domestic convenience, creates neuroses, particularly among mothers who must either have their toddlers forever about their feet or release them to play-areas perhaps twenty-five storeys below. Should a youngster find himself in trouble, it can take a mother quite a time to arrive with succour or comfort, especially if vandals have put a lift out of action, or trade unionists happen to be demonstrating the outmoded nature of their so-called rule books by taking euphemistically mis-named action the result of which is a withdrawal of the supply of electricity.

Even if serious doubts about the sociological viability of high-rise housing had not arisen, those probing towers that pierce and pillar the night sky with lights reflected against the silhouettes of the Clydeside hills, cannot for much longer be multiplied. Soon Glasgow will have no more vacant land at all, and new building within the city's boundaries will have to be confined to urban replacement.

Clearly, the character of a city depends to some extent upon the quality of its best buildings. With Glasgow in the turmoil of major redevelopment, it has become urgently necessary for thought to be given to the future of those buildings which, for architectural or historical reasons, must be conserved either through the listed building provisions of the Town and Country Planning Act (Scotland) 1969, or under the Civic Amenities Act of 1967. Sooner or later the question must arise as to how much of the splendid Victorian central area should be conserved, so that the life of a city that relies on commerce is not stultified, nor either the heritage which gives Glasgow its individuality and quality destroyed.

Glasgow Corporation has wisely insisted that certain listed buildings—the Royal Bank of Scotland, the former Western Club and Burnet's Stock Exchange Building, all in Buchanan Street, and Blythswood Square—could only be redeveloped behind their existing façades. On the other hand, while obviously every single listed building cannot reasonably be expected to survive, the disappearance of a building as distinguished as McGeoch's ware-house clearly indicated the need for a study of Central Glasgow.

The corporation therefore commissioned Lord Esher to undertake a study the first result of which is *Conservation in Glasgow: A Preliminary Report* (1971). The corporation has declared its willingness to allocate money for practical conservation, provided this expenditure is matched with an equal central government contribution.

Laws exist to enable a local authority to resist undesirable pressures from outside developers, whose motives, naturally, are not social but personal, and financial help from central government sources*, though modest at present, is also available. But the laws which relate to the conservation of our stone-and-mortar heritage are in this country permissive, not mandatory. Permissive laws, however, are only as good as the determination of a council or corporation to administer them.

The massive re-development which throughout the 60s has torn huge gaps in the city for new office and housing projects, ring roads and bridges; the declining population resulting from the redevelopment of slum or near-slum housing areas; the gradual seep southwards of the control of nearly all the main industries based on Glasgow; the unfortunate, sometimes violent, social consequences of such amenity-less post-1939-war housing concentrations as Easterhouse; these things have together combined to help produce a malaise, a serious faltering of self-confidence among Glaswegians, which is deeply disturbing.

One manifestation of this is the eagerness of some elected local authority representatives to grab at any project whatever which appears likely in the short term to produce more job opportunities, or to bring money into the area, regardless of the long-term social consequences, whether in the centre of Glasgow or on the Clyde estuary, Glasgow's traditional recreational playground.

As a result planning decisions that are inherently bad are liable to be taken out of sheer nervousness, lest the promise of what looks like prosperity vanish beneath discussion.

Glasgow has attracted to itself a bad environmental reputation in Europe. During the 60s, when it was first mooted that the Post Office Savings Bank workers were to be moved from the London area to Glasgow, the voices of panic and indignation were heard in vigorous protest. Undoubtedly it is the case that fast-expanding, unplanned industry in and around Glasgow did create very bad environmental conditions during the latter part of the

*The Historic Buildings Council for Scotland.

nineteenth century, conditions involving near-permanent despoliation, in some cases. The enormous effort being made to overcome these conditions and prevent their recurrence could be vitiated if lack of self-confidence were to result in hustling developers or industrialists being allowed to work their most easily profitable will under threat of removing their patronage elsewhere should amenity or other considerations of social concern be put in their way. As it happens, the Post Office Savings Bank is located in a green parkland area within the city, evidence of the strength which amenity lends to the cause of economic growth.

Unfortunately, the ability to relate cause and effect in the mind's eye is not a common attribute. Many of those upon whose political decisions the fate of our environment depends seem quite unable to envisage the ultimate results of what their deliberations may have unleashed.

The leader in *The Times* of 28th December 1970, commenting on such disappointments in European Conservation Year (1970) as the recommendation by the Roskill Commission of Cublington instead of Foulness as the site of London's third airport (a choice dissented from by the Commission's only professional planner, Professor Colin Buchanan), the fouling of our rivers with untreated sewage during the electricity workers' strike, and the scare over mercury poisoning in canned tuna, rightly declares:

The more developed a society the less can progress be measured in purely economic terms. Conservationists or environmentalists, call them what you will, do not deny that there is often an economic cost in the measures they propose. What they seek is a balancing of social and economic costs in the taking of decisions. . . .

Many of the most crucial decisions will be taken by men in public life whose political responses are more highly tuned than their aesthetic sense. This will always be so. Therefore the success of the environmentalists over a period of time will depend a great deal on their political muscle. . . .

Perhaps, after all, the main achievement of European Conservation Year will be to have provoked the disappointment that stimulates action. In almost all countries of the world there is now a much greater anxiety and determination to prevent the destruction of the patrimony before it is too late.

Glasgow has a wet climate (average rainfall 40 inches each year), an ethnical population mixture which produces a high violence rate, and an inherited environmental mess which it is

Sir Basil Spence's Glasgow Airport
The new Gorbals
(overleaf) *Approach roads to the Kingston Bridge, and the Inner Ring Road*

doing its best to clear up as quickly as possible. It also has a wide range of fine buildings which give it a unique character, a generality of easily approachable and kindly hearted citizens who welcome strangers to their midst, and glorious countryside on its doorstep. The good points have to be balanced against the bad. To a stranger who took the trouble to investigate them, the balance might seem to be equal. The problem is how to ensure that in the struggle to secure English, American or Continental economic patronage, now that the inclination and economic opportunity to generate self-help has largely vanished, the balance is not swung over to the debit side. If that were to happen, then Glasgow's reputation could only go further into decline, and it could become increasingly difficult to persuade those experts and executives, upon whom industrial initiative depends, to settle their factories and their families in or near our city.

In the technological age into which we are moving with accelerating rapidity and an increasing threat to health, if not possibly to the continuation of life itself on our space-ship Earth, it might perhaps be as well if we reminded ourselves from time to time that industry exists for the well-being of man, not the other way round. The ultimate human aim is presumably to create the best possible conditions in which the greatest number can enjoy the good life.

Environment is the basic condition from which alone the good life can be created. The greatest threat to environment, stripped of euphemistic verbiage, is short sighted economic greed. It was presumably an awareness of the virulence of this threat which inspired the drafting of the United Kingdom's first overall mandatory planning laws by the 1945 Labour government. There seems to me to be grounds for doubting if the resistance mechanisms in our civic body are operating healthily enough for us to be able to feel sure that the environmental future of the Glasgow region is secure.

Glasgow's future can no longer be that of a large, comparatively compact city. Inevitably, it must become the heart of a city region, like every comparable conurbation of its size in the United Kingdom.

When Comprehensive Development Areas necessarily shed 60 per cent of their population, so also do they have to shed some industries and the related job opportunities. During the past two decades, more than 100 firms have moved out of Glasgow to

Glasgow's Christmas Lights

resettle in places like Irvine, Kirkintilloch, Hamilton, East Kilbride and Cumbernauld. Even those industries that have stayed
and resettled within the city were offering only eighty jobs to
the acre as against the ninety to the acre offered in 1948, before
Comprehensive Development had taken place. These densities
are still falling.

On top of this inevitable job loss planned within the city, during
the same twenty-year period more than 70,000 jobs in Glasgow's
steel works, shipyards, heavy engineering shops and locomotive
building works have vanished. Furthermore, space can no longer
be found for the kind of acreage needed by industries that might
want to come into the city. Thus most new job opportunities are
now occurring outside Glasgow's boundaries, though many of
those who fill them commute from and to Glasgow. Glasgow is
already the shopping, recreational and entertainment centre for a
wide area round about.

The arrival of the Rootes Group (now Chrysler) at Linwood,
Renfewshire, in 1961, and of the British Motor Corporation (now
British Leyland) at Bathgate in 1963, brought the motor industry
back to Scotland. The failure of the Linwood factory to attract
the hoped-for manufacturers of component parts, the bad strike
record at Linwood and the poor profitability results at both
factories make one wonder whether these vital transplants are
going to take Scottish root.

The collapse of Fairfield of Govan in 1965, and its reorganization with other yards as Upper Clyde Shipbuilders, backed by
massive infusions of public money, raised hopes that those inter-
union feudings of the who-does-what variety which had long
made it difficult for Clyde yards to quote either prices likely to
prove profitable or accurate delivery dates, might be replaced by
twentieth century common sense. But U.C.S. went into complex
bankruptcy in 1971. The ensuing work-in led by James Reid—a
shop steward comparatively new to the shipbuilding industry and
on his own admission once a paid servant of the Communist
Party—may have had some effect in temporarily focussing attention on Scotland's economic difficulties, but has also created
abroad a somewhat damaging image of Clydeside's industrial
reliability. Not even his election as Lord Rector of Glasgow
University (from a total poll of less than 40 per cent) glosses the
absurdity of his shop stewards' resistance to the inevitability of
change, vividly reflected by the shipyard worker who told a tele-

vision interviewer: "On the Clyde, shipbuilding is our birthright."

The unacceptable human tragedy of mass employment can neither be cured by emotive one-sided action, nor by demanding more public money to paint up the corpses of dead possibilities. What Glasgow and Clydeside need now are lively new opportunities.

Perhaps the most important single industrial benefit to Scotland was the Government's decision in 1959 to site the nationalized steel industry's new steel strip-mill at Ravenscraig, where new steel works had been begun in 1954. Even although it was accepted that it had no immediate prospect of operating at full capacity, here at least is one major new venture which forms part of a success story.

Some other newcomers, like the I.B.M. factory at Greenock and Burroughs at Dumbarton, represent American investment on Scottish soil, usually on one or other of the Scottish industrial estates. Many of these 'foreign' firms have been persuaded into the Glasgow region by the Scottish Council (Development and Industry), formed in 1946 out of Tom Johnstone's war-time Scottish Council on Industry and the privately formed Scottish Development Council of 1930. The Scottish Council, though not a government agency, has done remarkable work in promoting the economic well-being of Scotland as a whole, and its advice is rightly listened to by the Secretary of State for Scotland of the day.

The dangers which are always present when a country has to rely on imported industries are obvious. When periods of economic recession affect America, England, Germany or Japan, it is likely to be in such distant outposts as Scotland that retrenchment will occur. Living constantly with this weakness and the inescapable fact that Scotland's unemployment level remains obstinately at about twice the United Kingdom average, together with an awareness of the fact that upwards of 20,000 Scots emigrate from their country every year (presumably because they are dissatisfied with the conditions of living it can offer) adds further to that running sense of uncertainty which is not just a Glasgow ailment, but a Scottish malaise.*

Squeezes and relaxations, the giving of Government grants and the declaring of development areas, are words on the television screen or headlines in the newspapers which, to most people, can only occasionally be seen to relate to day-to-day practical realities.

*Certainly about 6,000 come in, Sassenachs mainly, many of whom want to stay.

Fortunately, life goes on. New buildings appear. Festivals erupt happiness or add to information, and disappear into memory. Public tragedies briefly arouse intense communal concern, and then sink into limbo, since "we forget because we must, and not because we will". Books get written, plays staged, holidays taken and life enjoyed. In a sense, these things happening mean Glasgow for most of us.

It is not easy to point to many post-1946 buildings in Glasgow and say with conviction, "That is a great piece of architecture, which will undoubtedly be a listed building in 2070." Housing blocks like Hutchesontown-Gorbals Redevelopments Area B (1962) by Robert Matthew, Johnston-Marshall and Partners, and the Area C Redevelopment by Sir Basil Spence, Glover and Ferguson (1965), both already mentioned; the Ladywell Housing Scheme of Honeyman, Jack and Robertson, which went up in 1964 on the site of the former Duke Street prison for women: the Queen Mother's Hospital, Yorkhill, designed by J. L. Gleave and Partners in 1964; or the London architect William Whitfield's exciting university library and art gallery (its complex of towers a relief in the context of so many single high-rise towers), attract attention by their distinction in contemporary cosmopolitan terms, as also does Derek Stephenson and Partners' Heron House (1970), designed to blend with Thomson's St. Vincent Street Church, which it closely neighbours.

Strangely, in an age when support for the Church as an institution seems to be steadily waning, it is the best of the new religious buildings which seem to carry the strongest conviction. The finest that I have seen in or around Glasgow are Jack Coia's St. Brides at East Kilbride and the beautiful St. Charles Roman Catholic Church, Kelvinside Gardens, which has an exposed concrete frame with infill panels of rustic facing bricks and a free-standing tower. Inside, there is a delicate vaulted concrete ceiling and the sculptor Benno Schotz's "Stations of the Cross".

New ideas on schooling have resulted in the carrying through of an extensive rebuilding programme; not, however, extensive enough, since Glasgow has neither enough schools nor enough teachers. Indeed, some primary schools have had to resort to part-time education.

In by-gone days, urban schools were frequently cramped up into odd corners, the playing space for the children a few yards of dismal concrete surrounded by iron railings. Today, the regulations rightly insist that a two-stream primary school must have 4½ acres, while a secondary school for 1,000 children must have 14 acres, 7 for the school and 7 for playing fields. Because of Glasgow's land shortage, these need not necessarily be contiguous.

Since the Civic Trust award scheme was inaugurated in 1959 a number of awards or commendations have gone to Glasgow schools and educational buildings, among them the University's Institute of Virology (1963), the College of Nautical Studies (1969). The assessors for the Civic Trust Award scheme relate the good design of a building specifically to its environment.

The expansion of Glasgow University and the evolution in status of the Royal Technical College—housed in the handsome red sandstone Edwardian 'Tec' building—into Glasgow's second university, the University of Strathclyde, has resulted in the erection of some interesting though close-crowded new structures.

In Glasgow University, apart from the library already mentioned, which dominates the districts of Hillhead and Kelvinside, the Students Refectory Club of Frank Fielden has received a Civic Trust award. Already the half-completed Adam Smith building of Harvey, Scott and Associates promises a typical kind of Glaswegian stolid dignity.

The building of the University of Strathclyde offers a magnificent opportunity which carries with it a kind of poetic justice; for eventually the new university may take in the old site of Glasgow University, given over to goods trains since 1870. Appropriately, Fielden's School of Architecture is one of the most exciting buildings in a huge range eventually to include a quiet residential enclave which will use, in the words of the authors of *Glasgow at a Glance*,* "linked seven-storey blocks to form a series of planted piazzas punctuated by the point-blocks."

A. J. Jury's splendid restoration of the City Hall, and Bazaar—the Bazaar the work of J. Cleland *circa* 1817, the 1840 Hall itself by George Murray, with later additions—eventually come into possession of Strathclyde University when the planned concert-hall complex being designed by Sir Leslie Martin around the junction of Sauchiehall Street, Buchanan Street and West Nile Street is built. Whether or not this happens—and at present an argument between the custodians of two public purses puts the matter in doubt—this oldest surviving link with Glasgow's cultural history must certainly be conserved.

*Professor A. MacLaren Young and A. M. Doak.

Leaving aside such recurring inconveniences as strikes, official and unofficial, of which most Glaswegians have become heartily sick, public events have not lacked variety.

At the lowest level, there were the more sensational murders: for instance, the Pollokshields murder of 1946, when a man shot a clerkess and an office boy at Pollokshields East railway station. It took the police ten months to find him at Carlisle, during which period there was a deal of apprehension in the South Side. Charles Brown, a 20-year-old railway fireman, was tried and sentenced to death. It came out that he had a fondness for gangster films—he had seen one such film, *Scarface*, five times—and at parties was fond of pretending to be a gangster. While I am totally opposed to the kind of mealy-mouthed pietistic censorship which Mrs. Mary ('Whitewash') Whitehouse and others apparently seek to impose upon television, the endless diet of criminal violence now transferred from the cinema to the television screen and proliferated nightly, does seem to me an infliction upon society which cannot fail to have long-term harmful effects.

Another admirer of gangsters and gangster films, Peter Manuel, described by a senior police officer who had to do with the investigation of his crimes as "one of the worst and most horrible murderers ever to cross the scene of criminal history in Scotland, if not in Great Britain", was responsible, in all probability, for nine murders in the Glasgow district between 1956 and his execution in 1958. He was charged with murdering a 17-year-old girl, Anne Kneilands (he reduced her head "more or less to pulp", according to one report): with several cases of breaking-in and stealing; with the murder of a Mrs. Watt, whose husband was for some time in custody, one of Manuel's specialities being the planting of blame on others; with the murder of Watt's daughter; the murder of Isabelle Cooke, aged 17; the murder of Peter Smart, his wife and 11-year-old son, all shot at close range while asleep; and the theft of a motor-car. He was also strongly suspected of having murdered a taxi-driver in Northumberland but not charged with this offence. Manuel, who had produced a confession when the police arrested his father on minor charges, and who sacked his counsel at his trial, then, in the words of the judge, Lord Cameron, conducted his own defence "with a skill that is quite remarkable". On Lord Cameron's direction, Manuel was acquitted of the Kneilands murder because of lack of corroborative evidence, but found guilty of all the other major charges and hanged.

Manuel, the sex-maniac who stripped his young victims of their lower clothing without actually sexually assaulting them (although he first came to the notice of the police as a rapist as well as a housebreaker); the man who wanted to be thought a high-time crook in the eyes of Glasgow's criminal fraternity; whose whole sense of values was so deranged that his indignation at being accused of shooting an 11-year-old sleeping boy reflected his belief that it would have been in order had the victim been a man; Manuel, who was found sane and fit to plead, serves to remind us, in an age where sympathy often now seems to be more readily extended to the murderer than his victim and relatives, that, once again, in Lord Cameron's wise words, "badness need not necessarily mean madness".

The Festival of Britain was celebrated in Glasgow, as elsewhere, in 1951 with, among other things, an exhibition of industrial power held in the Kelvin Hall. During the same year Glasgow University celebrated its fifth centenary, and in 1970 it celebrated the anniversary of its final move from the High Street. In 1951 the Attlee Government went out and Churchill came back in, to be succeeded by Eden, the disaster of Suez, and Harold Macmillan's 'you've never-had-it-so-good winds-of-change' era. The fact was however that throughout the 50s, wages in Glasgow certainly were good and work was plentiful. When George VI died in 1952, and Queen Elizabeth came to the throne, some Glaswegians were involved in the dispute over the use of the numeral II following her name, the contention being that the previous Queen Elizabeth had no jurisdiction over the Scots, and indeed caused their own queen to be judicially murdered. Like most controversies over unessentials, it petered out.

Television came into Glasgow homes with the death of George VI in 1952, followed by the coronation of the Queen in the following year. The information and entertainment thus brought to people in their own armchairs soon had an effect on older methods of communication. For example, it quickly drove out of existence two newspapers, the *Evening News* (Neil Munro's old paper) in 1957, and *The Bulletin* in 1960. Soon, it brought about the closure of more than twenty-five cinemas, many of them in the suburbs.

Theatres, too, began to disappear; the 'Queens' in 1952, the 'Royalty' ('Lyric') in 1953, the 'Royal' in 1957 when it became

S.T.V.'s studio, the old 'Metropole'⋆ in 1961 and the 'Empire' in 1962. Glasgow's most disastrous entertainment loss was caused not by demolition, but by a fire probably started by a cigar butt left in a seat after a boxing match. St. Andrew's Halls went up in flames in 1962. The Scottish National Orchestra, homeless as a result, had for several years to use a concert hall hurriedly constructed out of a disused cinema on a site where the north-western approach to the Kingston Bridge (1970) now curves upwards.

Many of the provincial cinemas which were the centres of twice-weekly entertainment during the 30s turned to bingo in the struggle for survival during the 60s. It seems possible that the popularity of this most dreary and unimaginative of all gambling pastimes may now have passed its peak.

The Arts in Glasgow were by no means unproductive in those postwar decades. Most of Scotland's composers now in their forties neither come from Glasgow nor live in Scotland. But Thomas Wilson does both. His symphony has achieved several performances in and out of his native country, music which reveals powerful lyrical and dramatic gifts.

But it is on the performing side that Glasgow has excelled itself. The old part-time Scottish Orchestra gave place to the full-time Scottish National Orchestra in 1950. In 1959 Alexander Gibson was appointed Musical Director. Since then, he has built up the orchestra, numerically and qualitatively, until without any doubt it stands second to none in the United Kingdom. It has made several successful European tours and a number of recordings.

To Alexander Gibson, together with Robin Orr, Ian Rodger and those other visionary people who supported his ambition for Scotland, also goes the credit for bringing into being Scottish Opera, which now has its headquarters in the former Engineer's Institute in Elmbank Street. Scottish Opera, Scotland's first professional opera company, has played operas by Mozart, Rossini, Verdi, Beethoven, Wagner and Britten. The company's outstanding triumph† was perhaps their exciting performance of Berlioz's *The Trojans*, given on a single evening for the first time in English and without the usual cuts. *Full Circle*, a short Scottish opera by Robin Orr, Professor of Music at Cambridge and formerly the

⋆The present 'Metropole' at St. George's Cross, at the moment of writing up for sale, was originally the 'Empress'.

†To which has been added their first complete performance of Wagner's *Ring* in Glasgow since 1921.

incumbent of the Chair of Music at Glasgow University, is so far the only Scottish work to be performed. It is to be hoped that Scottish Opera will eventually be able to give Scottish composers the opportunity of presenting their stage works to the Scottish public.

If this ambition is to be achieved, then Scottish Opera will need more money. The Edinburgh-based Scottish Arts Council, though in theory autonomous, is ultimately dependent on a proportional cut of whatever monetary cake the government provides for the Arts Council as a whole. This sum is apt to depend upon political values, and can rarely be adjusted quickly enough to meet inflationary factors, or guaranteed far enough in advance to enable long-term plans involving international singers to be finalized. Inevitably, nowadays the Scottish Art Council, partnered to some extent by local authorities, has taken over the role of principal patron. The Arts cannot, and never have been able to, exist without patronage. They are not unique in this respect; schools, libraries and even council housing developments coming into the same category.

There is in some Glasgow quarters a tendency still to think of the Arts as a luxury benefiting only a privileged few, and that consequently money spent in their support would better be spent in helping house the homeless. Obviously, such arguments are fallacious both on practical and theoretical counts. Limitations of men and materials affect building possibilities. In any event, the needs and aspirations of society have to be considered as a whole if a state of well-being is to prevail. Primitive man revealed his fundamental psychological need for the kind of satisfaction to be derived from art by drawing and scratching on the walls of his damp caves.

John Davidson once declared all that ultimately mattered to be a satisfied imagination. He qualified this assertion by admitting that individual imaginations are satisfied at different levels. A raising of the level at which satisfaction can be obtained represents an advance in sophisticated civilization.

It is therefore disappointing that television in Scotland, most of which emanates from Glasgow, should have failed so lamentably to do much to help raise the level of imagination at which its viewers might attain satisfaction. The B.B.C. launched a magazine of the Arts, "Counterpoint",* in December 1958, from the first

*A venture with which George Bruce, Alan Rees and I were jointly associated.

edition of which emerged the head of 'Hugh MacDiarmid' by Benno Schotz, subsequently cast in bronze and now dignifying the main entrance of Broadcasting House, Queen Margaret Drive. After a lapse of almost a decade, when no real attempt to deal with the Scottish Arts on television was made, coverage in 1971 does not often achieve a level higher than visual journalism.

Scottish Television Limited has had less excuse for its failure to offer quality productions. In its earlier days, the famous Thomsonian 'licence to print money' resulted in a supply so plentiful that in about three or four years the lucky investor could expect to have recouped more than his original invested capital in dividends. Scottish Television has given generous support to various artistic enterprises in Scotland, including Scottish Opera: but its role should be to put out its quota of imaginative television programmes, not act the part of a secondary Arts Council by way of excuse for having failed to do so.

The average Glasgow viewer's imagination is no doubt satisfied at a fairly low level. Television undoubtedly has a duty to meet mass demand at any proper level: but it also has a duty to meet minority demand, and so gradually to help raise the level of imaginative satisfaction of its viewers over the years, as the B.B.C. did so successfully through radio with its music and current-affairs broadcasts throughout the 30s and 40s.

A different view can be taken, and is reflected in the pronouncement by the American Lee Loevinger of the American Federal Communications Commission: "T.V. is a golden goose that lays scrambled eggs and it is futile and probably fatal to beat it for not laying caviare. Anyway, more people like scrambled eggs than caviare. T.V. should be recognized for what it is, the literature of the illiterate, the culture of the low-brows, the wealth of the poor, the privilege of the under-privileged, the exclusive club of the excluded masses."

These are mighty fine-rounding sentiments. Analyse them, and they are seen to be humbug; an attempt at rationalizing licence to swamp the air with perpetual triviality, levelling standards to those of the lowest common denominator, and in the process securing to the programme operator the maximum financial return for the minimum expenditure.

Fortunately, real literature does not exist in this morass of double-think and smoothy-talk. During the 1939 war, and immediately after it, William Maclellan published from an address in

Hope Street the work of what Eric Linklater called the 'Second Wind' generation of writers of the 'Scottish Renaissance'. The banner was always a wide one, covering such diverse writers as, among the poets 'Hugh MacDiarmid' (its begetter), Sydney Goodsir Smith, Douglas Young, Ruthven Todd and George Bruce, and among the story-tellers, Fred Urquhart and Robin Jenkins. Myself apart, none of the group were actually native Glaswegians; but it was from Glasgow, through Maclellan's anthologies *Poetry Scotland* and the *Scottish Art and Letters*, and in club-rooms of the Scottish Arts Group in Blythswood Square and the Saltire Society in Wellington Street that much of the creative excitement then being generated was communicated to the public.

Almost all the poets who appeared under Maclellan's aegis are to be found today represented in the standard Scottish anthologies, while the work of such painters as Donald Bain, Andrew Taylor Elder, Isobel Brodie Babianska, Millie Frood, William Crosbie and Marie de Banzie, was thought of sufficient importance for the Scottish Arts Council to mount and circulate an exhibition of it as recently as 1969.

All that was a generation ago, and today's young tigers are apt to snarl at the sobriquet 'Scottish Renaissance', even although much of the habit of questioning accepted values and the insistence on honesty of expression which the movement practised has, perforce, rubbed off on them.

Post-Scottish Renaissance Glasgow poets like Edwin Morgan and Tom Buchan are wide in their range and usually have strongly radical leanings—in Buchan's case, sometimes pulling him towards disruptive violence of imagery. He sees Scotland (with some justice) as the "crèche of the soul", the "land of the millionaire draper, whisky vomit and the Hillman Imp", the "nirvana of the keelie imagination". Morgan's sympathies are altogether kindlier. He has the advantage of an energetic sense of humour, typified by his poem dealing with a hygiene problem which often causes owners of Glasgow buildings expense and those who line up in bus queues some annoyance, "The Starlings in George Square":

> The City Chambers are hopping mad.
> Councillors with rubber plugs in their ears!
> Secretaries closing windows!
> Window-cleaners want protection and danger money.
> The Lord Provost can't hear herself think, man.

What's that?
Lord Provost, can't hear herself think.

At the General Post Office
the clerks write Three Pounds Sterling in the savings-books.
Each telephone booth is like an aviary,
I tried to send a parcel to County Kerry but—
The cables to Cairo got fankled, sir,
What's that?
I said the cables to Cairo got fankled. . . .*

Although Glasgow has inspired no notable drama, it has acquired a civic theatre, the 'Kings', which is owned by Glasgow Corporation, and has been reconstructed to provide an orchestral pit large enough to accommodate a Wagner orchestra. The Citizens Theatre, brain-child of 'James Bridie', moved over to the old Princess's Theatre in the Gorbals in 1945 just before the necessary redevelopment of that notorious area began. The increasingly derelict nature of the surroundings of the 'Citizens' has made it difficult for any producer or company to retain capacity audiences. Eventually, the 'Citizens' will be housed in Sir Leslie Martin's Arts complex along with its experimental companion theatre, the 'Close'. For some inexplicable reason, the works of Bridie apart, scarcely a single play by a Scot that one would want to see produced a second time has been thrown up by the Citizens Theatre during its activities over more than three decades.

Novelists have been less inhibited, for since the war there have been published Nancy Brysson Morrison's *The Winnowing Years* (1949), Robin Jenkins's *Happy for the Child* (1953) and Archie Hinds' *The Dear Green Place* (1966), added to which might be listed Cliff Hanley's *Dancing in the Streets* (1958), an autobiographical account of a Glasgow upbringing. Literary agents state categorically that novels with a Glasgow setting are not easily marketable to publishers. Yet a surprising number of Glasgow writers concerned with other topics than sexual athletics do seem somehow to break through this formidable barrier, even if none of the results has yet turned out to be the late twentieth-century's Great Scottish Novel so diligently sought by newspaper reviewers.

Glasgow's reading habits have changed over a generation. Those little tuppence-a-night lending libraries to be found in every suburb, well-stocked with novels, have been driven out of business

*From *The Second Life* (1968).

by the paperback revolution. But the statistical evidence from the Corporation Library Department seems to show that year by year, more and more people are actually reading books, though fewer of these books are works of fiction—a decline which would undoubtedly have pleased that fastidious benefactor to Glasgow, Mr. Stirling.

A much thumbed non-fictional work in city libraries is the Glasgow volume of the Third Statistical Account (1958). It deals with many aspects of the city's way of life, though it is weak in its coverage of Glasgow's culture and sub-cultures. One of the most interesting sections is that in which the sociologist J. A. Mack, describes the various disorders which produce "socially incompetent families", Glasgow possessing a large minority of these. In these families, he tells us, the children

for a variety of reasons, are the victims of physical or moral or emotional neglect or of all three combined. . . . The organisation of many households is very loose indeed. The "official" inhabitants of a house are not clearly known from day to day. Temporary changes as a result of quarrels, reorientation of affections or simply convenience of sleeping arrangements are very common. In such households where there are children, there is strictly speaking no parental control. The parents may change partners, and one or other move out temporarily. Even without this type of instability, the large and ranging numbers of adults of different generations with different standards of behaviour, all taking turn, so to speak in disciplining or indulging the children, makes it impossible for the children to be brought up to any pattern of behaviour consistent with the wider society. These children may be normal as individuals. . . . But it is to be suspected that they provide a high proportion of these persistent young criminals whose criminality has nothing psychologically abnormal about it.

Then there are the children who live "from drinking-session to drinking-session", Edward Gaitens' Dance of the Apprentices (1948) depicts one such family, the Macdonnels, in the inter-war years. Idealized politics are discussed against "a background of seductive triviality" the "dispiriting background of the Gorbals".

When Jimmy, the sailor son, comes home from a voyage and gets engaged to a "good-living" girl, he promises to give up drink, a promise which horrifies father Macdonnel, who had been anticipating the usual drunken party on Jimmy's return until his sailor's pay was exhausted. But three hours later, brother Eddy, who had been inspired by Jimmy's unexpected conversion, looks out into the street to see Jimmy (wearing his Aunt Kate's hat), and their father staggering arm-in-arm, "large bottles of whisky waggled from the pockets of the two men. Behind them, laughing like witches, came Mrs. Macdonnel and Aunt Kate with the sailor's hat on, followed by six of Jimmy's pals who were carrying between them three large crates of bottled beer."

In the orgy which followed, Eddy decided that "human behaviour" had passed his understanding. "He was thinking of Jeannie Lindsay and wishing he might find her standing at her close mouth in South Wellington Street. But it was very late. He hurried round the corner in a queer emotional tangle of sexual shame and desire, his romantic thoughts of Jeannie mingled with the shameful memory of his mother dressing up in men's clothes and Bridget Delaney pulling up her skirts to the hips to show her bare legs to the men."

Methods of transport have changed equally dramatically over the last two decades. The sheer suburban spread of Glasgow has necessitated the introduction of extended bus services, although bus passenger-carrying returns show a fall-away in favour of the private car, a phenomenon common almost everywhere in the Western world. Electrified train services now connect places along both banks of the Clyde with Glasgow. The Cathcart Circle has also been electrified. A broad pattern of road development, including a circular city inner ring motorway, is in the course of construction.

Inevitably, the tramcar had to go, its centre-of-the-road lack of manœuvreability an increasing hazard in busy streets. A historic procession of Glasgow's trams from past decades wound its way through the streets for the last time on 4th September 1962. So affectionate did they feel towards the trams that some of those who turned out to see the procession—the old coloured trams (blue for Kirklee to Rutherglen, green for Dennistoun to Knightswood, yellow for Clarkston to Hyndland, white for Mosspark to the university, and so on, the still older open-ended cars, single deckers and the dignified 'Coronation' models, once the pride and boast of Glaswegians—actually wept!

The gradual reduction of the Clyde Steamer cruising fleet was no doubt as inevitable as the departure of the trams. Immediately after the nationalization of the railways in 1947 redundancies were declared and the scrapping of the older paddlers begun. By 1971, only two cruise steamers were left, the *Queen Mary II* and the *Waverley*, the last sea-going paddler in service in the United Kingdom. Service routes across the Firth are now operated by car ferries, since no holidaymaker nowadays wants to travel without his car. I have yet to meet the man who can develop any affection for a car ferry.

The beautiful Clyde estuary itself seems to be about to suffer drastic change, which may ultimately destroy its value as a recreational area. Deep water such as ships of large tonnage require, has been discovered off the Ayrshire coast. The construction of an electricity power-station has been authorized at Inverkip in the middle of an area of coastline designated as being of outstanding scenic beauty. An ore terminal and a general port at Hunterston could be the forerunners of what might yet become the western edge of a future central industrialized belt, an 'Oceanspan'* linking Clyde and Forth, Glasgow and Edinburgh.

Economic prosperity is the essential basis of modern urban life: but good environment is nowadays the basic essential of any kind of tolerable life. I sometimes wonder if, in their laudable search after economic prosperity, the advocates of industrialization at any cost get their human priorities wrong. Development for prosperity must be accepted; but industry cannot for ever be allowed to go on issuing ultimatums of the order 'either there, or else we go to the Continent', to those who have to make the planning decisions. If the industrialization of sections of areas of outstanding natural beauty is really inevitable in Scotland's economic interests,† then it may be necessary for the Government to accept as a public charge an element of social capital cost. This might meant that an oil company with its terminal on the estuary would have to agree to situate its refinery inland in the interests of amenity, the Government meeting the social cost element should the inland site be more costly to set up than a coastal site. If we are not willing to accept a measure of social control of this sort, and bear its inevitable financial implications, then strategic planning will be reduced to a kind of academic game, its reasoned decisions

*The title of the plan by Professor R. E. Nicoll and Sir William Lithgow advocating such a development.

†I say "Scotland's interests" rather than "the United Kingdom interest", since the latter could conceivably run counter to the former, as in the siting in the Holy Loch and the Gareloch of the American and British nuclear submarine bases.

constantly overthrown by commercial expediency or political convenience.

Everywhere there are visual signs that Glasgow is renewing herself, and significant signs that some of her citizens want to be associated with that renewal. Groups like the New Glasgow Society, which concern themselves with public participation in Glasgow's planning process, provide evidence of this kind of interest, as do more localized societies which have come into existence at Maryhill, Springburn and Govan. The Scottish Civic Trust, which exists to stimulate interest in, and concern for, the environment, has had its headquarters in Glasgow since it was set up in 1967. The National Trust for Scotland opened a Glasgow office in 1970.

Any portrait of Glasgow ought to end with something about Glasgow people, yet it is impossible to write meaningful generalities about a race who, out of one end of the genetical chance-mixer produce the worst possible ethnical mixture of dull Irish and dull Scot, a runted, stunted violent minority of low intelligence quotient who start fights at football matches, daub bus-shelters and buildings with aerosol paint sprays, slash the seats of railway-carriages, and generally indulge in the sort of mindless behaviour which leaps into television features and newspaper headlines, unjustly smearing the reputation of the whole city in the eyes of the world beyond.

Glasgow is thus sensitive in its appreciation of those who enhance its fair name. A Glasgow shoe manufacturer, A. P. Somerville—inventor of the square-toed shoe which let Glasgow men stand closer to the bar—bequeathed a large sum of money to the city so that a St. Mungo prize could be awarded tri-annually to whoever was deemed to have done the most for Glasgow's reputation in the three preceding years. Winners have included Lord Provost Sir Patrick Dollan; the man who, as curator of the art galleries, did much to make Glasgow picture-conscious; Dr. T. J. Honeyman, the founder-chairwoman of the Glasgow Treelovers Society; Dr. Mackenzie Anderson, a distinguished minister of Glasgow Cathedral and Moderator of the General Assembly of the Church of Scotland; the Reverend Dr. Neville Davidson; and the conductor of the Scottish National Orchestra, Alexander Gibson.

The majority of Glaswegians are couthy and kindly, easy-going and tolerant, perhaps not very sophisticated by London standards

but catching up fast, still more attached to the Church than their
English counterparts, and less willing to go fully along with the
so-called permissiveness of society. Glaswegians are the con-
sumers of more cakes and sweeter lemonade than any other people
in the United Kingdom. By modern standards, they are indus-
trious, although today they lack involved leadership, since those
citizens who in bygone days would have played a dominant part
in the policy-making of the city's organizations, no longer live in
Glasgow but commute from Helensburgh, Killearn or even
Edinburgh.

Most of these commuter dormitory towns or villages, and
perhaps even Edinburgh if 'Oceanspan' materializes, a century
hence may well find themselves pulled into Glasgow's orbit as
the reform of local government creates larger administrative units
and the City of Glasgow becomes officially a city-region.

Even so, I doubt very much if Glasgow humour will change.
Its flavour today is much the same as it was half a century ago.
Two examples must suffice here.

During the First World War, an English officer rode past a
Bantam H.L.I. lance corporal marching some twenty sturdy
German prisoners down a country lane.

"You all right there, Lance-Corporal?" the officer asked.

"Fine, sir," the Bantam answered. The officer remained
unconvinced.

"Sure you can manage all these men on your own?" he
inquired.

"D'ye ken whit's in my hand, sir?" the Bantam asked, opening
his palm. The officer found himself peering down at a common
type of hand grenade.

"Why yes, of course. A Mills bomb."

"Ay, sir, but whit they ken and I ken but you dinna is that the
pin's oot."

Forty years later, a middle-class father had been persuaded to
take his football-daft son to the annual ritualistic Rangers versus
Celtic match.

Those who have never attended a football match along with
perhaps thirty thousand others may not have had cause to appreciate that the sheer press of numbers makes the provision of
normal sanitary arrangements impossible.

To this particular father's dismayed astonishment, a little
Glaswegian beside him suddenly stopped shouting, unbuttoned

and relieved himself. The father, a little startled, instinctively stepped back.

"Whit's the matter wi' you, heh?" came the indignant query. "Shoes leakin', or somethin'?"

That, ultimately, is Glasgow: utterly realistic and down to earth.

I was born in Glasgow. I believe in it. I like its unappreciated marvellous buildings and its cheerfully average people; its balanced attitude to life and its occasional flight of imaginative achievement; its temperate climate and its neighbourly hills and lochs. When, at different periods of my life, I have had to live away from it, sooner or later, I have been overwhelmed by a compelling nostalgia. Though Glasgow often infuriates me, back I have always come.

The loquacious but humourless St. Paul is neither an author whose works lie by my bedside, nor one of my favourite men. But I have often found myself silently quoting his proud answer to the Roman Tribune, before whom he was defending himself:

> "I am a citizen of no mean city."

By that, in the end, I stand.

INDEX

Abbotsford Place, 69, 70
A.B.C. Company, 135
Achaius, John, Bishop of Glasgow, 23
Acme Wringer Company, 135
Across the Tweed, 124
Active Society, 192
Adam, James, 38, 64–5
— John, 65
— Robert, 64–5
— William, 65
Adelphi Theatre, 115
Advertiser, 80. See also *Glasgow Herald, The*
Aeronautics, 135–6
Albert, Prince, 122–3, 163,
Albion Company, 135
Alcoholism, 19, 117, 168–9
Alexander, John Henry, 110, 114–15, 117
Alexandra Park, 171
Alhambra Theatre, 144, 156, 188
Ali, Tariq, 19
Alison, Sir Archibald, Sheriff of Lanarkshire, 121, 123
Allan, Dot, 194
Allen, Milner, 153
American Civil War, 86, 94
American War of Independence, 46
Anderson, George, 52n
— Sir John, 203
— John, 119
— Dr. Mackenzie, 232
— Sir Robert Rowand, 65, 145
Anderson (actor-manager), 115–16
Andersonian University, 119
Anderson's College, 126
Anderson, 52, 57, 73, 211
Anderston Club, 53

Annals of Commerce, 54–5
Annals of Glasgow, 66n
Annals of the Parish, 109
Annan, Rev. William, 31
Antonine Wall, 21
Archbishop's Castle, 26
Architecture of Glasgow, 23n, 67, 104
Argyll, Duke of, 42
— Marquis of, 32, 33
Argyll Furnace Company, 87
Argyll Motor Company, 135, 136
Argyll Street, 73, 74, 79, 100
Arkwright (inventor of spinning frame), 58
Arran, James Hamilton, Duke of Chatelherault and Earl of, 27–8, 32
Arrol-Johnston Company, 135
Art, 158–9, 195–6
Ashley, Lord (later Earl of Shaftesbury), 125
Assembly Rooms, 64, 79, 121
Athenaeum (Ingram Street), 121
Athenaeum (St. George's Place), 121, 144
Athenaeum Theatre, 144, 145
Athenia, 200
Atlantic Chambers, 144
Auden, W. H., 201
Aunt Bel, 104
Aytoun, W. E., 111

Babcock and Wilcox, 133
Bailie, 189
Baillie, Joanna, 82
Baird, John, 101, 138, 141
— John (weaver), 63

Baird and Company, William, 126
Baldwin, Stanley, 185
Ballochney Railway, 89
Band of Hope Union, 168
Bank Tavern, 117
Barclay, Hugh and David, 143
Barke, James, 194
Barony North Church, 142
Barr, Professor, 134
— the Reverend James, 183
Barrie, James Matthew, 159
Bartholomew, Hugh, 127
Bathgate, 126, 127
Bartok, Bela, 192
Baynham, Walter, 114
Beardmore, William, 127
Beaton, Archbishop James, 25, 27, 29, 32
Belgians, King of the, 152n
Bell, Henry, 74–5
— James Joy, 152, 155, 162, 195
— J. and P. 103
Bellahouston Park, 192
Benmore, 715
Bergius Company, 135
Berkeley Hall, 192
Beside the Bonnie Briar Bush, 160
Binnie, Thomas, 70
Binyon, Lawrence, 177–8
Bishop's Forest, 26. See also Glasgow Green
Black, William, 160–61
Black Bull Hotel, 82
Blackie and Son, 192
Blake, George, 184
Blind Harry, 24
Bliss, Sir Arthur, 211n
Blochairn Works, 127
Blue Riband, 129, 130
Blythswood New Town, 66–9, 79
Blythswood Square, 68, 214

235